C000213280

The Life of the
Brigadier Gerard

The Young Hussar

The Life of the Real
Brigadier Gerard

The Young Hussar

Volume 1:
A French Cavalryman of the Napoleonic Wars
at Marengo, Austerlitz, Jena, Eylau & Friedland

1782 - 1807

Jean-Baptiste de Marbot

LEONAUR

The Life of the Real Brigadier Gerard
The Young Hussar
Volume 1:
A French Cavalryman of the Napoleonic Wars
at Marengo, Austerlitz, Jena, Eylau & Friedland
1782 - 1807
by Jean-Baptiste de Marbot

Published by Leonaur Ltd

First Edition

Copyright © 2006 Leonaur Ltd

ISBN (10 digit): 1-84677-058-0 (hardcover)
ISBN (13 digit): 978-1-84677-058-6 (hardcover)

ISBN (10 digit): 1-84677-045-9 (softcover)
ISBN (13 digit): 978-1-84677-045-6 (softcover)

http://www.leonaur.com

Publisher's Notes

In the interests of authenticity, the spellings, grammar and place names
used have been retained from the original editions.

The opinions of the authors represent a view of events in which he
was a participant related from his own perspective,
as such the text is relevant as an historical document.

The views expressed in this book are not necessarily
those of the publisher.

Contents

Chapter 1
About My Family

I was born on the 18th August 1782 at my father's Château of Larivière, in the beautiful valley of Beaulieu, on the borders of Limousin and Quercy--now the department of Corrèze--where my father owned a considerable property.

The family of Marbot was of noble origin, although for a long time they had not preceded their name by any title. They lived nobly, that is to say on the income from their estates, without engaging in any form of employment.

My father was born in 1753. He had a rather fiery temperament, but he was so good-hearted that, after a first outburst, he always sought to make one forget any hasty words which he might have uttered. He was a fine figure of a man, very tall and well built, with handsome, manly features.

My grandfather had become a widower when my father was still at school. His house was run by one of his elderly cousins, the oldest of the demoiselles Oudinet of Beaulieu. She gave unstinting care to my grandfather, who, having become almost blind as a result of a flash of lightning, which had struck near him, no longer went out of his manor. Thus my father, when he reached manhood, faced by an infirm old man and an aunt devoted to his least wishes, could have played fast and loose with the family fortune. He did not, however, abuse his position, but as he had a great fancy for a military career, he accepted a proposal which was made to him by colonel the Marquis d'Estresse, a neighbour and close friend of the family, which was to have him enrolled in the bodyguard of the king, Louis XV.

Being under the auspices of the Marquis d'Estresse, he was received in a number of houses; notably that of lieutenant-general the Comte de Schomberg, the inspector-general of cavalry, who, recognising my father's worth, had him posted to his regiment of dragoons as captain, and took him as his aide-de-camp.

On the death of my grandfather my father was still unmarried, and his fortune, as well as his place in the Royal Bodyguard, put him in a position to choose a wife, without the likelihood of being refused.

There lived at that time, in the Château de Laval de Cère, about a league from Larivière, a family of noble rank but without much money, named de Certain. The head of this house was stricken by gout and so his affairs were managed by Madame de Certain, an admirable woman.

The de Certains had three sons and a daughter, and as was the custom at that time they added to their family name that of some estate. Thus the eldest son was given the name Canrobert: this eldest son was, at the time of which I write, Chevalier de St. Louis and a captain in the infantry regiment of Penthièvre; the second son who was called de L'Isle was a lieutenant in the same regiment; the third son, who had the surname La Coste served, like my father, in the Royal Bodyguard; the daughter was called Mlle. Du Puy, and she was my mother.

My father became a close friend of M. Certain de La Coste, and it would have been difficult to do otherwise, for quite apart from the three months which they spent in quarters at Versailles during their period of duty, the journeys which they made together, twice a year, were bound to make a bond between them.

At that time public coaches were very few in number, dirty, uncomfortable, and travelled by very short stages; also it was considered not at all fashionable to ride in them. So, gentry who were old or in poor health travelled by carriage, while the young and officers in the armed forces went on horseback. There was an established custom among the Bodyguard, which today would seem most peculiar. As these gentlemen did only three months on duty, and as in consequence the corps was split into four almost equal sections, those of them who lived in Brittany, the Auvergne, Limousin and other parts of the country where there were good small horses had bought a number of these at a price not exceeding 100 francs, which included the saddle and bridle. On a fixed day all the Bodyguards from the same province, who were called to go and take up their duties, would meet, on horseback, at an agreed spot and the cheerful caravanserai would take the road for Versailles.

They made twelve to fifteen leagues each day, sure of finding every evening, at an agreed and reasonable price, a good lodging and a good supper at the inns previously arranged as stopping places. They went happily on their way, talking, singing, putting up with bad weather or heat as they did with accidents and laughing at the stories which all, in turn, had to tell as they rode along. The group grew in size by the arrival of Bodyguards from the provinces through which they passed until, at last, the various parties arrived from all parts of France to enter Versailles on the day on which their leave expired, and, in consequence, at the moment of departure of those guards whom they had come to relieve. Then each of these latter bought one of the ponies brought by the new arrivals, for which they paid 100 francs, and forming fresh groups they took to the road for their paternal châteaux, where they turned the horses out to grass for nine months, until they were taken back to Versailles and handed over to other comrades-in-arms.

My father, then, was a close friend of M. Certain de La Coste, who shared the same quarters and belonged, like him, to the company de Noailles. On their return to the country they saw much of each other, and he made the acquaintance of Mlle. Du Puy. Mlle. Du Puy was pretty and high spirited, and although she would have little in the way of dowry, and although several rich matches were offered to my father, he preferred Mlle. Du Puy, and he married her in 1776.

We were four brothers: the eldest Adolphe, myself the second, Théodore the third and Félix the last. There was a gap of about two years between our ages. I was very sturdy and suffered only some minor illness.

Chapter 2
The Storm of Revolution

While my childhood was rolling by peacefully, the storm of revolution which had been growling in the distance, drew ever nearer, and it was not long before it broke. We were in 1789. The assembly of the States General stirred up all manner of passions, destroyed the tranquillity enjoyed by the province in which we lived and introduced divisions into all families, particularly into ours; for my father, who for a long time had railed against the abuses to which France was subjected, accepted, in principle, the improvements which were mooted, without foreseeing the atrocities to which these changes were going to lead; while his three brothers-in-law and all his friends rejected any innovation. This gave rise to animated discussions, of which I understood nothing, but which distressed me because I saw my mother in tears as she tried to keep the peace between her brothers and her husband. For my part, although I did not understand what was going on, I naturally took sides with my father.

The Constituent Assembly had revoked all feudal rents. My father possessed some of these which his father had purchased. He was the first to conform to the law. The peasantry who had been waiting to make up their minds until my father gave them a lead, refused to continue paying these rents once they knew what he had done.

Shortly after this, France having been divided into departments, my father was named administrator for the Corrèze and then a member of the Legislative Assembly.

My mother's three brothers, and nearly all the nobility of the county had hurriedly emigrated. War seemed to be imminent, so, to persuade all citizens to take up arms, and also, perhaps, to find out up to what point they could count on the populace, the government arranged for the rumour to be spread throughout all the communes of France, that the "Brigands" led by the émigrés, were coming to destroy all the new institutions. The tocsin was rung by all the churches; everyone armed themselves with whatever they could lay hands upon; a National Guard was organised; the country turned into an armed camp while it waited for these imaginary "Brigands" who, in every commune, were said to be in the one next door. Nothing ever appeared, but the effect remained: France found herself in arms and had shown that she was prepared to defend herself.

We children were then alone in the country with our mother. This alert, which was called "The day of fear" surprised me and would probably have alarmed me, had I not seen my mother remain so calm. I have always thought that my father had discreetly warned her of what was about to happen.

All went well at first, without any excess on the part of the peasants, who, in our part of the country, retained much respect for the ancient families; but soon, stirred up by demagogues from the towns, the country-dwellers invaded the houses of the nobles, under the pretext of looking for hidden émigrés, but in fact to exact money and to seize the title deeds of feudal rents, which they burned in a big bonfire. From the height of our terrace, we saw these ruffians, torches in their hands, running towards the Château d'Estresse, from which all the men had emigrated and which was occupied only by women. These were my mother's best friends, and so she was greatly upset by this spectacle. Her anxiety was redoubled by the arrival of her own aged mother, who had been driven out of her château, which was declared national property because of the emigration of her three sons...!

Up until then, my father's property had been respected; largely because his patriotism was known, and because, to give further proof of it, he had taken service in the army of the Pyrenees as captain in the Chasseurs des Montagnes, at the end of his term in the legislative assembly. But the revolutionary torrent swept over everyone; the house at St. Céré, which my father had bought ten years before, was confiscated and declared national property because the deed of sale had been signed privately and the seller had emigrated before ratifying the deal before a notary. My mother was given a few days to remove her linen, then the house was put up for auction and was bought by the president of the district who had himself arranged for its confiscation!

At last, the peasants, stirred up by some agitators from Beaulieu, came in a body to my father's château and insisted, though with some politeness, that they had to burn the deeds of feudal rents which we still had, and make sure that émigrés were not concealed in the château.

My mother received them with fortitude, handed over the deeds and pointed out to them that, knowing her brothers to be sensible people, they should not suppose that they would emigrate only then to come back to France and hide in her château.

They accepted the correctness of this line of reasoning, ate and drank and having burned the deeds in the centre of the courtyard, they left without doing any further damage, shouting "Long live France and citizen Marbot!" And charging my mother to write to him to say that they liked him very much and that his family was quite safe among them.

In spite of this assurance, my mother felt that her position as the sister of émigrés might expose her to a great deal of unpleasantness from which even her position as the wife of a defender of the country would not protect her. She decided to go away for the time being. She told me later that she took this step because she was convinced that the revolutionary storm would last only for some months. There were many people who thought this!

My grandmother had had seven brothers, all of whom, as was usual in the Verdal family had been soldiers and knights of St. Louis. One of them, a former battalion commander in the infantry regiment of Penthièvre, had married, on retirement, the rich widow of counsellor of the parliament of Rennes. My mother decided to go and stay with her and was counting on taking me with her, when I was smitten by a number of large and very painful boils. It was impossible to travel with a child of eight in such a state, and my mother was in great perplexity. She was extricated by a worthy lady, Mlle. Mongalvi, who was much devoted to her and whose memory will always be dear to me. Mlle. Mongalvi lived at Turenne and ran boarding establishment for young ladies of which my mother had been one of the first occupants. She offered to take me into her house for the few months of my mother's absence. My father's agreement having been obtained, I left and was installed there. "What!" you may say, "A boy amongst young ladies?" Well yes, but do not forget that I was a quiet, peaceable, obedient child, and I was only eight years old.

The boarders who stayed with Mlle. Mongalvi, where my mother had once been one of them, were young persons of some sixteen to twenty years of age; the youngest being at least fourteen, and were sensible enough to let me mingle with them.

On my arrival, all this little feminine flock gathered about me and received me with such cries of pleasure and warm caresses that, from the first instant, I thought myself lucky to have made this trip. I figured that it would not last long and I believe that, secretly, I even regretted that I would have only a short time to spend with these nice young ladies, who did everything to please me and argued as to who was to hold my hand.

However, my mother left and went to stay with my uncle. Events moved forward rapidly. The terror bathed France in blood. Civil war broke, out in the Vendée and in Brittany. Travel there became absolutely impossible, so that my mother, who had thought to spend two or three months at Rennes, found herself stuck there for several years. I was sent as a boarder at the home of Mlles. Mongalvi.

My father continued on active service in the Pyrenees and in Spain, where his ability and courage had raised him to the rank of divisional general; while I, having gone as a boarder for a few months, stayed for some four years, which were for me years of much happiness, clouded only, from time to time, by the memory of my parents.

I recall, that on hearing of the horrible execution of Louis XVI, Mlle. Mongalvi had all the boarders on their knees, to recite prayers for the repose of the soul of the unfortunate king. The indiscretion of any one of us could have brought down disaster on her head, but all the pupils were of an age to understand, and I felt that it was something I should not talk about; so no one knew anything about it. I stayed in this pleasant retreat until November 1793.

Chapter 3
I Enter Military College

When I was eleven and a half years old, my father was given command of a camp which was set up at Toulouse. He took advantage of a few days leave to come and see me and to arrange his affairs, which he had not been able to do for several years. He came to Turenne, to the house of one of his friends, and hurried to my lodging. He was in the uniform of a general officer, with a big sabre, his hair cut short and unpowdered and sporting an enormous moustache, which was in remarkable contrast to the costume in which I was used to seeing him when we lived peacefully at Larivière.

I have said that my father, in spite of his stern masculine looks, was a kind man, and particularly toward children, whom he adored. I saw him again with the keenest transports of delight, and he overwhelmed me with caresses. He stayed for several days at Turenne; he warmly thanked the good mesdames Mongalvi for the truly maternal care they had taken of me; but when he asked me a few questions, it was easy for him to see that though I had a good knowledge of prayers and litanies and lots of hymns, my remaining education was limited to some notions of history, geography, and spelling. He considered also, that, being now in my twelfth year, it was time to give me an education which was more masculine and more extensive. He had resolved therefore, to take me with him to Toulouse, to where he had also brought Adolphe, and to place us both in the military college of Sorèze, the sole great establishment of this kind which the revolutionary turmoil had left standing.

I left, after bidding a tender farewell to my young friends. We headed for Cressensac, where we were joined by Captain Gault, my father's aide-de-camp. While the coach was being got ready, Spire, my father's old servant, who knew that his master intended to travel day and night, made up packages of food.

At this moment a new spectacle was presented to me: a mobile column, composed of gendarmes, national guards and volunteers, entered the town of Cressensac with a band playing at its head. I had never seen anything like it, and it seemed to me quite superb, but I was unable to understand why, in the midst of all these soldiers, there was a dozen coaches filled with old men, women and children, all of whom looked extremely sad. This sight infuriated my father. He drew back from the window and, striding about with his aide-de-camp, whom he could trust, I heard him burst out, "These miserable members of the convention have ruined the revolution which could have done so much good. There you see yet more innocent people who are being thrown into gaol because they are landowners or are related to émigrés; it is disgusting!"

Why, you may ask, did my father continue to serve a government which he despised? It was because he thought that to confront the enemies of France was honourable, but did not mean that the military condoned the atrocities which the convention committed in the interior of the country.

What my father had said, had interested me in the people in the coaches. I gathered that they had been, that morning, seized from their châteaux and were being led away to the prisons of Souilhac. They were old men, women and children, and I was wondering to myself how these frail people could present any danger to the country, when I heard several of the children asking for food. One lady begged a national guard to let her get out to go and buy something to eat. He refused her, rudely, and when the lady produced an "assignat" and pleaded with him to go and buy some bread, he replied, "Do you take me for one of your former lackeys?" This brutality angered me. I had noticed that Spire had placed in the pockets of the coach, a number of bread-rolls in the centre of which was a sausage; I took two of these rolls, and drawing near to the coach holding the child prisoners, I threw them in, when the guards were not looking. The mothers and the children made signs to me of such gratitude that I resolved to give food to all the other prisoners, and piece by piece, I gave them all the provisions which Spire had made for the two days journey to Toulouse, which we were about to make. We left, at last, without Spire having any suspicion of the distribution which I had just made. The little prisoners blew me kisses and their parents waved to me; but no sooner were we some hundred paces from the post-house than my father, who had been in haste to get away from a spectacle which distressed him, and had not wished to eat at the inn, felt hungry, and asked for the provisions. Spire pointed to the pockets in which he had placed them. My father and M. Gault rummaged through all the interior of the coach, but found nothing. My father grew angry with Spire, who from the height of his seat, swore by all the saints that he had stuffed the coach with food for two days. I was somewhat embarrassed; however, I did not want poor Spire to be blamed any longer, so I admitted what I had done. I expected to be scolded for acting without authority, but my father put his arm round me in the most affectionate manner, and many years after he still spoke with pleasure of my conduct on this occasion.

From Cressensac to Toulouse the road was full of volunteers, going to join the army of the Pyrenees, and making the air ring with patriotic songs. I was charmed by this bustling spectacle and would have been happy had it not been for my physical suffering. I had never made a long journey by coach before, and I was sea-sick throughout the trip, which decided my father to stop every night to allow me some repose. I arrived at Toulouse feeling very tired, but the sight of my brother, from whom I had been parted for four or five years, gave me so much joy that I very soon recovered.

My father, with the rank of divisional general, commanding the camp situated at Miral, close to Toulouse, was entitled to a billet, and the municipality had assigned to him the fine town house of Rességuier, whose owner had emigrated. Madame de Rességuier and her son had retreated to the most distant rooms, and my father gave orders that the strictest regard was to be given to their unhappy position.

My father's house was much frequented. Every day there were visitors, and he had a great deal of expense, for although at that time a divisional general received eighteen rations of all kinds, and his aides-de-camp a similar amount, it was not enough. He had to buy a host of things and as the state gave to a general officer what it gave to a sous-lieutenant, that is eight francs a month in cash, the rest being made up in assignats, the value of which diminished daily, and as my father was very generous, entertained many of the officers from the camp, had numerous domestic servants (at that time called servitors), had eighteen horses, a coach, a box at the theatre etc...He spent the savings which he had accumulated at Larivière, and it was from the time of his re-entry into military service that the decline of his fortune began.

Although the "Terror" was now at its height and class distinction was greatly weakened in France, from whence all good manners seemed to have removed themselves forever, my father knew so well how to impose them on the many officers who came to his quarters, that the most perfect politeness ruled in his salon and at his table.

Among the officers employed at the camp, my father had taken a great liking to two, who were invited more often than the others. One was named Augereau and was the adjutant-general, that is to say colonel of the general staff, the other was Lannes, a lieutenant of Grenadiers, in a battalion of volunteers from the department of Gers.

They became Marshals of the Empire and I have been aide-de-camp to both of them.

At this period Augereau, after escaping from the prison of the Inquisition at Lisbon, had come to fight in the Vendée, where he was noticed for his courage and his quality of leadership. He was an excellent tactician, a skill which he had learned in Prussia, where he had served for a considerable time in the Foot-guards of Frederick the Great; hence his nick-name of "The Big Prussian." He had an irreproachable military turn-out, spick and span, curled and powdered, with a long pig-tail, big, highly polished riding boots and withal, a very martial bearing. This smart appearance was the more remarkable because, at this time it was not something on which the French army could pride itself, being almost entirely made up of volunteers not used to wearing uniform and very careless of their grooming. However nobody made fun of Augereau about this, for he was known to be a brave and accomplished duelist, who had given even the celebrated Saint-George, the finest swordsman in France, a run for his money.

I have said that Augereau was a good tactician; because of this, my father had appointed him to direct the training of the battalions of new levées, of which the division was largely composed. These men came from Limousin, Auvergne, the Basque country, Quercy,

Gers and Languedoc. Augereau trained them well, and in so doing he was unaware that he was laying the foundations of his own future fame, for these troops, which my father then commanded, formed later the famous Augereau division which did such fine things in the Pyrenees and in Italy.

Augereau came almost daily to my father's house, and seeing that he was appreciated, he devoted to him a friendship which never wavered and of which I felt the benefit after the death of my mother.

As for Lieutenant Lannes, he was a very lively young Gascon, intelligent and cheerful, without education or training but anxious to learn at a time when no one else was. He became a very good instructor, and since he was very vain, he accepted with the greatest delight the praises which my father lavished on him, and which he deserved. By way of recompense, he spoiled, as much as he could, his general's children.

One fine morning, my father received the order to strike his camp at Miral and to lead his division to join the army corps of General Dugommier, which was laying siege to Toulon, which the English had captured in a surprise attack. My father then said to me that he was taking me, the next day, to the military college of Sorèze, where he had already arranged a place for me and my brother.

The road was covered with troops and guns, which my father passed in review at Castelnaudary. This spectacle, which a few days earlier would have delighted me, now failed to lessen the anxiety which I felt about the teachers in whose presence I was about to find myself.

We stayed overnight at Castelnaudary, where my father learned of the evacuation of Toulon by the English (18th Dec 1793), and was ordered to go with his division, to the eastern Pyrenees. Whereupon he decided to deposit us, the very next day, at Sorèze, to stay there for a few hours only, and to set off immediately for Perpignon.

On leaving Castelnaudary, my father ordered the coach to stop at a famous tree under which the Constable Montmorency had been taken prisoner by the troops of Louis XIII, following the defeat of the supporters of Gaston d'Orléans, who had rebelled against his brother. He chatted about this event with his aides-de-camp, and my brother-- who was already well informed--took part in the conversation. As for me, I had only the vaguest notions of the general history of France and knew nothing of the details. It was the first time I had heard of the battle of Castelnaudary, of Gaston, of his revolt and of the capture and execution of the Constable de Montmorency. I realised that my father did not ask me any question on the subject because he was quite certain that I would be unable to reply. This made me feel ashamed, and I concluded that my father was right in taking me to the college to be educated. My regrets then changed into a resolution to learn all that I needed to know.

Nevertheless, my heart sank at the sight of the high sombre walls of the cloister in which I was to be enclosed. I was eleven years and four months old when I entered this establishment.

Chapter 4
The Coming of Bonaparte

I reached the age of sixteen in August 1798. Six months later, towards the end of February, I left the college of Sorèze.

My father had a friend named M. Dorignac, who offered to take me with him to the capital. It took us eight days to reach Paris, where we arrived in March 1799, on the day when the Odéon theatre was burned down for the first time. The flames were visible far off on the Orleans road, and I thought, in my simplicity, that the light came from furnaces operating in the city. My father, at that time, occupied a fine mansion in the Faubourg-St-Honoré road, number 87, on the corner with the little Rue Vert. I arrived there at dinner time: all the family were gathered there. It would be impossible for me to describe the joy which I felt at seeing them all together! This was one of the happiest days of my life!

We were now in the spring of 1799. The Republic still existed, and the government was now composed of the Directorate of five members, and two chambers, one of which was called the Council of Elders, and the other the Council of Five Hundred.

My father entertained many members of society. There I made the acquaintance of his intimate friend, General Bernadotte, and some of the outstanding men of the period, such as Joseph and Lucien Bonaparte, and also Napper-Tandy, the Irish leader, who had taken refuge in France. At my mother's house I frequently saw Madame Bonaparte and sometimes Madame De Staël, already celebrated for her literary works.

I had been in Paris for only about a month, when the term of the legislature expired. It was necessary to hold new elections. My father, fed up with the constant wrangling of political life, and regretting that he was not taking any part in the army's achievements, declared that he would no longer accept nomination as a deputy, and that he wished to return to active service. Events turned out in his favour. On the assembly of the new Chambers there was a change of minister. General Bernadotte became minister for war. He had promised my father that he would send him to the army of the Rhine, and my father was about to set off for Mainz, when the directory, learning of the defeat suffered by the army of Italy, commanded by Scherer, appointed as his successor, General Joubert, who commanded the 17th division in Paris.

This post having now become vacant, the directory, realising that its great political importance required that it should be filled by someone of capacity and determination, instructed the minister for war to offer it to my father. My father who had resigned from the legislature only to resume active service, turned the offer down; but on Bernadotte showing him the letter of appointment, already signed, and saying that as a friend, he begged him to accept, and as a minister, he ordered him, my father gave in, and the next day he went to install himself in the headquarters of the Paris division, situated, at that time in the Quai Voltaire, at the corner of the Rue de Saint-Pères, and which has since been demolished. My father took as his chief of staff his old friend Col. Ménard. I was delighted by all the military suite with which my father was surrounded. His headquarters were never empty of officers of all ranks. A squadron of cavalry, a battalion of infantry and six field-guns were stationed before his portals, and one saw a crowd of orderlies coming and going. This seemed to me much more entertaining than the exercises and translations of Sorèze.

France, and in particular Paris, were, at this time, in a state of much agitation. We were on the brink of catastrophe. The Russians, commanded by the celebrated Souwaroff, had just entered Italy, where our army had suffered a major defeat at Novi, where General Joubert had been killed. The victor, Souwaroff, was heading for our army of Switzerland, commanded by Masséna.

We had few troops on the Rhine. The peace conference begun at Rastadt had broken down and our ambassadors had been assassinated; now all Germany was arming once more against us, and the Directory, fallen into disfavour, had neither troops nor the money to raise them. In order to procure funds it decreed a forced loan, which had the effect of turning everyone against it. All hopes were pinned on Masséna's ability to stop the Russians and prevent them from entering France. The directory, impatient, sent him courier after courier, ordering him to join battle; but this latter-day Fabius, unwilling to risk the safety of his country, was waiting for some false move, on the part of his impetuous adversary, to give him the opportunity for victory.

At this point, I shall relate an anecdote which demonstrates on how fine a thread sometimes hangs the destiny of states and the reputation of generals. The directory, exasperated to see that Masséna did not obey the repeated commands to engage in battle, resolved to relieve him of his post; but, as it was feared that this general would take no notice of the order and simply stuff it in his pocket, if it was sent by an ordinary courier, the minister for war was ordered to send a staff-officer, charged to deliver, publicly, to Masséna his demotion, and to give to his chief of staff, Chérin, the official letter which would confirm him as commander-in-chief of the army.

When the minister told my father, in confidence, about these plans, my father disapproved, saying that it would be dangerous, on the eve of a decisive action, to deprive the army of Switzerland of a general in whom it had confidence, and give the command to a general who was more used to administration than the direction of troops in the field. In addition, the position of the armies might change; and he thought it essential that the mission was given to a man with enough wisdom to assess the state of affairs, and who would not hand Masséna his dismissal on the eve of, or in the middle of a battle.

My father, eventually persuaded the minister to give the task to M. Gault, his aide-de-camp, who, under the ostensible pretext of going to see if the suppliers had delivered the number of horses stipulated in their contract, would proceed to Switzerland with the authority to retain or to hand out the order for the dismissal of Masséna, and the installing of general Chérin, according to the circumstances which might lead him to judge whether this would be useful or dangerous. This was an enormous responsibility to confide to the prudence of a simple captain, but M. Gault fully justified the faith my father had in him.

Arriving at the headquarters of the army of Switzerland five days before the battle of Zurich, he found the troops so full of confidence in Masséna, and Masséna himself so calm and deter-

24

mined, that he had no doubts of success, and, maintaining the deepest silence about his secret powers, he took part in the battle of Zurich and then returned to Paris, without Masséna suspecting that this modest captain had in his hands the authority which could have deprived him of the glory of one of the finest victories of the century.

Had Masséna been rashly dismissed, this would probably have led to the defeat of General Chérin and the invasion of France by the Russians, followed by the Germans, and perhaps finally to the overrunning of Europe. General Chérin was killed at Zurich, without being aware of the intentions of the government towards him.

The victory of Zurich, although, it prevented the advance of the enemy into the country, gave the Directory only a momentary respite. The government was everywhere crumbling; no one had confidence in it. The treasury was bankrupt; the Vendée and Brittany were in open revolt; the interior stripped of troops; the Midi in turmoil; the chamber of deputies squabbling among themselves, and with the executive. In short, the state was on the verge of disaster.

Everyone in politics recognised that a major change was necessary and inevitable; but although all agreed on this point, opinions differed as to the remedy to be employed. The old Republicans, who upheld the constitution of year III, then still in force, believed that it would be sufficient to change several members of the Directory. Two of them were removed and replaced by MM. Gohier and Moulins; but this was the feeblest of palliatives for the calamities which afflicted the country, and it continued to be shaken by anarchy.

It was then that several members of the Directory, amongst whom was the well-known Sieyès, thought, as did many of the deputies and the great majority of the public, that to save France it was necessary to put the reins of government in the hands of someone resolute and already distinguished by services given to the state. It was realised, also, that this would have to be a soldier who had great influence in the army, and who was able, by re-arousing national enthusiasm, to lead our banners to victory and chase away the foreigners who were preparing to cross our frontiers.

To speak like this was to point to General Bonaparte, but at this moment he was in Egypt, and the need was pressing. Joubert had been killed in Italy. Messéna, though famous for several victories, was an excellent general at the head of an army in the field, but in no way a politician. Bernadotte did not seem to have the capacity or the wisdom to repair the country's fortunes. The eyes of the reformers then turned to General Moreau; although the weakness of his character and his indecisive conduct on the 18th Fructidor raised some fears about his ability to govern. It is certain, however, that lacking an alternative, he was asked to head the party which intended to overthrow the Directory, and was offered the title of President or Consul. Moreau, a good fighting soldier, lacked political courage, and perhaps doubted his own ability to cope with affairs in such a mess as were those of France. Also he was self-centered and indolent and worried little about the future of the country, preferring the repose of private life to the agitation of politics. He refused the offer and retired to his estate of Grosbois, to devote himself to hunting, of which he was passionately fond.

Abandoned by the man of their choice, Sieyès and those with him, who wished to change the form of the government, not feeling themselves to be sufficiently strong or popular to achieve their aim without the support of a general whose name would rally the army to their side, were forced to turn their thoughts to General Bonaparte. The leader of this enterprise, Sieyès, flattered himself that, having been placed in power, Bonaparte would busy himself with the management and re-organising of the army, and leave to him the conduct of the government, of which he would be the master and Bonaparte but the nominal head. Events showed how badly he was mistaken.

Imbued with this notion, Sieyès, through the intermission of the Corsican deputy, Salicetti, sent a reliable secret agent to Egypt, to inform General Bonaparte of the troubled state of France, and propose to him that he should come back and place himself at the head of the government. Having no doubt that Bonaparte would accept readily and return promptly to Europe, Sieyès put everything in motion to assure the execution of the coup d'état which he was planning.

It was easy for him to convince his fellow director, Roger-Duclos, that their power was slipping away daily, and that the country being on the brink of complete disorganisation, the public welfare, and their personal interests, demanded that they should take part in the establishment of a strong government, in which they would contrive to place themselves in a less precarious and more advantageous position.

Roger-Duclos promised his agreement to the proposed changes; but the other three directors, Barras, Gohier and Moulins were unwilling to give up their positions, so Sieyès and the leaders of his party resolved to go over their heads, and to sacrifice them after the event.

However, it would be difficult, not to say dangerous, even with the presence of General Bonaparte, to overthrow the Directorate, change the constitution and establish a new government, without the support of the army, and, above all, that of the division which occupied Paris. To be able to rely on this, it was necessary to be sure of the co-operation of the minister for war and of the general commanding the 17th division.

President Sieyès then sought to win over Bernadotte and my father, by having them sounded out by several deputies who were their friends and also supporters of Sieyès's plans. I have learned since that my father replied to the vague overtures which were put to him on behalf of the crafty Sieyès by saying that he agreed that the country's misfortunes demanded a drastic remedy, but that, having sworn to maintain the constitution of year III, he would not use the authority he had over his troops to lead them to its overthrow. He then went to Sieyès and handed in his resignation as commander of the Paris division, and requested a posting to a division on active service. Sieyès hastened to fall in with his wishes, being only too glad to get rid of a man whose devotion to what he saw as his duty, might abort the projected coup. The minister, Bernadotte followed my father's example, and was replaced by Dubois-Crance.

President Sieyès was, for some days, at a loss to find a successor to my father. In the end, he gave the command to general Lefebvre, who, having recently been wounded in the army of the Rhine, was at that moment in the capital. Lefebvre was a former sergeant in the Guards, a brave soldier, a good, workmanlike general, provided that he was closely supervised, but credulous in the extreme, with no understanding of the political situation in France. So, by careful use of the words "Glory," "Motherland," and " Victory, " One could be sure of making him do whatever one wished. This was just the sort of commander that Sieyès was looking for. He did not even take the trouble to win him over, or to warn him of what was about to happen, so sure was he that on the day Lefebvre would not resist the influence of General Bonaparte, and the cajoleries of the president of the directorate.

He had made an accurate assessment of Lefebvre, for on the 18th Brumaire, he placed himself and all his troops under the command of General Bonaparte, to march against the Directorate and the Councillors, to throw down the established government and create the Consulate. This action made him, later, one of the Emperor's greatest favourites. He was made a marshal, Duke of Danzig and senator and was showered with riches.

I have rapidly outlined these events, because they explain some of the reasons which led my father to Italy: a move which had such a profound effect on his destiny and mine.

Chapter 5
I Join the 1st Hussars

After handing over his command to General Lefebvre, my father returned to his house in the Faubourg St. Honoré and busied himself with preparations for his departure to Italy.

A man's destiny is often influenced by the smallest of events. My father and mother were very friendly with M. Barairon, the director of registration, and one day, when they were going to dine with him, they took me along. The talk was of my father's coming departure, and the progress of my two younger brothers. At last, M. Barairon asked, "And Marcellin, what are you going to make of him?" "A sailor," replied my father, "Captain Sibille has agreed to take him with him to Toulon." Then the good Mme. Barairon, towards whom I have always felt the warmest gratitude, observed to my father that the French navy was in complete disarray, that the poor state of the country's finances would not allow its rapid refurbishment, and, furthermore, its inferiority vis-à-vis the English navy was such that it would spend most of its time in harbour. She said that she could not think why he, a divisional general, would put his son into the navy, instead of placing him in a regiment, where the name and services of his father would make him welcome. She ended by saying, "Take him to Italy, sooner than send him to die of boredom, in a vessel shut up in Toulon harbour."

My father, who had been briefly enticed by Capt. Sibille's proposition, was too intelligent not to appreciate Mme. Barairon's reasoning. "Well then," he asked me, "Do you want to come to Italy with me and serve in the army?" I put my arms round him and accepted, with a joy which my mother shared, for she had not been in favour of my father's first idea.

As, at that time, there was no military academy, and one could join the army only as a private soldier, my father took me right away to the municipality of the first arrondissment, in the Place

29

Beauvau, and had me enlisted in the 1st Hussars, (formerly the Bercheny), who were part of the division which he was going to command in Italy. It was September the 3rd, 1799.

My father took me to a tailor, who had the job of making official army uniforms, and ordered for me a complete outfit for a Hussar of the 1st. As well as all the arms and equipment.

There I was!....A soldier!......And was I not happy? But my happiness was somewhat lessened when I reflected that this was going to upset my brother Adolphe, two years older than me, and still stuck in college. I then had the idea that I would not tell Adolphe about my enlistment without telling him, at the same time, that I wanted to spend with him the period which would have to pass before my departure. I then asked my father if he would allow me to be installed close to Adolphe, at Sainte-Barbe, until the day when we would take the road for Italy. My father understood the reason for my asking, and thought well of me for it. He took me, the next day to stay with a M. Lanneau.

Can you imagine my arrival at college?...It was a recreation period. All games stopped. All the pupils, big and small, surrounded me. They vied with each other to touch part of my equipment.... In short, the Hussar was a complete success!

The day of the departure arrived....I said farewell to my mother and my three brothers with the greatest sadness, in spite of the pleasure I felt on starting a military career.

Chapter 6
An Encounter with General Bonaparte

After my father had accepted a command in Italy, a division became vacant in the army of the Rhine, which he would have preferred; but an inescapable fate drew him towards the country where he would find his grave.

One of his compatriots, and a personal friend, M. Lachèze, whom I might call his evil genius, had for a long time been French consul at Leghorn and Genoa, where he had business interests. This wretched man, in order to lure my father to Italy, was forever painting the most exaggerated picture of the country's beauties, and pointing out the credit which might be gained by dealing successfully with the difficult situation in the army there, whereas there would be little opportunity to acquire distinction in the army of the Rhine, where all was well. My father was swayed by this specious reasoning, and believing that there was more merit in going to the more dangerous post, he persisted in his intention of going to Italy, in spite of the objections of my mother, who had a secret presentiment which made her wish for my father to go to the Rhine. This presentiment was not false. She never saw her husband again!

To his present aide-de-camp, Captain Gault, my father now added another officer, M. R★★★ who had come to him from his friend General Augereau. M. R★★★ had the rank of major. He was a member of a Maintenon family and had some ability and some education, which he very rarely employed; for in a stupid manner, which was then quite common, he swaggered about, forever cursing and swearing, and talking of running people through with his sabre. This bully-boy had only one virtue, very rare at this time: he was always turned out with the greatest elegance. My father, who had taken on M. R★★★ without knowing anything about him, now much regretted it; but he could not send him back without upsetting his old friend, Augereau. Although my father disliked him, he thought, perhaps rightly, that a general should make use of the military qualities of an officer, without worrying too much about his personal manners; but, as he did not care to have the company of M. R★★★ on a long journey, he had given him the job of taking his coaches and horses from Paris to Nice, having under his orders the old stud-groom, Spire, a highly responsible man, used to the management of stables. The stable was large: my father had fifteen horses, which with those of his aide-de-camp and of his chief-of-staff and his assistants, together with those for the wagons and so on, made up a fairly large group of which R★★★ was the leader.

They left a month before we did.

My father took in his coach the fatal M. Lachèze, Captain Gault and me. Colonel Ménard, the chief-of- staff, followed, with one of his assistants, in a post-chaise. A big rascal, my father's valet, went ahead as a courier. We travelled in uniform. I had a fine forage cap which pleased me so much that I wore it all the time, but, as I put my head out of the coach window frequently, because the coach made me travel-sick, it so happened that during the night, when my companions were asleep, the cap fell into the road. The coach, drawn by six vigourous horses, was going at top speed. I did not dare have it stopped and so I lost my cap. A bad omen! But I was to suffer far worse things in the terrible campaign which we were about to undertake. This incident upset me a good deal, but I said nothing about it for fear of being chaffed about the way the new soldier was looking after his kit.

My father stopped at Mâcon, at the house of an old friend. We spent twenty-four hours there and then continued our journey to Lyons. We were not more than a few leagues from there, and were changing horses at the post-house of Limonest, when we noticed that all the postilions had decorated their hats with tricolour ribbons, and that there were flags of the same colours hanging from all the windows. We asked the reason for this demonstration, and were told that General Bonaparte had just arrived in Lyons...!

My father, who was certain that Bonaparte was still in the depths of Egypt, treated this news as absurd, but he was taken aback when, having sent for the post master, who had just returned from Lyons, he was told, "I saw General Bonaparte, whom I know very well, because I served under his command in Italy. He is staying in some hotel in Lyon, and has with him his brother Louis, Generals Berthier, Lannes and Murat, as well as a great, number of officers, and a Mameluke."

This could hardly have been more positive; however the revolution had given rise to so many falsehoods, and factions had been so cunning in inventing stories which would serve their ends, that my father was still in doubt when we entered the suburbs of Lyon. All the houses were draped with flags. Fireworks were going off. The crowd filled the streets to the point of preventing our coach from moving. There was dancing in the public squares and the air rang with cries of "Vive Bonaparte. Saviour of the country!" It was evident that Bonaparte was indeed in Lyon. My father said, "I was well aware that he was to be sent for, but I did not think it would be so soon. The coup has been well organised, and there are great events to come. I feel sure that I was right to leave Paris. At least, in the army I can serve the country without taking part in a coup, which, however necessary, I find repugnant." Having said this, he fell into a deep reverie, which lasted for the long time it took us to work our way through the crowds to the hotel where our rooms had been prepared.

The nearer we got to the hotel, the thicker the crowd became, and when we reached the door we saw that it was hung about with Chinese lanterns and guarded by Grenadiers. It was here that General Bonaparte was staying, in rooms that had been booked a week before for my father.

Although quick-tempered, my father did not say a word when the hotelier, who had been compelled to obey the orders of the municipality, came with some embarrassment to make his excuses. The inn-keeper having added that he had arranged for our accommodation at another hotel....very good, though of second grade.... and run by one of his relatives, my father simply asked Capt. Gault to tell the postilion to take us there.

When we arrived, we were met by our courier, a lively fellow, who, heated by the long journey he had just made and the numerous drinks he had downed at each post-house had complained most loudly when he found that the rooms booked for his master had been given to General Bonaparte. The latter's aides-de-camp hearing this uproar and learning the cause, went to warn their master that General Marbot had been displaced to make room for him, and, at the same time, General Bonaparte saw through his open window my father's two coaches pull up at the door.

He had not been aware, until then, of the shabby way in which my father had been treated; and as General Marbot, recently commandant of Paris, and now a divisional commander in Italy was too important a man to be treated unceremoniously, and also as General Bonaparte had good reason to make himself popular with everybody, he ordered one of his officers to go down straight away and ask General Marbot to come, as a fellow soldier, and share his accommodation. Then, seeing the coaches leave before his aide-de-camp could speak to my father, Bonaparte went immediately, on foot, to offer his regrets in person.

The crowd which followed him set up a great noise of cheering, which, as it drew near our hotel, should have warned us, but we had heard so much since coming to the town that it did not occur to one of us to look out of the window. We were all in the drawing-room where my father was striding up and down, deep in thought, when the valet-de-chambre, opening the double doors, announced, "The General Bonaparte."

On entering, he hurried to embrace my father, who received him very politely, but coolly. They had known each other for a long time.

The explanations about the lodgings could be disposed of in a few words between two such people, and so they were. They had much else to talk about; so they went alone into the bedroom, where they remained in conference for more than an hour.

During this time, the officers who had come with General Bonaparte chatted with us in the drawing-room. I never tired of examining their martial appearance, their sun-bronzed faces, their strange uniforms and their Turkish sabres, hung from cords. I listened with interest to their stories of the campaign in Egypt, and the battles which were fought there. I took pleasure in hearing them talk of such celebrated places as the Pyramids, the Nile, Cairo, Alexandria, Acre, the desert and so on. What delighted me most, however, was the sight of the young Mameluke, Rustum. He had stayed in the ante-chamber, where I went several times to admire his costume, which he showed me willingly. He already spoke reasonable French, and I never wearied of asking him questions.

General Lannes recalled having let me fire his pistols, when, in 1793, he was serving under my father in the camp at Miral. He was very friendly toward me, and neither of us then foresaw that one day I should be his aide-de-camp, and that he would die in my arms at Essling. General Murat came from the same region as we did, and as he had been a shop-assistant to a silk merchant at Saint-Céré during the period when my family spent the winter there, he had often come to the house, bringing purchases to my mother. My father, also, had rendered him a number of services, for which he was always grateful. He gave me a hug, and reminded me that he had often held me in his arms, when I was an infant.

General Bonaparte and my father having come back into the room, they presented to one another the members of their suites. Generals Lannes and Murat were old acquaintances of my father, who welcomed them with great affability. He was a little distant with General Berthier, whom, however he had seen before, when he was in the bodyguard and Berthier was an engineer.

General Bonaparte, who knew my mother, asked me, very politely, for news of her. He complimented me most warmly on having, while yet so young, taken up a military career, and taking me gently by the ear, which was always the most flattering caress which he bestowed on those with whom he was pleased, he said to my father, "One day this will be a second General Marbot." This prediction came true, although at that time I had no expectation of it. However I was very proud of these words. It takes so very little to make a child feel pleased with himself.

When the visit was over, my father disclosed nothing of what had been said between him and General Bonaparte; but I learned later that Bonaparte, without stating his objectives clearly, had sought, by the most adroit cajolements, to win my father over to his side, and that, my father had always dodged the issue.

Disgusted at seeing the people of Lyon running in front of Bonaparte, as if he was already the sovereign of France, my father declared that he wanted to leave at dawn the next day; but as his coaches needed some repairs, he was forced to spend an entire day at Lyon. I profited from this to have a new forage cap made, and, enchanted with this purchase, I took no notice of the political conversations, about which, to tell the truth, I understood little.

My father went to return the visit he had received from General Bonaparte. They walked alone for a very long time in the hotel's little garden, while their suites remained respectfully at a distance. We saw them sometimes gesture with warmth, and at other times speak more calmly; then Bonaparte, with a wheedling look, went up to my father and put his arm through his in a friendly fashion, probably so that the officials who were in the courtyard and the many spectators who hung out of neighbouring windows might conclude that General Marbot agreed with the plans of General Bonaparte; for this crafty man neglected nothing to achieve his aims.

My father came away from this second conversation even more pensive than he had been after the first, and on coming back to the hotel, he ordered our departure for the next day. Unfortunately, the next day, General Bonaparte was to make an excursion round the town to inspect the heights suitable for fortification, and all the post-horses were reserved for him. I thought that at this blow my father would become angry, but he contented himself by saying, "There is the beginning of omnipotence." And told his staff to see if they could hire any horses, so keen was he to get away from the town and from the sights which offended him. No spare horses could be found. Then Col. Ménard, who was born in the Midi, and knew the district perfectly, observed that the road from Lyon to Avignon was in such a poor state of repair that the coaches might be badly damaged if they attempted it, and it would be better to embark them on the Rhône, the descent of which would offer us an enchanting spectacle. My father, who was no great lover of the picturesque, would, at any other time, have rejected this advice, but as it gave him the opportunity to leave the town a day earlier, he agreed to take to the Rhône.

Col. Ménard then hired a large boat, the coaches were put on board, and the next day, early in the morning, we all embarked: a decision which was very nearly the end of us.

It was autumn. The water was very low. All the time the boat touched and scraped along the bottom. One feared that it might be torn open. We slept the first night at Saint-Péray, next at Tain, and took two days to get as far down as the junction with the Drôme. There we had much more water, and went along rapidly; but a

36

dangerous high wind called the Mistral hit us when we were about a quarter league above the bridge known as Pont Saint-Esprit. The boatmen were unable to reach the bank. They lost their heads, and set themselves to praying instead of working, while a furious wind and a strong current were driving the boat towards the bridge! We were about to crash against the pier of the bridge and be sunk, when my father and all of us, taking up boat-hooks, hurried forward to fend off from the pier which we were about to strike.

The shock was so severe that it knocked us into the thwarts, but the push had changed the direction of the boat, which, by a miraculous piece of good fortune, shot through under the arch. The boatmen then recovered a little from their terror and resumed some sort of control of their boat; but the Mistral continued, and the two coaches offering a resistance to the wind made any manoeuvre almost impossible. At last, six leagues above Avignon, we went aground on a very large island, where the bow of the boat dug into the sand in such a way that it would not be possible to get it out without a gang of labourers, and we were listing over so far that we feared being swamped at any moment. We put some planks between the boat and the shore and, with the help of some rope, we all got ashore without accident, though with some difficulty.

There could be no thought of re-embarking in the very high wind, (although without rain), and so we pushed on into the interior of the island, which we thought at first was uninhabited; but eventually we came across a sort of farm, where we found some good folk who made us very welcome. We were dying of hunger, but it was impossible to go back to the boat for food, and all we had was a little bread.

We were told that the island was full of poultry, which was allowed to run wild, and which the peasants shot, when they wanted some. My father was very fond of shooting, and he needed some relaxation from his problems, so we borrowed guns from the peasants, some pitch-forks and sticks, and we set off on a hen shoot. We shot several, though it was not easy to hit them as they flew like pheasants. We also picked up many of their eggs in the woods. When we returned to the farm, we lit a big fire in the middle of a field, around which we set up a bivouac, while the valet, helped by the farmer, prepared the eggs and the chickens in a variety of ways.

We supped well and then bedded down on some hay, no one daring to accept the beds which the good peasants offered us, as they seemed to us to be far from clean.

By day-break the wind had dropped, so all the peasants and the boatmen took spades and picks, and after several hours of hard work they got the boat afloat, enabling us to continue our journey towards Avignon, which we reached without any further accidents. Those that had befallen us were so embroidered in the telling, that the rumour reached Paris that my father and all his staff had been drowned.

The approach to Avignon, particularly when one comes down the Rhône, is very picturesque. The old Papal Château; the ramparts by which the city is surrounded; its numerous steeples and the Château de Villeneuve rising opposite, combine to make a fine prospect. At Avignon we met Mme. Ménard and one of her nieces, and we spent three days in the town, visiting the charming outskirts, including the fountain of Vaucluse. My father was in no hurry to leave, because M. R*** had written to say that the very hot weather, still persisting in the Midi, had forced him to slow the pace of his march and my father did not wish to arrive before his horses.

From Avignon we headed for Aix, but when we reached Bompart, on the banks of the Durance, which, at that time, was crossed by a ferry, we found the river so swollen by flood, that it would not be possible to cross for at least five or six hours. We were debating whether to return to Avignon, when the operator of the ferry, a gentlemanly sort of person, who owned a charming little castle on the height some five hundred paces from the river bank, came and begged my father to rest there until the coaches could be embarked. He accepted, hoping that it would be for a few hours only; but it appeared that there had been heavy storms in the Alps, where the Durance has its source, for the river continued to rise all day, and we were compelled to accept lodging for the night, which was offered most cordially by the owner of the castle. The weather being fine we spent the day walking. It was a break in our travels which I enjoyed.

The next day, seeing that the flood-water was running even more rapidly than the evening before, our host, who was a devout Republican, and who knew the river well enough to judge that we would not be able to cross for twenty-four hours, hurried off, unknown to us, to the little town of Cavaillon, which is about two leagues from Bompart, on the same bank of the river. He had gone to inform all the "Patriots" of the locality that he had in his house divisional General Marbot. He then returned to the castle, where, an hour or so later, we saw the arrival of a cavalcade composed of the keenest "Patriots" of Cavaillon, who had come to beg my father to accept an invitation to a banquet, which they offered him in the name of all the notables of the town, "Always so staunchly Republican."

My father, who found these sort of occasions far from agreeable, at first refused; but these "Citoyens" were so insistent, saying that everything had been organised and that the guests had gathered, that my father gave in and went off to Cavaillon.

The best hotel had been decked with garlands, and was graced by the presence of the local dignitaries from the town and its outskirts. After an interminable number of compliments, we took our places at a table laden with the most exclusive dishes. Above all, there were ortolans, birds which thrive well in this part of the country.

A great many toasts were drunk. Virulent speeches were made, denouncing the "Enemies of liberty" and the dinner did not end until ten o'clock in the evening. It was a little late to return to Bompart, and anyway, my father could not with politeness leave his hosts the moment the meal was over. He decided then to spend the night at Cavaillon, and the rest of the evening was passed in rather noisy talk. Eventually, one by one, the guests went home and we were left alone.

The next morning, M. Gault asked the inn-keeper how much my father owed for his part in the immense feast of the night before, which he assumed was a communal meal in which each paid for his own share. The inn-keeper presented him with a bill of more than 1500 francs. The good "Patriots" not having paid a single sou!...We were told that though some had expressed a wish to pay, the great majority had replied that this would be "An insult to General Marbot"....!

Capt. Gault was furious at this procedure, but my father, who at first could not get over his astonishment, burst into laughter, and told the inn-keeper to go and collect the money at Bompart, to where we returned straight away, without saying a word of this to the chatelaine; whose servants we tipped handsomely, and then, taking advantage of the fall in the water level, we at last crossed the Durance and made our way to Aix.

Although I might not yet be of an age to discuss politics with my father, what I had heard him say led me to believe that his Republican ideas had been much modified over the preceding two years, and what he had experienced as a supposed guest of honour at Cavaillon had severely shaken them, but he did not display any ill-feeling on the subject of this banquet, and was even amused at the anger of M. Gault, who said repeatedly, "I am not surprised that, in spite of their cost, these scoundrels produced so many ortolans, and ordered so many bottles of good wine!"

After spending a night at Aix, we left for Nice. This was the last stage of our journey. While we were travelling through the mountain and the beautiful forest of Esterel, we encountered the Colonel of the 1st Hussars, who, escorted by an officer and several troopers, was taking some lame horses, returned by the army, back to the depot at Puy-en-Velay. This colonel was named M. Picart and had been given his command because of his administrative ability. He was sent frequently to the depot to arrange for the equipment of men and horses, which he then forwarded to the fighting units, where he appeared but rarely and did not stay for long.

When he saw Col. Picart, my father had the coach stopped and got out, and after presenting me to my colonel, he took him on one side, and asked him to name an intelligent and well educated non-commissioned officer who might be made my mentor. The Colonel named Sergeant Pertelay. My father made a note of the name, and we continued on our way to Nice; where we found M.R★★★ settled in an excellent hotel, with our coaches and horses in first-class order.

Chapter 7
I Almost Fight a Duel

The town of Nice was full of troops, among which was a squadron of the 1st Hussars, to which regiment I belonged. In the absence of its colonel, the regiment was commanded by a Major Muller. On learning that the divisional general had arrived, Muller came to see my father, and it was agreed between them that, after a few days rest, I should begin my service in the seventh company, commanded by Capt. Mathis.

Although my father was very good to me, I was so much in awe of him that I was very shy in his presence, a shyness which he thought was greater than was really the case; he said I should have been a girl, and often called me madamoiselle Marcellin, which annoyed me very much, especially now that I was a Hussar. It was to overcome this shyness, that my father wished me to serve in the ranks, and in any case, as I have already said, one could not join the army except as a private soldier. My father, it is true, could have attached me to his personal staff, since my regiment was part of his division, but, quite apart from the notion which I have described above, he wanted me to learn how to saddle and bridle my own horse and to look after my arms and equipment; also, he did not want his son to enjoy the least privilege, as this would have had a bad effect on the rest of the troops. It was already enough that I was to be allowed to join a squadron without undergoing a long and wearisome period of training at the depot. I passed several days with my father and his staff, travelling about the district round Nice, which was very beautiful, but the moment for my entry into the squadron having arrived, my father asked Major Muller to send him Sergeant Pertelay.

Now, there were two brothers of this name in the regiment, both of them sergeants, but having nothing else, physically or mentally in common, the elder being something of a scamp, while the younger was thoroughly respectable. It was this latter whom the colonel had intended to appoint as my mentor, but in the short time which he and my father had spent together, Col. Picart had forgotten, when naming Pertelay, to add the younger: furthermore, this Pertelay was not in the part of the squadron which was stationed in Nice, while the elder was in the very company, the seventh, which I was about to join.

Major Muller believed that the colonel had named the elder to my father and that this wild character had been chosen to open the eyes of an innocent and shy young man, which I then was. So he sent us the elder Pertelay.

This example of the old type of Hussar was a rowdy, quarrelsome, swashbuckling, tippler, but also brave to the point of foolhardiness; for the rest, he was completely ignorant of anything that was not connected with his horse, his arms and his duties in the face of the enemy. Pertelay the younger, on the other hand, was quiet, polite, and well-educated. He was a handsome man and just as brave as his brother, and would surely have gone far had he not, while still very young, been killed in action.

Now to return to the elder. He arrived at my father's quarters, and what did we see? A fine fellow, very well turned out it is true, but with his shako tipped over one ear, his sabre trailing on the ground, his red face slashed by an immense scar, moustaches six inches long, which, stiffened by wax, curled up into his ears, two big plaits of hair, braided from his temples, which, escaping from his shako, hung down to his chest, and with all this an air...! An air of rakishness which was increased by his speech, which was rattled out in a sort of Franco-Alsatian patois. This last did not surprise my father, as he knew that the 1st Hussars were the former regiment of Bercheny, which in earlier days recruited only Germans, and where, until 1793, all the orders were given in German, which was the language generally used by the officers and men, almost all of whom came from the provinces bordering the Rhine. My father was however exceedingly surprised by the style and manner of my proposed mentor.

I learned later that he had hesitated to put me in the hands of this bravo, but M. Gault having reminded him that Colonel Picart had described him as the best N.C.O. in the squadron, he decided to try it. So off I went with Pertelay, who, taking me by the arm without ceremony, came to my room, showed me how to pack my kit into my valise, and conducted me to a small barracks, situated in a former monastery, and now occupied by a squadron of the 1st Hussars.

My mentor made me saddle and unsaddle the pretty little horse which my father had bought me; then he showed me how to put on my cloak and my arms, giving me a complete demonstration, and having decided that he had explained to me all that was necessary, he thought it time to go for dinner. My father, who wished me to eat with my mentor, had given us extra money to meet the expense.

Pertelay took me to a small inn, which was crammed with Hussars, Grenadiers and soldiers of every sort. We were served with a meal, and on the table was placed an enormous bottle of red wine of the most violent nature. Pertelay poured me a glassful. We clinked glasses. My man emptied his and I raised mine without putting it to my lips, for I had never drunk undiluted wine and I found the smell of this liquid disagreeable. I admitted this to my mentor, who shouted, in a stentorian voice, "Waiter! Bring some lemonade for this boy who never drinks wine." A gale of laughter swept through the room. I was mortified, but I could not bring myself to taste this wine, and as I did not dare to ask for water, I dined without a drink.

A soldier's apprenticeship has always been hard going. It was particularly so at the time of which I write. I had, therefore, some unhappy experiences to suffer. A thing I found unbearable was the requirement to share my bed with another Hussar. The regulations allotted only one bed for two soldiers. N.C.O.s alone were allowed to have a bed each. On the first night which I spent in the barracks, I had already gone to my bed when a tall, ungainly Hussar, who arrived an hour after the others, approached it, and seeing that it was occupied, he unhooked a lantern and stuck it under my nose to examine me more closely. Then he got undressed. As I watched him, I had no idea that he intended to get in beside me; but I was soon disillusioned, when he said to me roughly, "Shove over, conscript!" And got into the bed, taking up three-quarters of it, and began to snore loudly. I was unable to sleep a wink, largely because of the revolting odour arising from a large package which my comrade had placed under the bolster, to raise his head. I could not think what this could be, so to find out, I slid my hand gently toward this object and found it to be a leather apron impregnated with cobbler's wax, which shoemakers use to treat their thread. My amiable bed companion was one of the men employed by the regimental bootmaker. I was so disgusted that I got up, got dressed, and went to the stables where I bedded down on a heap of straw. The next day I told Pertelay of my misadventure, and he reported it to the sub-lieutenant commanding the platoon. He was a well-educated man named Leisteinschneider (in German, a stone-worker) who was later killed in action. He understood how painful it must be for me to have to sleep with a bootmaker, and he took it on himself to arrange for me to have a bed in the N.C.O's room, something which pleased me greatly.

Although the revolution had produced a great relaxation in the general turn-out of troops, the 1st Hussars had kept theirs exactly as it was when they were Bercheny's Hussars; so except for the physical differences imposed by nature, all troopers had to resemble one another in their appearance, and as the regiments of Hussars of that period had not only pig-tails, but long plaited tresses which hung from their temples and turned-up moustaches, it was the rule that everyone belonging to the regiment must have moustache, pig-tail and tresses. Now, as I had none of these things, my mentor took me to the regimental wig-maker where I bought a false pig-tail and tresses, which were attached to my own hair, already fairly long, as I had let it grow since my enlistment. These embellishments embarrassed me at first but I got used to them in a few days, and it pleased me to imagine that they gave me the appearance of a seasoned trooper. It was a different matter when it came to the moustache I had no more of a moustache than a girl, and as a hairless face would have spoiled the ranks of the squadron, Pertelay, as was the custom of Bercheny, took a pot of black wax, and with his thumb he gave me an enormous curling moustache, which covered my upper lip and reached almost to, my eyes. The shakos of the time did not have a vizor, so that, when I was on guard duty, or during an inspection, when one has to remain perfectly still, the Italian sun, shining hotly onto my face, sucked the moisture out of the wax of which my moustache was made, and, as it dried it pulled at my skin in a most disagreeable manner. However, I did not blink. I was a Hussar! A word that had for me an almost magical significance; besides which, having engaged in a military career, I understood very well that my first duty was to obey the regulations.

My father and part of his division were still in Nice, when we heard of the events of the 18th Brumaire, the overthrow of the Directorate and the establishment of the Consulate. My father had too much contempt for the Directorate to regret its downfall, but he feared that, intoxicated by power, General Bonaparte, after re-establishing order in France, would not restrict himself to the modest title of consul, and he predicted to us that in a short time he would aim to become king. My father was mistaken only in the title, four years later Napoleon made himself emperor.

Whatever his misgivings about the future, my father congratulated himself on not having been in Paris on the 18th Brumaire, and I believe that had he been there he might well have opposed the actions of General Bonaparte, but in the army, at the head of a division facing the enemy, he was content to adopt the passive obedience of the soldier. He even rejected proposals, which were made to him by a number of generals and colonels, to march on Paris at the head of their troops. "Who," he said to them, "will defend our frontiers if we abandon them? And what will become of France if, to the war against foreigners, we add the calamity of civil strife?" By these wise observations he calmed down the hot-heads; but he was, nonetheless, very disturbed by the coup which had just taken place: he adored his country and would have greatly preferred that it could have been saved without being submitted to the yoke of a dictator.

I have said that my father's principle reason for making me enlist as a lowly Hussar had been to rid me of the simple notions of a schoolboy, which had not been changed by my short acquaintance with the world of Paris. The result exceeded his expectations, for living amongst swaggering Hussars, and having as a mentor a sort of brigand who laughed at my innocence, I began to howl with the wolves, and for fear that I might be mocked for my timidity, I became a real devil. This, however, was not enough for me to be accepted into a sort of brotherhood, which under the name of the clique, had members in all the squadrons the 1st Hussars.

The clique was made up of all the biggest rogues, but, at the same time, some of the bravest men in the regiment. The members of the clique supported one another against all opposition, particularly in the face of the enemy. They called themselves the Jokers, and recognised one another by a notch cut into the metal of the first button on the right hand row of the pelisse and dolman. The officers were aware of the existence of the clique, but as its worst crimes were limited to the adroit theft of chickens or sheep, or some trick played on the local inhabitants, and as the Jokers were always at the forefront in any action, they turned a blind eye. I was young and feckless, and I longed desperately to belong to this raffish society, which I thought would raise my standing amongst my comrades; but it was in vain that I frequented the salle-d'armes to practice swordsmanship and the use of the pistol and carbine, and that I dug my elbows into anyone who got in my way: allowed my sabre to trail on the ground and tipped my shako over one ear, the members of the clique regarded me as a child and refused to admit me to their society. However, an unforeseen event led to my being accepted unanimously.

The army of Italy was at this time in Liguria and spread out on a front of more than sixty miles in length, the right of which was in the Gulf of Spezzia, beyond Genoa, and the left at Nice and Var, that is to say on the frontier of France. We had, therefore, the sea at our backs, and we faced Piedmont, which was occupied by the Austrian army, from which we were separated by that branch of the Apennines which runs from Var to Gavi: a bad position, in which the army ran the risk of being cut in two, which, in fact, happened some months later.

My father, having been ordered to concentrate his division at Savona, a small town, by the sea, ten leagues towards France from Genoa, set up his headquarters in the bishop's palace. The infantry was spread out among the market towns and villages of the neighbourhood to keep watch on the valleys from which emerged the roads which led to Piedmont. The 1st Hussars, who had come from Nice to Savona, were encamped on a plain known as the Madona. The outposts of the enemy were at Dego, four or five leagues from us, on the forward slopes of the Apennines, whose summits were covered in snow, whereas Savona and its surroundings enjoyed the mildest of climates.

Our encampment would have been delightful if the rations had been more plentiful; but there was at that time no main road from Nice to Genoa; the sea was covered by English warships, so the army had to live on what could be brought by detachments of mules along the Corniche, or by small boat-loads, which could slip unnoticed along the coast. These precarious supplies were scarcely enough to provide, from day to day, sufficient food to support the troops; but, happily, the country produced plenty of wine, which enabled them to bear their privations with more resignation.

One fine day I was walking along the beach with my mentor when we came on a "taverna," where there was a charming garden planted with orange and lemon trees, under which were tables at which sat soldiers of all kinds. He suggested that we went there, and although I had never overcome my distaste for wine, I agreed, simply to please him.

In those days the cavalryman's belt did not have a hook, so that when we went on foot, it was necessary to hold up the scabbard of the sabre with one's left hand, and one could allow the end to trail on the ground. This made a noise on the pavement, and looked rather dashing, so of course I had to adopt this way of doing things. Thus it happened that as we went into this garden, the end of my scabbard came in contact with the foot of an enormous horse-gunner, who was sprawled on his chair with his legs sticking out. The horse artillery had been formed at the beginning of the revolutionary wars from men taken from the companies of Grenadiers, who took advantage of the occasion to get rid of their most troublesome characters. The men of the flying artillery, as it was then called, were known for their dash, but also for their love of quarreling.

The one whose foot the end of my scabbard had touched, shouted to me in a very rude tone of voice, "Hussar, your sabre drags too much!" I was going to walk on without saying any thing, when master Pertelay, nudging me with his elbow, whispered, "Tell him to come and lift it up." So I said to the gunner "Come and lift it up then!" "That will be easy!" he replied. Then, at another whisper from Pertelay, "I'd like to see you do it!" I said. On these words, the gunner, or this Goliath, for he was at least six feet tall, sat up straight with a threatening air... But my mentor pushed himself between him and me. All the gunners who were in the garden came to support their comrade, but a crowd of Hussars gathered beside Pertelay and me. There was a lot of angry shouting with everyone talking at once; I thought there was going to be a general melée. However as the Hussars were in a majority of at least two to one, they took the matter the more calmly, while the gunners realised that if they started something they would get the worst of it, so in the end the giant was made to understand that in brushing his foot with my scabbard, I had in no way insulted him, and that should be the end of the matter.

During the tumult, however, a trumpeter from the artillery, of about twenty years of age, had offered me some insults, and in my indignation I had pushed him so roughly that he had fallen into a muddy ditch. It was agreed that this lad and I should fight a duel with our sabres.

We left the garden, followed by all the assistants, and found ourselves by the edge of the sea, on fine solid sand, ready for battle. Pertelay knew that I was quite a good swordsman; however he gave me some words of advice on how I should attack my adversary, and fastened the hilt of my sabre to my hand with a large handkerchief, which he rolled round my arm.

My father hated duelling. Not only because of his own conclusions about this barbarous custom, but also, I believe, because in his youth, when he was a member of the bodyguard, he had acted as second for a comrade of whom he was very fond, and who was killed in a duel over the most trivial matter. However that may be, when my father took command, he ordered the police to arrest anyone caught engaging in swordplay and bring them before him.

Although the trumpeter and I both knew of this order, we had, nevertheless, taken off our dolmans and taken up our sabres. I had my back to the town of Savona, my adversary was facing it, and we were about to begin our combat when I saw the trumpeter duck to one side, pick up his dolman and make off at top speed.

"Coward!....Runaway!" I shouted, and was about to, pursue him when two iron hands grasped me by the collar. I turned my head and found myself facing some eight to ten police! I understood then why my antagonist had cleared off, followed by all the assistants, including master Pertelay, whom I saw disappearing into the distance, as fast as their legs could carry them, for fear of being arrested and brought before the General.

There I was! Disarmed and a prisoner! I picked up my dolman, and looking very sheepish, followed my captors, to whom I had not given my name, as they led me to the Bishop's palace where my father was installed. He was at that moment with General Suchet, who had come to Savona to confer with him on service matters. They were walking in a gallery which overlooked the courtyard. The police put me up before General Marbot, without any idea that I was his son. The sergeant explained why I had been arrested. Then my father, looking very severe, gave me a lively dressing down, after which admonition, he said to the sergeant, "Take this Hussar to the citadel." I left without saying a word, and without General Suchet, who did not know me, suspecting that the scene he had just witnessed had taken place between a father and his son. It was not until the next day that he learned the truth, and he has often spoken to me since, with laughter, about the episode.

On my arrival at the citadel, an ancient Genoese building situated near the harbour, I was locked into a big room lit by a high window, which faced toward the sea. I recovered slowly from my fright. The reprimand which I had received seemed to me to be deserved; however I was less concerned at having disobeyed the General than I was at having upset my father. I passed the rest of the day sadly enough.

In the evening, an old ex-soldier of the Genoan force brought me a jug of water, a piece of ration bread, and a bale of straw, on which I lay down, without being able to eat. I could not go to sleep; at first because I was too upset, and later because of the arrival of some large rats, which ran about me and soon made off with my piece of bread. I was lying in the dark, a prey to my sad reflections, when, at about ten o'clock, I heard the bolts of my prison being drawn and I saw Spire, my father's old and faithful servant. He told me that after my despatch to the citadel, Capt. Gault, Col. Ménard, and all my father's officers had asked him to pardon me. The General had agreed, and had sent him, Spire, to find me and take the order for my release to the governor of the fort. I was taken before the governor, General Buget, an excellent man, who had lost an arm in battle. He knew me and was very fond of my father. He felt it his duty, after giving me back my sabre, to give me a long lecture, to which I listened patiently, but which made me reflect that I would get a much worse telling-off from my father. I did not have the courage to face this and decided to evade it, if that were possible. At last we were let out of the gates of the citadel. The night was dark, and Spire went in front with a lantern. As we walked through the narrow twisting streets, the good fellow, delighted to be bringing me back, recounted all the comforts which would await me at headquarters. "But," he said, "you must expect a severe ticking-off from your father." This last remark put an end to my doubts, and in order to let my father's anger cool off, I decided it would be better not to appear before him for a few days and that I would return to my bivouac at Madona. I could easily have slipped away without playing any trick on poor Spire; but fearing that he might be able to pursue me by the light of his lantern, I gave it a kick which sent it flying ten paces from him, and ran off while the good man, groping for his lantern, shouted, "Ah...! You little blighter! I shall tell your father!"

After wandering for some time in the deserted streets, I found at last the road to Madona, and made my way to the regimental camp. All the Hussars thought I was in prison. As soon as one of them recognised me by the light of the fires, I was surrounded and questioned. There was much laughter when I described how I had got away from Spire. The members of the clique were so satisfied with my behaviour that they decided unanimously to admit me into their society, which was preparing an expedition to go, that very night, to the gates of Dego and steal a herd of cattle which belonged to the Austrian army. The French Generals and even the corps commanders were obliged to ignore these raids, which, in the absence of regular rations, the soldiers carried out beyond the advance posts in order to obtain food. In each regiment the boldest soldiers had formed marauding bands who were marvellously skilled at finding out where supplies were being assembled for the enemy, and using ruse and audacity to lay hands on them.

A rascally horse-dealer had told the clique that a herd of cattle which he had sold to the Austrians was in a meadow a quarter of a league from Dego, and now sixty Hussars, armed only with their carbines, were on their way to capture it. Avoiding the main road, we went several leagues into the mountain by winding and atrociously rough tracks. We surprised five Croats, who had been left to guard the herd, asleep in a shed. To prevent them from going to waken the garrison at Dego, we tied them up and left them there. We drove away the herd without a shot being fired and returned to the camp, tired out, but delighted to have played such a successful trick on the enemy, and at the same time acquired some food.

This event illustrates the already wretched condition of the army of Italy, and demonstrates to what a state of disorganisation such neglect will bring troops; whose officers are obliged not only to tolerate these sort of expeditions, but to take advantage of the supplies they procure without seeming to know whence they come.

Chapter 8
Sergeant Marbot, 1st Hussars

Happy in my military career, I had not even reached the rank of corporal when I was raised immediately to that of sergeant. This is how it came about.

On the left of my father's division was that commanded by General Séras, whose headquarters were at Finale. This division, which occupied the part of Liguria where the mountains are steepest, was composed solely of infantry, the cavalry being unable to operate, except in small detachments, on the few open spaces which at this point separate the shore of the Mediterranean from the mountains of Piedmont. General Séras, having been ordered to push forward with the greater part of his division to reconnoitre the area of Mount Santa-Giacomo, beyond which there were several valleys, wrote to my father requesting the loan of a detachment of fifty Hussars for this expedition; a request which could not be turned down. So my father agreed and named Lt. Leisteinschneider as commander of this detachment, of which my platoon was a part.

We left Madona to make our way to Finale. There was, at that time, only a very bad road along the sea coast, known as the Corniche. The lieutenant badly injured his foot as a result of a fall from his horse, and so the command passed to the next in seniority who was a sergeant named Canon, a handsome young man, capable and well-trained, and full of self-assurance.

General Séras, at the head of his division, advanced next day onto the snow-clad slopes of Mount Santa-Giacomo, where we encamped. He had intended to go forward the next day, with he almost certain expectation of making contact with the enemy; but in how great a number? On this subject the General had absolutely no information, and as his orders from the commander-in-chief were to reconnoitre the Austrian positions at this point of the line, but not to engage in combat if he found the enemy in strength, General Séras reflected that if he advanced his infantry division into the middle of the mountains, where often one could not see enemy troops until one found oneself face to face with them at a bend in a gorge, he might be led, in spite of his wishes, into a major battle against superior forces, and obliged to carry out a dangerous retreat.

He decided therefore to proceed with caution, and to push out, three or four leagues in front of him, an advance party which could probe the country and, most importantly, take some prisoners, from whom he hoped to get some information; for the peasantry either knew nothing or would not talk. As a small body of infantry would be endangered if he advanced them too far, and as, also, men on foot would take too long to return with the information which he so urgently needed, it was to the fifty Hussars that he gave the task of going ahead and exploring the terrain. Then, as the country was very broken, he gave a map to our sergeant, briefed him, in front of the detachment and sent us off, two hours before daylight, repeating that it was essential that we went ahead until we made contact with the enemy outposts, from which he would very much like us to capture a few prisoners.

Sergeant Canon managed his detachment according to the book. He sent out a small advance-guard, put scouts on the flanks and took all the precautions usual in partisan warfare. When we had gone some two leagues from the camp, we came on a large inn. Our sergeant questioned the inn-keeper and was told that, a good hour's march away, was a body of Austrian troops, the size of which he did not know, though he knew that the leading regiment contained some very unpleasant Hussars, who had maltreated a number of the local inhabitants.

Having gathered this information, we set off once more, but hardly had we gone a hundred paces, when Sergeant Canon, writhing on his horse, declared that he had the most dreadful pain and could not go any further. He handed the command to Sergeant Pertelay, who was next in seniority. Pertelay, however pointed out that he was an Alsatian and was unable to read French, and could not, in consequence, understand the map or the written instructions given by the general. He did not wish to accept the command. All the other sergeants, old Bercheny Hussars, refused for the same reason, as did the corporals. In vain, as a matter of duty,

I offered to read the general's instructions and explain our route on the map for any of the sergeants who would take over; they all refused anew; then, to my great surprise, these old sweats turned to me and said "Take command yourself. We'll follow you and obey all your orders."

The rest of the party expressed the same wish, and it was clear that if I refused, we would go no further and the honour of the regiment would be blemished; for it was essential that the general's orders were carried out, above all when it was perhaps a matter of avoiding a disaster for his division. So I accepted the command, but not without asking Sergeant Canon if he felt able to continue. At which point he began to complain once more, left us and returned to the inn. I promise you I thought he was really ill, but the men of the detachment, who knew him better, made some very disparaging remarks about him.

I think I can say, without boasting, that nature has endowed me with a good stock of courage. I might even add that there was a time when I enjoyed facing danger. My military record and the thirteen wounds I have received in the wars are, I believe, sufficient proof. So, on taking command of fifty men, placed under my orders in such extraordinary circumstances, -- me, a simple Hussar, seventeen years of age -- I resolved to prove to my comrades that if I had neither experience nor military talent, I was at least brave; and placing myself resolutely at their head I set off in the direction where I knew we would encounter the enemy.

We had been marching for a long time when our scouts spotted a peasant who was trying to hide. They hastened to capture him and bring him back. I questioned him. He came, it seemed, from four or five leagues away, and claimed that he had not seen any Austrian troops. I was sure he was lying, either from fear or from cunning, because we were very close to the enemy cantonments. I remembered then that I had read in a book about partisan warfare, which my father had given me to study, that to persuade the inhabitants of a country in which one is fighting to talk, it is sometimes necessary to frighten them. So I roughened my voice, and, trying to give my boyish face a ferocious look, I shouted, "What! You rascal! You have been wandering about in a country occupied by a great body of Austrian troops, and you claim you have seen nothing? You are a spy! Come on lads, let's shoot him right away."

I ordered four Hussars to dismount, indicating to them not to harm the fellow, who, finding himself held by the troopers whose carbines had just been loaded in front of him, was overcome by such terror that he swore that he would tell me all he knew. He was a servant in a monastery, who had been given a letter to take to relatives of the Prior, and he had been told that if he ran into the French, he was not to tell them where the Austrians were; but now that he was forced to speak, he told us that a league from us there were several regiments of the enemy billeted in the villages, and that about a hundred of Barco's Hussars were in a hamlet which was only a short distance away. Questioned about the defensive precautions taken by these Hussars, he said that before one reached the houses, they had posted a picket-guard which was in a garden surrounded by hedges, and that when he went through the hamlet, the remainder were preparing to water their horses at a little pond on the far side of the buildings.

Having received this information, I had now to make a plan of action. I wished to avoid passing the picket-guard who, being entrenched behind hedges, could not be attacked by cavalry, while the fire from their carbines would perhaps kill several of my men and give warning of our approach. To do this required that we go round the hamlet, so as to reach the pond, and fall, unexpectedly, on our enemies. But how were we to pass without being seen? I then ordered the peasant to lead us on a detour, and promised to set him free as soon as we reached the other side of the hamlet, which we could see: when he refused to do so, I had him taken by the scruff of the neck by one Hussar while another held a pistol to his ear, which made him change his mind. He guided us very well; some large hedges hid our movements, and we got completely round the village to see, at the edge of a small pond, the Austrian squadron peacefully watering their horses. All the riders were carrying their arms, which is the usual practice for outposts, but those in command had neglected a precaution which is essential in war, that is, to allow only one troop at a time to unbridle their horses and enter the water, while the remainder stay on the bank ready to repel any attack. Confident that there were no French about and relying on the watchfulness of the guard posted at the entry to the village, the enemy commander had thought this precaution unnecessary. This was to be his downfall.

When I was some five hundred paces from the pond, I ordered the peasant to be released, who ran off as fast as his legs could carry him; then, sabre in hand, and having forbidden my comrades to utter any war-cry, I advanced at full gallop on the enemy Hussars, who did not see us until a moment before we arrived at the pond. The pond's banks were too high for the horses to climb out, and there was only one practicable way in, which was the one that served as the village drinking place. It is true that this was a wide area, but there were more than a hundred horsemen crowded together there, all with their bridles in their hands and their carbines slung, so unconcerned that some of them were singing. You may imagine their surprise!

I attacked them immediately with carbine fire, which killed several, wounded many and knocked out a lot of their horses. The confusion was total! Nevertheless, their captain, rallying some men who were nearest to the outlet, tried to force a passage to get out of the water, and opened fire on us, which although not sustained, wounded two of my men; they then engaged us, but Pertelay having killed the captain with a blow from his sabre, the rest crowded back into the pond. To escape from the carbine fire, many tried to reach the other bank; several lost their footing and a good number of men and horses were floundering in the water. Those who reached the other side found that their horses could not clamber up the steep edge and so they abandoned them, and pulling themselves up by the aid of trees growing along the bank, they fled in disorder into the countryside.

The twelve men of the picket-guard came running at the sound of firing. We attacked them with the sabre and they also took to flight. However there remained about thirty men still in the pond, afraid to try to escape because we occupied the only way out. They shouted to us that they were surrendering; I accepted this and as they came to the bank, made them throw down their arms. Most of these men and horses were wounded, but as I wished to have some trophy from our victory, I chose seventeen horses and riders who were fit, and placing them in the middle of the detachment, I abandoned the rest and went off at the gallop, going round the village, as before.

It was just as well that I made a rapid retreat, for as I had foreseen, the fugitives had run to warn the nearby troops who had already been alerted by the sound of gunfire, and within half an hour there were five hundred horsemen on the banks of the little pond and some thousands of infantrymen close behind them. We, however, were two leagues away, our wounded having been able to sustain a full gallop. We stopped for a short time on top of a hill to bandage their wounds, and we laughed to see in the distance several enemy columns following our trail, since we knew that they had no hope of catching us, because in their fear of falling into an ambush they were feeling their way forward very slowly. Being now out of danger, I gave Pertelay two of the best-mounted troopers and sent him off post-haste to inform general Séras of the success of our mission; then marshalling the detachment into good order, with our prisoners in the centre and well guarded, I set off at a slow trot down the road to the inn.

It would be impossible for me to describe the joy of my companions and the praises which they heaped on me during this journey. It could be summed up in these words, which in their minds was the highest commendation, "You are truly worthy to serve in Bercheny's Hussars, the finest regiment in the world."

Meanwhile, what had been happening at Santo-Giacomo during my absence? After several hours of waiting, General Séras, impatient for news, saw some smoke on the horizon; his aide-de-camp put his ear to a drum placed on the ground, a common expedient in wartime, and heard the distant sound of gunfire. General Séras was uneasy, and having no doubt that the cavalry detachment was at grips with the enemy, he took a regiment of infantry with him as far as the inn. When he arrived there, he saw, under the cart-shelter, a Hussar's horse tied up to the rail; it was Sergeant Canon's. The inn-keeper appeared and was questioned. He replied that the sergeant of Hussars had gone no further than the inn, and had been, for several hours, in the dining room. The General went in, and what did he find but Sergeant Canon asleep by the fireside with, in front of him, an enormous ham, two empty bottles and a coffee cup! The wretched sergeant was woken up; he attempted once more to make the excuse of a sudden indisposition, but the accusing remains of the formidable meal which he had just eaten, gave the lie to his claims of illness, so General Séras was very short with him. The General's anger was increasing at the thought that a detachment of fifty cavalrymen handed over to the command of a young soldier had probably been wiped out by the enemy, when Pertelay and the two troopers who were with him arrived at the gallop to announce our victory and the approaching arrival of seventeen prisoners. As General Séras, in spite of this happy outcome, continued to berate Sergeant Canon, Pertelay said to him, in his bluff outspoken way, "Don't scold him, mon General, he's such a coward that if he'd been in charge we wouldn't have succeeded!" A remark which did nothing to improve the awkward position of Sgt. Canon, who was now placed under arrest.

I arrived in the midst of these goings-on. General Séras broke poor Sgt. Canon, and made him take off his chevrons in front of a regiment of infantry and fifty Hussars. Then, coming to me, whose name he did not know, he said, "You have carried out successfully a mission which would normally be given only to an officer. I am sorry that the powers of a divisional commander do not allow me to promote you to sous-lieutenant, only the commander-in-chief can do that, and I shall ask him to do so, but in the meantime I promote you to sergeant." He thereupon ordered his aide-de-camp to announce this in front of the detachment. In order to carry out this formality, the aide-de-camp had to ask my name, and it was only then that General Séras learned that I was the son of his comrade, General Marbot. I was very pleased about this, because it demonstrated to my father that favouritism had nothing to do with my promotion.

Chapter 9
Against the Austrians in Piedmont

The information which General Séras obtained from the prisoners having decided him to push forward, he ordered his division to come down from the heights of Mont Santa-Giacomo, and to encamp that evening near to the inn. The prisoners were sent to Finale, and as for the horses they belonged by rights to the Hussars. They were all of good quality, but, according to the custom of the time, which was aimed at favouring poorly mounted officers, captured horses were always sold for five louis. This was a fixed price and was paid in cash. As soon as the camp was established the sale began. General Séras, the officers of his staff, the colonels and battalion commanders of the regiments in his division soon took up our seventeen horses, which produced the sum of 85 louis. This was handed over to my detachment, who, not having had any pay for six months, were delighted with this windfall, for which they gave me the credit.

I had some money, so I did not pocket my share from the sale of the horses, but to celebrate my promotion, I bought from the inn-keeper two sheep, an enormous cheese and a load of wine, with which my detachment had a feast. This was one of the happiest days of my life.

General Séras, in his report to General Championet included a most flattering reference to my conduct, and said the same sort of thing to my father; so when, several days later, I brought the detachment back to Savona, my father welcomed me with the greatest show of affection. I was highly delighted; I rejoined the camp where all the regiment was united; my detachment had arrived there before me and had told of what we had done, giving me always the leading part in our success, so I was heartily welcomed by the officers and soldiers and also by my new comrades, the non-commissioned officers, who handed me my sergeant's stripes.

It was on this day that I met the younger Pertelay for the first time, he had come back from Genoa, where he had been stationed for some months. I became friendly with this excellent man, and regretted not having had him as my mentor at the beginning of my career, for he gave me much good advice, which steadied me up and made me break away from the wild men of the clique.

The commander-in-chief, Championet, intended to carry out some operations in the interior of Piedmont, but having very little in the way of cavalry, he ordered my father to send him the 1st Hussars, who could no longer stay at Madon, in any case, because of the shortage of fodder. I parted from my father with much regret and left with the regiment.

We went along the Corniche as far as Albenga. We crossed the Apennines, in spite of the snow, and entered the fertile plains of Piedmont. The commander-in-chief fought a number of actions in the area round Fossano, Novi and Mondovi, some of which were successful and others not.

In one of these actions I had the opportunity of seeing Brigadier-general Macard, a soldier of fortune whom the revolutionary upheavals had carried almost straight from the rank of trumpet-major to that of general! He was a good example of a type of officer created by luck and their personal courage who, although displaying much bravery before the enemy, were nevertheless incapable of occupying effectively a senior position because of their lack of education.

This extraordinary character, a veritable colossus, was well known for one peculiarity. When about to lead his troops in a charge against the enemy, it was his custom to shout "Let's go! I'll put on my animal dress." Then he took off his uniform, his jacket and shirt and retained only his plumed hat, his leather breeches and his big boots! Thus, naked to the waist, he displayed a torso almost as hairy as that of a bear, which gave him a very strange appearance indeed. Once in his animal dress, as he called it, General Macard, sabre in hand, hurled himself at the enemy horsemen, swearing like a pagan; but it so happened that he rarely reached any of them, for at the unexpected and terrible sight of this kind of giant, half naked and covered in hair rushing toward them uttering the most fearsome yells the enemy often fled in all directions, not knowing if they had to deal with a man or some extraordinary wild beast.

General Macard was entirely ignorant, which sometimes amused the more educated officers under his command. One day one of them came to ask permission to go into a neighbouring town to order a pair of boots. "Parbleu!" said the general, "This has come at just the right time; since you are going to the bootmaker, sit down and take the measurements of my boots and order a new pair for me." The officer, much surprised, said that he could not take the measurements as he had no idea how to do this, having never been a boot-maker. "What!" exclaimed the general loudly, "I see you sometimes spend whole days sketching and drawing lines opposite the mountains and when I ask what you are doing, you say you are measuring the mountains. How is it that you can measure objects which are more than a league away, and yet you cannot measure a pair of boots which are under your nose? Come on, take the measurements quickly and no more nonsense." The officer assured him that this was impossible. The general insisted; swore; got angry; and it was only with great difficulty that other officers, attracted by the noise, were able to put an end to this ridiculous scene. The general could never understand how a man who could measure mountains could not measure a pair of men's boots.

You should not think, as a result of this anecdote, that all the general officers in the army of Italy were like the good general Macard. Far from that, they contained in their number many men distinguished by their education and manners; but at this time there were still some senior officers who were completely out of place in the higher ranks of the army. They were being weeded out little by little.

The 1st Hussars took part in all the battles fought at this time in Piedmont, and suffered many losses in encounters with the Austrian heavy cavalry. After some marching and countermarching, and a series of almost daily minor engagements, General Championet, having concentrated the centre and left of his army between Coni and Mondovi, attacked, at the end of December, several divisions of the enemy army.

The encounter took place on a plain dotted with small hills and clumps of trees. The 1st Hussars, attached to General Beaumont's brigade, were positioned on the extreme right of the French army. As the number of officers and men who make up a squadron is laid down in the regulations, our regiment, having suffered casualties in the previous affairs, instead of putting four squadrons into the line could put only three; but having done this, there were some thirty men left over, of which five were sergeants. I was one of this number, as were both the Pertelays. We were formed into two sections and Pertelay the younger was put in command. General Beaumont merely instructed him to scout on the right flank of the army, and act as the situation seemed to require. We then left the regiment and went to explore the countryside.

In the meanwhile, a fierce battle commenced between the two armies, and an hour later, when we were returning to our own lines without having spotted anything on the flank, young Pertelay saw, opposite us, and consequently on the extreme left of the enemy line, a battery of eight guns whose fire was raking the French ranks. Very unwisely, this Austrian battery, in order to have a better field of fire, had advanced onto a small hillock some seven or eight hundred paces in front of the infantry division to which it belonged. The commander of this artillery believed that he was quite safe because the position he occupied dominated the whole French line, and he thought that if any troops set out to attack him, he would see them and would have time to regain the safety of the Austrian lines. He had not considered that a little clump of trees, close to where he was, could conceal a party of French troops, and had thought no more about it. But young Pertelay resolved to lead his men there, and from there to fall upon the Austrian battery.

Pertelay, knowing that on the battlefield no one takes much notice of a single horseman, explained his plan to us, which was for us to go individually, a detour by a sunken road, to arrive one by one behind the wood on the left of the enemy battery, and from there to make a sudden assault on it, without the fear of cannon-balls, because we would be approaching from the side. We would capture the guns and take them to the French lines. The first part of this plan was executed without the Austrian gunners noticing; we reached the back of the little wood, where we re-formed the sections. Pertelay put himself at our head. We went through the wood, and sabre in hand, threw ourselves on the enemy battery at the moment when it was directing a murderous fire on our troops. We sabred some of the gunners, but the rest hid under their ammunition wagons, where our sabres could not reach them. As instructed by Pertelay, we did not kill or wound the men on the limbers, but forced them at sword point to make their horses pull the guns toward the French lines. This order was obeyed in respect of six guns whose riders had remained on horseback, but the riders for the two other guns had dismounted, and although some of the Hussars took the horses by the bridle, they refused to move.

The enemy infantry were running to the aid of their battery; minutes seemed like hours to us; so young Pertelay, satisfied to have captured six guns, ordered us to leave the others and to head, with our booty, at the gallop, for the French lines.

This was a prudent measure, but it proved fatal to our leader, for hardly had we begun our retreat, when the gunners and their officers emerged from their hiding places under the wagons, loaded the two guns which we had not taken with grape-shot and discharged a hail of bullets into our backs.

You can well imagine that thirty horsemen and six artillery pieces, each drawn by six horses and ridden by three transport riders, all proceeding in a state of disorder, presented a target which the grape-shot could hardly miss. We had two sergeants and several Hussars killed or wounded, as well as two of the transport riders. Some of the horses were also put out of action, so that most of the teams were so disorganised that they could not move. Pertelay, keeping perfectly cool, ordered the traces of the dead or injured horses to be cut and Hussars to take the place of the dead transport riders, and we continued quickly on our way. However, the commander of the Austrian battery made use of the few minutes we had taken to do this to direct a second volley of grape-shot at us, which caused further casualties, but we were so resolved not to abandon the six guns which we had captured that we repaired the damage as well as we could, and kept on the move. We were already in touch with the French lines and out of the range of grape-shot, when the enemy artillery officer changed projectiles and fired two cannon-balls at us, one of which shattered the back of poor young Pertelay.

However, our attack on the Austrian battery and its outcome had been seen by the French generals who moved the line forward. The enemy drew back, which allowed the remnants of the 1st

Hussars to revisit the area where our unfortunate comrades had fallen. Almost a third of the detachment were killed or wounded. There were five sergeants at the beginning of the action; three had perished; there remained only Pertelay the elder and myself. The poor fellow was wounded but suffered almost more mentally, for he adored his brother, whom we all bitterly regretted. While we were paying him our last respects and picking up the wounded, General Championet arrived with General Suchet, his chief-of-staff. The commander-in-chief had witnessed the actions of the platoon. He gathered us round the six guns which we had just captured, and after praising the courage with which we had rid the French army of a battery which was causing them the most grievous losses, he added that to reward us for having saved the lives of so many of our comrades, and contributed to the day's success, he intended to use the power which a recent decree of the First Consul had given him to award "Armes d'honneur" and that he would award three sabres of honour and one promotion to sous-lieutenant to the detachment, who should decide amongst themselves who the recipients should be. We then regretted even more keenly the loss of young Pertelay, who would have made such a fine officer.

The elder Pertelay, a corporal and a Hussar were awarded the sabres of honour, which, three years later gave the right to the Cross of the Legion of Honour. It remained to be decided which of us would be sous-lieutenant. All my comrades put my name forward, and the commander-in-chief, recalling that General Séras had written to him about my conduct at Santa-Giacomo, designated me sous-lieutenant...! I had been a sergeant for only a month! I have to admit, however, that during the capture of the guns, I had done no more than the rest of my companions; but as I have already said, these good Alsatians did not feel that they had the qualities to take command and become officers. They were unanimous in choosing me, and General Championet, as well as noting the favourable comments of General Séras, was perhaps also glad to be able to please my father.

My father, however, was less than pleased with what he considered to be my over-rapid promotion, and he wrote to me instructing me to refuse it. I would have obeyed; but my father had written in the same strain to General Suchet, the chief-of-staff, and this latter had replied that the commander-in-chief would be very put out to find that one of his divisional generals had taken it upon himself to disapprove of a promotion which he had made. My father then authorised me to accept, and I was gazetted sous-Lieutenant in December 1799.

I was one of the last officers promoted by General Championet, who, not being able to remain in Piedmont in the face of superior forces, was compelled to re-cross the Apennines and lead his army back to Liguria. He was greatly distressed to see his force breaking down, because he was not given enough supplies to support it, and he died two weeks after he had made me an officer. My father, who was now the most senior divisional general, was made provisional commander-in-chief of the army of Italy, whose headquarters were at Nice. He therefore went there and immediately sent back to Provence the few remaining cavalry, as there was no longer any fodder in Liguria. So the 1st Hussars went back to France, but my father kept me behind to become his aide-de-camp.

While we were at Nice, my father received an order from the war ministry to go and take command of the advance guard of the army of the Rhine, where his chief-of-staff Col. Ménard would join him. We were very pleased at this, since want of supplies had reduced the army of Italy to such a state of disorder that it seemed impossible that it could be kept in Liguria. My father was not sorry to be leaving an army which was disintegrating, and was likely to be pushed back across the Var and into France. He prepared to move as soon as General Masséna, who had been nominated to replace him, had arrived. He sent M. Gault, his aide-de-camp, to Paris to buy maps and make various preparations for our operations on the Rhine. But fate had decreed otherwise, and my unfortunate father's grave was destined to be in Italy.

When Masséna arrived he found no more than the shadow of an army: the soldiers, without pay and almost without clothing and footwear, existing on a quarter of the normal ration, were dying of malnutrition as well as an epidemic of disease, the result of the intolerable privations which they were suffering. The hospitals were full but had no medicines. Some groups of soldiers, and even whole regiments, were daily abandoning their posts and heading for the bridge across the Var, where they forced a passage to get into France and spread themselves over Provence, although saying that they were willing to return if they were given food! The generals were unable to remedy this appalling state of affairs. They became, daily more discouraged, and all were requesting leave or retiring on the grounds of ill-health. Masséna had expected that he would be joined in Italy by several of the generals who had helped him to defeat the Russians in Switzerland, among them, Soult, Oudinot and Gazan, but none of them had yet arrived, and it was essential to do something about the serious situation.

Masséna, who was born in La Turbie, a village in the little principality of Monaco, was one of the most crafty Italians that ever existed. He did not know my father, but he decided on their first meeting that he was a big-hearted man who loved his country, and, to persuade him to stay, he played on these sensitive areas, his generosity and his patriotism, suggesting to him how much nobler it would be for him to continue to serve in the unhappy army of Italy rather than go to the Rhine. He said that he would take the responsibility for the failure to carry out the orders given to my father by the government if he would agree to stay. My father, beguiled by these speeches and not wishing to leave the new commander in a mess, consented to remain with him. He did not doubt that his chief-of-staff, Col. Ménard, his friend, would also give up the idea of going to the Rhine; but this was not to be. Ménard stuck to the order he had been given, although he was assured that it would be cancelled if he wished. My father felt very badly about this desertion. Ménard hurried off to Paris, where he took the job of chief-of-staff to general Lefebvre.

My father went to Genoa, where he took command of the three divisions which composed the right wing of the army. Despite all the shortages, the winter carnival was quite gay in the town, the Italians being so pleasure-loving! We were lodged in the Centurione Palace, where we spent the end of the winter 1799-1800. My father had left Spire at Nice with the greater part of his baggage. He now took on Col. Sacleux as his chief-of-staff, an admirable man, a good soldier, with a very pleasant personality, if somewhat solemn and serious-minded. He had as his secretary a young man by the name of Colindo, the son of a banker, Signor Trepano of Parma, whom he had picked up after a series of adventures too long to relate here, who became my very good friend.

Early in the spring of 1800, my father was told that General Masséna intended to give the command of the right wing to General Soult, who had just arrived, and was much my father's junior, and he was ordered to go back to Savona and head his old division, the third. My father obeyed, though his pride was hurt by this new posting.

Chapter 10
The Siege of Genoa

A serious situation was developing in Italy. Masséna had received some reinforcements; he had established a little order in his army, and the campaign of 1800, which led to the memorable siege of Genoa and the battle of Marengo, was about to begin.

The snows which covered the mountains separating the two armies having melted, the Austrians attacked us, and their first efforts were directed upon my father's division, the third, stationed at the right of the French line, which they wished to separate from the centre and the left by driving them back from Savona to Genoa.

As soon as hostilities commenced, my father and Col. Sacleux sent all the non-combatants to Genoa; Colindo was among them. As for me, I was thoroughly enjoying myself, exhilarated as I was by the sight of marching troops, the noisy movements of artillery and the excitement of a young soldier at the prospect of action. I was far from suspecting that this war would become so terrible and would cost me so dear.

My father's division, fiercely attacked by greatly superior forces, defended for two days positions at Cadibone and Montenotte, but eventually, seeing themselves on the point of being outflanked, they had to retire to Voltri, and from there to Genoa, where they shut themselves in, together with the two other divisions of the right wing.

I had heard all the well-informed generals deploring the circumstances which forced our separation from the centre and the left, but I had at that time so little understanding of the principles of warfare that I took no notice. I understood well enough that we had been defeated, but as I personally had overcome, before Montenotte, an officer of Burco's Hussars, and taking the plume from his shako, had fastened it proudly to the head-band of my bridle, it seemed to me that I was like a knight of the middle-ages returning laden with the spoils of the infidel.

My childish vanity was soon crushed by a dreadful event. During the retreat, and at a moment when my father was giving me an order to take, he was hit by a bullet in the left leg, which had been wounded once before, in the army of the Pyrenees. The injury was serious, and my father would have fallen from his horse if he had not leaned on me. I took him out of the battle area. His wound was dressed. I shed tears as I saw his blood flow, but he tried to calm me, saying that a soldier should have more courage. My father was carried to the Centurione Palace in Genoa, where he had lived during the preceding winter. Our three divisions having entered Genoa, the Austrians blockaded it by land, and the English by sea.

I can hardly bring myself to describe the sufferings of the garrison and the population of Genoa during the two months for which this siege lasted. Famine, fighting and an epidemic of typhus did immense damage. The garrison lost ten thousand men out of sixteen thousand, and there were collected from the streets, every day, seven or eight hundred of the bodies of the inhabitants, of every age, sex, and condition, which were taken behind the church of Carignan to an immense pit filled with quick-lime. The number of victims rose to more than thirty thousand.

For you to understand just how badly the lack of food was felt by the inhabitants, I should explain that the ancient rulers of Genoa, in order to control the populace, had from time immemorial exercised a monopoly over grain, flour and bread, which was operated by a vast establishment protected by cannons and guarded by soldiers, so that when the Doge or the Senate wished to prevent or put down a revolt, they closed the state ovens and reduced the people to starvation. Although by this time the constitution of Genoa had been greatly modified and the aristocracy now had very little influence, there was not, however a single private bakery, and the old system of making bread in the public ovens was still in operation. Now, these public bakeries, which normally provided for a population of a hundred and twenty thousand souls, were closed for forty-five days out of the sixty for which the siege lasted. Neither rich nor poor could buy bread. The little in the way of dried vegetables and rice which was in the shops had been bought up at the beginning of the siege at greatly inflated prices. The troops alone were given a small ration of a quarter of a pound of horse flesh and a quarter of a pound of what was called bread. This was a horrible mixture of various flours, bran, starch, chalk, linseed, oatmeal, rancid nuts and other evil substances. General Thibauld in his diary of the siege described as "Turf mixed with oil."

For forty five days neither bread nor meat was on sale to the public. The richest were able (at the start the siege only,) to buy some dried cod, figs and some other dried goods such as sugar. There was never any shortage of wine, oil and salt, but what use are they without solid food? All the dogs and cats in the town were eaten. A rat could fetch a high price! In the end the starvation became so appalling that when the French troops made a sortie, the inhabitants would follow them in a crowd out of the gates, and rich and poor, women, children and the old would start collecting grass, nettles, and leaves, which they would then cook with some salt. The Genoese government mowed the grass which grew on the ramparts, which was then cooked in the public squares and distributed to the wretched invalids, who had not the strength to go and find for themselves and prepare this crude dish. Even the soldiers cooked nettles and all sorts of herbage with their horse flesh. The richest and most distinguished families in the town envied them this meat, disgusting as it was, for the shortage of fodder had made nearly all the horses sick and even the flesh of those dying of disease was distributed.

During the latter part of the siege, the desperation of the people was something to fear. There were cries that, as in 1756 their fathers had massacred an Austrian army, they should now try to get rid of the French army in the same way; and that it was better to die fighting than to starve to death, after watching their wives and children perish. These threats of revolt were made more serious by the fact that if they were carried out, the English by sea and the Austrians by land would have rushed to join their efforts to those of the insurgents, and would have overwhelmed us.

Amid such dangers and calamities of all sorts, Masséna remained immovable and calm, and to prevent any attempt at an uprising, he issued a proclamation that French troops had orders to open fire on any gathering of more than four people. Regiments camped in the squares and the principal streets. The avenues were occupied by cannon loaded with grape-shot. It being impossible for them to come together, the Genoese were unable to revolt.

It may seem surprising that Masséna was so determined to hold on to a place where he could not feed the inhabitants and could scarcely maintain his own troops; but Genoa was, at that time, of great importance. Our army had been cut in two. The centre and the left wing had retired behind the Var. As long as Masséna occupied Genoa, he kept part of the Austrian army occupied in besieging him and prevented them from employing all their forces against Provence.

Masséna knew also that the First Consul was assembling at Dijon, Lyon, and Geneva, an army of reserve, with which he proposed to cross the Alps by the St. Bernard pass, to enter Italy and to surprise the Austrians by falling on their rear while they were directing their efforts at taking Genoa. We therefore had the greatest interest in holding the town for as long as possible. These were the orders of the First Consul, and were subsequently justified by events.

To return to the siege. When he heard that my father had been brought to Genoa, Colindo Trepano hurried to his bedside, and it was there that we met once more. He helped me most tenderly to care for my father, for which I am even more beholden to him because, in the midst of these calamities my father had no one about him. All his staff officers had been ordered to go and attend the commander-in-chief; soon rations were refused to our servants, who were forced to go and take up a musket and line up with the combatants to have a right to the miserable ration which was distributed to the soldiers. No exception was made, apart from a young valet, named Oudin, and a young stable-lad, who looked after the horses; but Oudin deserted us as soon as he knew that my father had typhus.

My father fell ill with this dreadful disease, and at a time when he was in the greatest need of care, there was no one with him except me, Colindo and the stable lad Bastide. We did our best to follow the doctor's instructions, we hardly slept, being endlessly busy massaging my father with camphorated oil and changing his bedclothes and linen.

My father could take no nourishment except soup and I had nothing with which to make it but rotten horse-meat. My heart was breaking.

Providence sent us some help. The huge buildings of the public ovens were next to the walls of the palace where we were living. The terraces were almost touching. It was on the immense terraces of the public ovens that the crushing and mixing took place of all sorts of chicken food which was added to the rotten flour to make the garrison's bread. The stable lad Bastide had noticed that when the workmen of the bakery left the terraces, they were invaded by horde of pigeons who had their nests in the various church towers of the town, and were in the habit of coming to pick up the small amounts of grain which had spilled onto the flagstones. Bastide, who was a very clever lad, crossed the narrow space which separated the terraces, and on that of the public ovens he set up snares and other devices with which he captured pigeons which we used to make soup for my father, who found it excellent, compared to that made from horse.

To the horrors of famine and typhus were added those of a merciless and unceasing war, for the French troops fought all day on land against the Austrians, and when nightfall put an end to the Austrian assaults, the English, Turkish, and Neapolitan fleets, which were protected by darkness from the port's cannons and the batteries on the coast, drew close to the town, into which they hurled a great number of bombs which did fearful damage.

The noise of the guns and the cries of the wounded and dying reached my father and greatly disturbed him. He lamented his inability to place himself at the head of the men of his division. This state of mind worsened his condition. He became more gravely ill from day to day, and progressively weaker. Colindo and I did not leave him for a moment. Eventually, one night when I was on my knees by his bedside, sponging his wound, he spoke to me, perfectly lucidly, and placed his hand caressingly on my head, saying, "Poor child, what will happen to him, alone and without support in the horrors of this terrible siege?" Then he mumbled some words, among which I could distinguish the name of my mother, dropped his arms and closed his eyes...

Although very young and without much length of service, I had seen many dead on various battlefields, and above all on the streets of Genoa; but they had fallen in the open, still in their clothes, which gave them a very different appearance to someone who had died in bed. I had never witnessed this last sad spectacle and I believed that my father had fallen asleep. Colindo knew the truth but had not the heart to tell me, so I was not aware of my error until some time later, when M. Lachèze arrived and I saw him pull the sheet over my father's face, saying, "This is a dreadful loss for his family and friends". Only then did I understand that my father was dead.

My grief was so heartbroken that it touched even General Masséna, a man not easily moved, particularly in the present situation when he had need of such resolution. The critical position in which he found himself drove him to behave toward me in a way which I thought atrocious, although now I would do the same in the same circumstances.

To avoid anything that could lower the morale of the troops, Masséna had forbidden any funeral ceremonies, and as he knew that I had been unwilling to desert the mortal remains of my much-loved father, and thought it was my intention to go with him to his graveside, he feared that his troops might be adversely affected by the sight of a young officer, scarcely more than a boy, following, in tears, his father's bier. So he came the next day before dawn to the room where my father lay, and taking me by the hand, he led me under some pretext or other to a distant room, while, on his orders, twelve Grenadiers, accompanied only by one officer and Col. Sacleux, took the body in silence, and placed it in a provisional grave on the rampart facing the sea. It was only after this mournful ceremony was over that General Masséna told me of it and explained his motives for this decision. I was overcome by misery. It seemed to me that I had lost my poor father for a second time; that he had been deprived of my last services. My protests were in vain and there was nothing I could do but go and pray by my father's grave. I did not know where it was, but Colindo had followed the burial party, and he led me there. This good young man gave me the most touching evidences of sympathy, and this at a time when everyone thought only of themselves.

Nearly all the officers of my father's staff had been killed or carried off by typhus. Out of the eleven which we were at the start of the campaign, there remained only two; the commandant R★★★ and me! But R★★★ was interested only in himself, and instead of offering support to his general's son, he lived alone in the town. M. Lachèze abandoned me also. Only the good Col. Sacleux showed any interest in me, but having been given the command of a brigade, he was constantly outside the walls combatting the enemy. I stayed alone in the huge Centurione Palace with Colindo, Bastide, and the ancient concierge.

A week had scarcely passed since my father's death when General Masséna, who needed a large number of officers in attendance because some were killed or wounded almost every day, ordered me to come and serve as aide-de-camp, as did R★★★ and all the officers on the staff of those generals who were dead or unable to mount a horse. I obeyed. I followed the general all day in battle, and when I was not detained at headquarters, I went back to the Palace, and at nightfall, Colindo and I, passing among the dying and the dead bodies of men, women, and children which littered the streets, went to pray at my father's tomb.

The famine in the town continued to worsen. An order went out forbidding any officer from having more than one horse, the rest were to be butchered. There were several of my father's left and I was most unhappy at the thought of these poor beasts being killed. I managed to save their lives by proposing that I should give them to officers of the general staff in exchange for their worn out mounts, which I then sent to the butchery. These horses were later paid for by the state, on production of an order for their delivery. I have kept one of these orders as a curiosity; it bears the signature of General Oudinot, Masséna's chief-of-staff.

The cruel loss which I had just suffered, the position in which I found myself, and the sight of the truly horrible scenes in which I was involved every day, taught me more in a short time than I would have learned in a number of happier years. I realised that the starvation and disaster of the siege had made egoists of all those who a few months before had been smothering my father with attention.

I had to find within myself the courage and resource not only for my own needs but to look after Colindo and Bastide. The most pressing requirement was to find something for them to eat, since they were given no food from the army stores. I had, it is true, as an officer, two rations of horse meat and two rations of bread, but all this added together did not amount to more than a pounds weight of very bad food, and we were three! We very rarely caught pigeons now, for their numbers had infinitely diminished.

In my position as aide-de-camp to the commander-in-chief, I was entitled to a place at his table, where once a day was served some bread, some roast horse and some chick peas; but I was so embittered at General Masséna having deprived me of the sad consolation of attending my father's burial, that I could not bring myself to sit down at his table, although all my comrades were there and a place was reserved for me. But at last the wish to help my two unfortunate companions decided me to go and eat with the commander-in-chief. From then on Colindo and Bastide had each a quarter of a pound of horse meat and the same amount of bread. As for me, I did not have enough to eat, for the portions served at the general's table were exceedingly small, and I was worked hard. Often I had to lie on the ground to stop myself from fainting.

Providence came once more to our aid. Bastide had been born in the region of Cantal, and he had met, the previous winter, another Auvergnian whom he knew, and who was living in Genoa where he had a small business. Bastide went to visit this friend, and was surprised, on entering the house, to smell the odour which floats around a grocer's shop. Bastide remarked on this and asked his friend if he had some food. His friend admitted that he had, and begged Bastide to keep this a secret, since all food found in private hands was confiscated and taken to the army stores. The shrewd Bastide then offered to arrange the purchase of any surplus provisions by someone who would pay cash and would keep the secret inviolate. He came to tell me of his discovery. My father had left me some thousands of francs, so I bought, and brought back to our dwelling at night, a quantity of dried cod, cheese, figs, sugar, chocolate etc. All of which was extremely expensive, and the Auvergnian had most of my money. However I was happy to pay whatever he asked, for I heard daily at general headquarters suggestions that the siege would continue and the famine get worse. Sadly, this in fact happened. My joy at having procured some food was increased by the thought that I had thereby saved the life of my friend Colindo, who, without it, would have assuredly died of starvation, for he knew no one in the army except me and Col. Sacleux, who was shortly to be struck down by a dreadful misfortune.

Masséna, attacked on all sides, seeing his troops worn down by continual battle and famine, forced to hold down a large population, driven to despair by hunger, found himself in a most critical position, and believed that to maintain good order in the army he needed to impose iron discipline. So any officer who did not execute his orders immediately was dismissed, under the power which the law gave at that time to the commander-in-chief.

Several examples of this kind had already been made when, during a sortie which we had pushed forward some six leagues from the town, the brigade commanded by Col. Sacleux was not in position at the time ordered in a valley where it was meant to block the passage of the Austrians, who thus escaped.

The commander-in-chief, furious at seeing his plans come to nothing, dismissed poor Col. Sacleux by publishing his dismissal in an order of the day. Sacleux may well not have understood what was expected of him, but he was a very brave man. Assuredly he would have blown his brains out, had he not been determined to restore his honour. He took up a musket and joined the ranks as a private soldier! He came to see us one day, Colindo and I were sore at heart to see this excellent man dressed as a simple infantryman. We said our good-byes to Sacleux who, after the surrender of the town, was restored to his rank of colonel at the request of Masséna himself, who had been impressed by Sacleux's courage. But the following year, when peace had been made in Europe, Sacleux, perhaps wishing to rid himself completely of the stigma with which he had been so unjustly branded, asked to be posted to the war in Santa-Dominica, where he was killed at the moment when he was about to be promoted to brigadier-general! There are men who, in spite of their merits, have a cruel destiny; of which he was an example.

Chapter 11
Aide-de Camp to Masséna

I shall discuss only briefly the conduct of the siege or block-ade which we sustained. The fortifications of Genoa consisted at that time of a plain wall, flanked by towers; but what made the place well suited for defence was the fact that it is surrounded at a short distance by mountains, the summits and flanks of which are dotted with forts and strong-points. The Austrians continually attacked these positions. When they took one, we went to retake it, and the next day they came to take it again. If they managed to do so, we went to chase them out once more. There was an end-less shuttling back and forth, with varying results, but in the end, we remained in control of the terrain. These encounters were often very fierce. In one of them, General Soult, who was General Masséna's right hand man, was climbing up Monte Corona at the head of his men to retake a fort of that name, which we had lost the day before, when his knee was struck by a bullet at a moment when the enemy, who greatly outnumbered his party, were run-ning down from the top of the mountain. It was impossible with the few troops we had at this point to resist the avalanche, and a retreat was called for. The soldiers carried General Soult for some way, on their muskets, but the intolerable pain which he suffered decided them that he should be left at the foot of a tree, where his brother and one of his aides-de-camp stayed with him to pro-tect him from being attacked by the first enemy troops to arrive. Luckily there were among these some officers who had much respect for their illustrious prisoner.

The capture of General Soult having encouraged the Aus-trians, they pushed us back to the city wall, which they were preparing to attack when a heavy storm darkened the blue sky, which we had had since the beginning of the siege. The rain fell in torrents. The Austrians halted and most of them sought shelter in the blockhouses or under the trees. Then General Masséna, one of whose principal gifts was the ability to turn to advantage the unforeseen incidents of warfare, addressed his men, rekindled their spirit, and having reinforced them with some troops from the town, he ordered them to fix bayonets and led them, at the height of the storm, against the erstwhile victorious Austrians who, taken by surprise, retired in disorder. Masséna pursued them with such effect that he cut off some three thousand Grenadiers, who laid down their arms.

This was not the first time that we had taken numerous prisoners, for the total of those we had captured since the beginning of the siege amounted to more than eight thousand; but having no food for them, Masséna had always sent them back, on the condition that they would not be used against us for a period of six months. Although the officers held religiously to their promise, the wretched soldiers, who went back to the Austrian camp ignorant of the undertaking that their leaders had made on their behalf, were transferred to other regiments and forced to fight against us once more. If they fell again into our hands, something that often happened, they were once more sent back and transferred anew; so that there were very many of these men who, on their own admission, had been captured four or five times. Masséna, angered at the lack of good faith on the part of the Austrian generals, decided that this time he would retain both officers and men of the three thousand Grenadiers whom he had captured; and so that the duty of guarding them would not fall on his troops, he had the unfortunate prisoners loaded into floating hulks moored in the middle of the harbour with the guns of the harbour mole aimed at them. He then sent an envoy to General Ott, who commanded the Austrian troops before Genoa, to reproach him for his failure to keep his word, and to warn him that he did not consider himself bound to give the prisoners more than half the ration of the French soldier; but that he would agree to an arrangement which the Austrians might make with the British, whereby vessels might bring, every day, food for the prisoners, and not leave until they had seen it eaten, so that it could not be thought that Masséna was using this pretext to bring in food for his own men. The Austrian general who may have hoped that a refusal would compel Masséna to send back the three thousand soldiers, whom he probably intended to use again, turned down this philanthropic proposal, and Masséna then carried out his threat.

The French ration was composed of a quarter of a pound of disgusting bread and an equal amount of horse flesh; the prisoners were given only half this amount! This was fifteen days before the end of the siege. For fifteen days, these poor devils remained on this regime!. Every two or three days Masséna renewed his offer to the enemy general; he never accepted, perhaps out of obstinacy, or perhaps because the English admiral, Lord Kieth, was unwilling to employ his long-boats for fear, it is said, that they would bring typhus back to the fleet. However that may be, the wretched Austrians were left howling with rage and hunger in their floating prison. It was truly appalling! In the end, having eaten their boots and packs, and perhaps some dead bodies, they nearly all died of starvation! There were hardly more than seven or eight hundred left when the place was surrendered to our enemies. The Austrian soldiers, when they entered the town, hurried to the harbour and gave food to their compatriots with so little caution that many of them died as a result.

I have described this horrible episode, firstly as an example of the sort of ghastly event which war brings in its train, but principally to brand with shame the conduct and lack of good faith of the Austrian general, who forced soldiers who had been captured and released on parole, to take up arms against us once more, although he had promised to send them back to Germany.

In the course of the fighting which took place during the siege, I ran into a number of dangers but I shall limit myself to mentioning two of the more serious.

I have already said that the Austrians and the English took it in turns to keep us constantly in action. The first attacked us at dawn, on the landward side, and we fought them all day; at night, Lord Kieth's fleet would begin its bombardment, and try, under cover of darkness, to seize the harbour; which forced the garrison to keep a keen look-out on the seaward side, and prevented it from having any rest or relaxation. Now, one night, when the bombardment was more violent than usual, the commander-in-chief was warned that the light of Bengal flares burning on the beach had disclosed numerous boat loads of English soldiers heading for the harbour breakwater. Masséna, his staff, and the squadron of guides which went everywhere with him, immediately mounted their horses. We were about a hundred and fifty to two hundred horsemen when, passing through a little square called Campetto, the general stopped to speak to an officer who was returning from the harbour. Someone shouted "Look out for bombs!" And at that moment, one fell onto the crowded square.

I and several others had pushed our horses under a balcony which overhung the door of an hotel, and it was on this balcony that the bomb fell. It reduced the balcony to rubble, and bounced onto the road, where it exploded with a fearful bang in the middle of the square, which was lit for an instant by its malevolent light, after which there was complete darkness. One expected many casualties. There was the most profound silence, which was broken by the voice of General Masséna, asking if anyone was hurt. There was no reply, for by some miracle, not one of the horses or men had been hit by the flying fragments. As for those who, like me, had been under the balcony, we were covered with dust and bits of building material, but nobody was injured.

I have said that the English bombarded us only at night. However, one day, when they were celebrating some occasion or other, their ships, dressed overall, approached the town in broad daylight, and amused themselves by hurling at us a large number of projectiles. Those of our batteries which were in the best position to reply to this fire, were located near the breakwater on a big bastion in the form of a tower, known as the Lanterne. The general ordered me to take a message to the officer in charge of this battery, instructing him to direct all his efforts on an English brig, which had insolently anchored a short distance from the Lanterne. Our gunners fired with such accuracy that one of our large bombs fell on the English brig, piercing it from deck to keel so that it sank almost immediately. This so infuriated the English admiral that he had all his guns trained on the Lanterne, on which they now opened a violent fire. My mission being completed, I should have returned to Masséna; but it is rightly said that young soldiers, not recognising danger, confront it more coolly than those with more experience. The spectacle of which I was a witness, I found very interesting.

The platform of the Lanterne was floored with flagstones and was the size of a small courtyard. It was equipped with twelve cannons on enormous wooden mountings. Although it may be very difficult for ship at sea to aim its fire with sufficient accuracy to hit such a small target as was the platform of the Lanterne, the English managed to land several bombs there. As these bombs descended, the gunners took shelter behind or underneath the massive timbers of the gun mountings. I did the same; but this shelter was not entirely safe, because the flagstones presented a great resistance to the bombs, which, being unable to bury themselves, rolled unpredictably about the platform in all directions, and the fragments from their explosion could pass under or behind the mountings. It was, therefore, absurd to stay there when, like me, one was not obliged to do so. But I experienced a fearful pleasure, if one can describe it thus, in running here and there with the gunners whenever a bomb fell, and emerging with them as soon as the fragments from its explosion had settled. It was a game which could have cost me dear. One gunner had his legs broken, others were wounded by bomb fragments, lumps of metal which did terrible damage to anything they hit. One of them sliced through the thick timber baulk of a mounting behind which I was sheltering. However, I remained on the platform until Col. Mouton, who later became Marshal the Comte de Lobeau, and who, having served under my father, took an interest in me, while passing, caught sight of me. He came over to the Lanterne and ordered me sharply to come down and return to my post beside General Masséna. He added, "You are still very young, but you should realise that, in war, it is stupid to expose yourself to needless danger. Would you be any better off if you had a leg smashed for no good reason?"

I never forgot this lesson, and I have often thought of the difference it would have made to my life, if I had lost a leg at the age of seventeen.

Chapter 12
The Battle of Marengo

The courage and tenacity with which Masséna had defended Genoa would have very important results. Major Franceschi, sent by Masséna to contact the First Consul, had managed to slip through the enemy fleet at night, both in going and coming. On arriving back in Genoa he said that he had left Bonaparte descending the St. Bernard at the head of the army of reserve. Field-marshal Mélas was so convinced of the impossibility of bringing an army across the Alps, that while part of his force, under General Ott was blockading us, he had gone with the remainder fifty leagues away, to attack General Suchet on the Var. This gave the First Consul the opportunity to enter Italy without resistance, so that the army of reserve had reached Milan before the Austrians had ceased to regard its existence as imaginary. The First Consul, once in Italy, would have liked to go straight away to the aid of the town's brave garrison, but to do that it was necessary for him to unite all the elements of his force, such as the artillery and military supplies, whose passage across the Alps had proved extremely difficult. This delay gave Marshal Mélas the time to hurry with his main force from Nice in order to oppose Bonaparte, who was then unable to continue his march towards Genoa without defeating the Austrian army.

While Bonaparte and Mélas were engaged in marches and countermarches in preparation for a battle which would decide the destiny of France and Italy, the garrison of Genoa found itself reduced to its last extremity. The typhus epidemic was raging. The hospitals had become ghastly charnel houses; starvation was at its worst. Nearly all the horses had been eaten, and though for a long time the soldiers had had no more than half a pound of rotten food daily, the distribution for the following day was not assured. There was absolutely nothing left when, on the 15th Prairial Masséna gathered all his generals and colonels together and announced that he had decided to attempt a breakout with those remaining men who were fit for duty, to try to reach Livorno; but his officers declared unanimously that the troops were no longer in a state to engage in combat, or even a simple march, unless they were given sufficient food to restore their strength, and the stores were completely empty! General Masséna then considered that, having carried out the orders of the First Consul and facilitated his entry into Italy, that it was his duty to save the remains of a garrison which had fought so valiantly, and which it was in the country's interest to preserve. He therefore resolved to treat for the evacuation of the place, for he would not allow the word capitulation to be uttered. The English admiral and General Ott had, for more than a month, been making proposals for a parley, which Masséna had always turned down; but now, compelled by circumstance, he told them that he would accept. The conference took place in the little chapel which is situated in the middle of the bridge of Conegliano, and which is, as a result, between the sea and the French and Austrian lines. The French, English, and Austrian staffs occupied each end of the bridge. I was present at this most interesting event.

The foreign generals treated Masséna with much respect and consideration, and although he demanded favourable conditions, Admiral Kieth said more than once that the defense had been so heroic that they did not wish to refuse them. It was then agreed that the garrison would not be made prisoners, that they could retain their weapons and could go to Nice, and that having reached there they would be free to engage in further hostilities.

Masséna, who realised how important it was that the First Consul should not be led into making any false move because of his anxiety to go to the aid of Genoa, asked that the negotiations should permit the safe passage of two officers through the Austrian lines, whom he proposed to send to Bonaparte to inform him of the evacuation of the town by the French. General Ott opposed this because he intended to leave with some twenty-five thousand men of the blockading force to go and join Field-marshal Mélas, and he did not want these French officers to warn General Bonaparte of his movements. But Admiral Kieth overruled this objection. The treaty was about to be signed when, from far away, in the midst of the mountains, came the distant sound of gunfire. Masséna held up his pen, saying, "That is the First Consul, who has arrived with his army." The foreign commanders were much taken aback, but after a long pause it was realised that the sound was that of thunder, and Masséna appended his signature.

It is to be regretted that the garrison and its commander were deprived of the fame which would have been theirs if they had been able to hold Genoa until the arrival of Bonaparte; and furthermore, Masséna would have liked to hold out for a few more days, to delay the departure of General Ott's men to join in the battle, which was inevitable, between the First Consul and Fieldmarshal Mélas. In the event, General Ott was unable to join the main Austrian army until the day after the battle of Marengo, the result of which might have been very different if the Austrians, whom we had great difficulty in overcoming, had had twenty-five thousand more men with which to oppose us. The Austrians took possession of Genoa on the 16th Prairial (May) after a siege which had lasted two whole months.

Masséna, as has been said, considered it so important that the First Consul was informed immediately about the situation that he had demanded a safe conduct for two aides-de-camp, so that if any thing untoward befell one of them, the other could carry his despatch. As it would be useful if an officer going on such a mission spoke Italian, Masséna chose a Major Graziani, an Italian who was in the French service, but being a most suspicious man, Masséna feared that a foreigner might be corrupted by the Austrians and delay his journey, so he sent me to make sure that he made all possible haste. This precaution was unnecessary as Major Graziani was a man of probity who knew the urgency of his mission.

On the 16th Prairial we departed from Genoa where I left Colindo, whom I expected to collect in a few days time, as we knew that the First Consul's army was not very far away. Major Graziani and I reached it the next day at Milan.

General Bonaparte spoke to me with sympathy about the loss which I had suffered, and promised that he would be a father to me if I behaved myself well, a promise which he kept. He asked us endless questions about the events which had occurred in Genoa, and about the strength and movements of the Austrian forces we had come through to reach Milan; he kept us by him, and had horses provided for us from his stable, since we had travelled on post mules.

We followed the First Consul to Montebello and then to the battlefield of Marengo, where we were employed to carry his orders. I shall not go into any details about this battle, where I ran into no danger; one knows that we were on the brink of defeat, and might have fallen if General Ott's men had arrived in time to take part in the action. The First Consul, who feared that he might see them appear at any moment, was very anxious, and did not relax until our cavalry and the infantry of General Desaix, of whose death he was still unaware, had ensured victory by overwhelming the Grenadiers of General Zach. Seeing that the horse which I was riding was slightly wounded on a leg, he took me by the ear, and said, laughing, "I lend you my horses, and look what happens to them!" Major Graziani having died in 1812, I am the only French officer who was present at the siege of Genoa and the battle of Marengo.

After this memorable affair, I went back to Genoa, which the Austrians had left as a result of our victory at Marengo. There I rejoined Colindo and Major R★★★. I visited my father's grave, then we embarked on a French brig, which in twenty-four hours carried us to Nice. Some days later, a ship from Leghorn brought Colindo's mother, who had come in search of her son. This fine young man and I had come through some very rough times together, which had strengthened the friendship between us, but our paths were divergent and we had to part, albeit with much regret.

I have said earlier, that about the middle of the siege, Franceschi, carrying despatches from General Masséna to the First Consul, had reached France by passing through the enemy fleet at night. He took with him the news of my father's death. My mother had thereupon nominated a council of guardians, who sent to the aged Spire, who was at Nice with the coach and my father's baggage, an order to sell everything and return to Paris, which he then did. There was now nothing to detain me on the banks of the Var, and I was in a hurry to rejoin my dear mother; but this was not so easy; public coaches were, at the time, very scarce; the one that ran from Nice to Lyon went only every second day and was booked up for several weeks by sick or wounded officers, coming, like me, from Genoa.

To overcome this difficulty, Major R★★★, two colonels, a dozen officers and I decided to form a group to go to Grenoble on foot, crossing the foothills of the Alps by way of Grasse, Sisteron, Digne and Gap. Mules would carry our small amount of baggage, which would allow us to cover eight to ten leagues every day. Bastide was with me and was a great help to me, for I was not accustomed to making such long journeys on foot, and it was very hot. After eight days of very difficult walking, we reached Grenoble, from where we were able to take coaches to Lyon. It was with sorrow that I saw once more the town and the hotel where I had stayed with my father in happier times. I longed for and yet dreaded the reunion with my mother and my brothers. I fancied that they would ask me to account for what I had done with her husband and their father! I was returning alone, and had left him in his grave in a foreign land! I was very unhappy and had need of a friend who would understand and share my grief, while Major R★★★, happy, after so much privation, to enjoy once more, abundance and good living, was madly jolly, which I found most wounding; so I decided to leave for Paris without him; but he claimed, now that I had no need of him, that it was his duty to deliver me to the arms of my mother, and I was forced to put up with his company as far as Paris, to where we went by mail coach.

There are scenes which are perhaps better left to the imagination, so I shall not attempt to describe my first heartbreaking meeting with my widowed mother and my brothers.

Chapter 13
An Interlude as a Supernumerary

The end of the autumn of 1800 was approaching; my mother went back to Paris, my young brothers went back to school, and I was ordered to join Bernadotte at Rennes.

Bernadotte had been my father's best friend, and my father had helped him in various ways on many occasions. In recognition of the debt owed to my family, he had written to me saying that he had reserved a place for me as his aide-de-camp. I received this letter at Nice when I returned from Genoa, and on the strength of it, I refused an offer from General Masséna to take me on as a permanent aide-de-camp, and to allow me to spend several months with my mother before joining him and the army of Italy.

My father had arranged that my brother Adolphe should continue his studies in order to enter the polytechnic; so he was not a soldier when my father died; but on hearing this sad news, he rebelled at the thought that his younger brother was already an officer, and had been in action, while he was still on a school bench. He gave up the studies required for the technical arms, and opted to join the infantry instead, which allowed him to leave school.

He was presented with a good opportunity. The government had ordered a new regiment to be raised in the department of the Seine. The officers for this regiment were to be selected by General Lefebvre, who, as you know, had replaced my father in command of the Paris division. General Lefebvre was only too pleased to do something for the son of one of his old companions who had died in the service of his country; he therefore awarded my brother the rank of sous-lieutenant in this new unit. So far, so good! But instead of going to join his company, and without waiting for my return from Genoa, Adolphe hurried off to General Bernadotte, who, without further ado, handed the vacant post to the first brother to arrive, as if it was the prize in a race! So when I went to join the general staff at Rennes, I learned that my brother had been gazetted as permanent aide-de-camp, and I was only a supernumerary, that is to say temporary. I was very disappointed, because, had I expected this, I would have accepted the proposal made by General Masséna. But this opportunity had now passed. It was in vain that General Bernadotte assured me that he would obtain an increase in the establishment of his aides-de-camp, I did not think this likely, and was convinced that I would soon be moved elsewhere.

Bernadotte's staff was made up of officers who nearly all reached senior positions; four were already colonels. The most outstanding was, undoubtedly, Gérard. He was very clever, brave and had a natural talent for warfare. He was under the command of Marshal Grouchy at Waterloo, and gave him some sound advice, which could have led us to victory. Out of the eleven aides-de-camp attached to Bernadotte's staff, two became marshals, three lieutenant-generals, four were brigadiers and one was killed in action.

In the winter of 1800, Portugal, backed by the English, had declared war on Spain, and the French government had resolved to support the latter. In consequence, troops were sent to Bayonne and Bordeaux, and the companies of Grenadiers who belonged to various regiments scattered throughout Brittany and the Vendée were gathered together at Tours. This corps d'élite was intended to be the nucleus of the so-called army of Portugal, which Bernadotte was destined to command. The general had to move his headquarters to Tours; to where had to be sent all his horses and equipment, as well all that was required for the officers attached to his service. But the general, partly to receive his final orders from the First Consul and partly to take Madame Bernadotte back, had to go to Paris; and as it was customary in these circumstances during the absence of the general for the officers of his staff to be permitted to go and take leave of their families, it was decided that all the permanent aides could go to Paris, and that the supernumeraries would go to Tours with the baggage to supervise the servants, pay them every month, arrange with the supply commission for the distribution of forage, and the allotment of lodgings for the great number of men and horses. This disagreeable duty fell to me and my fellow supernumerary Lieutenant Maurin.

In the depths of winter and the most atrocious weather, we made on horseback the long eight days journey from Rennes to Tours, where we had all sorts of difficulties in setting up the headquarters. We had been told that we would not be there for much more than a fortnight, but we stayed there, bored stiff, for six weary months, while our comrades were disporting themselves in the capital.

Chapter 14
To Spain with the 25th Chasseurs

The First Consul now changed his mind about the army of Portugal. He gave the command to his brother-in-law, General Leclerc, and kept General Bernadotte in command of the army of the west. In consequence, the general staff, which my brother and the other aides-de-camp had just joined at Tours, was ordered to return to Brittany and betake itself to Brest, where the commander-in-chief was to be stationed. It is a long way from Tours to Brest, but the weather was fair, we were a young crowd, and the trip was great fun. I was unable to ride on horseback, because of an accident, so I rode in one of the commander-in-chief's coaches. We found him awaiting us at Brest.

The harbour at Brest held at that time not only a great number of French vessels, but also the Spanish fleet, commanded by Admiral Gravina, who was later killed at Trafalgar. When we arrived in Brest, the two allied fleets were expected to take to Ireland, General Bernadotte and a large invading force of French and Spanish troops; but while we awaited this expedition, -- which never actually took place -- the presence of so many army and naval officers greatly animated the town of Brest. The commander-in-chief, the admirals and several of the generals entertained daily. The troops of the two nations mingled on the best of terms, and I made the acquaintance of several Spanish officers.

We were thoroughly enjoying ourselves at Brest, when the commander-in-chief decided it would be a good idea to move his headquarters to Rennes, a dismal town, but more in the centre of his command. We had hardly arrived there when what I had foreseen happened. The First Consul cut the number of aides-de-camp allotted to the commander-in-chief. He was allowed only one colonel, five officers of lower rank and no additional officers. As a result I was told that I was to be posted to a regiment of light cavalry. I would have resigned myself to this, if it had been to return to the first Hussars, where I was known and whose uniform I wore; but it was more than a year since I had left the regiment, and I had been replaced, so I was ordered to join the 25th Chasseurs, who had just gone to Spain and were on the frontier with Portugal around Salamanca and Zamora. I felt increasingly bitter about the way I had been treated by General Bernadotte, for without his false promises I would have been an aide-de-camp to Messéna and regained my place in the 1st Hussars.

So I was much discontented....But one must obey. Once I had got over my resentment -- which does not last long at that age -- I could not wait to get on the road and leave General Bernadotte, of whom I thought I had good reason to complain. I had very little money. My father had often lent money to Bernadotte, in particular when he bought the estate of Lagrange; but although he knew that, scarcely recovered from an injury, I was about to cross a large part of France and all of Spain and, what is more, had to buy a new uniform, he never offered to advance me a sou; and not for anything in the world would I have asked him to do so. Very luckily for me my mother had, at Rennes, an elderly uncle, M. de Verdal of Gruniac, a former major in the infantry of Ponthièvre, with whom she had spent the first years of the revolution. This old man was a little eccentric, but very good-hearted; not only did he advance me the money which I desperately needed, but he gave it to me out of his own pocket.

Although, at this period, the Chasseurs wore the same dolman as the Hussars, theirs was green. I was foolish enough to shed a few tears when I had to discard the Bercheny uniform, and renounce the name of Hussar to become a Chasseur!

My farewell to General Bernadotte was somewhat cool; however he gave me letters of introduction to Lucien Bonaparte, our ambassador at Madrid, and to General Leclerc, our commander in Portugal.

On the day of my departure, all the aides-de-camp joined me in a farewell luncheon; then I set out with a heavy heart. I arrived at Nantes after two days of travel, dog tired, with a pain in my side, and quite sure that I would not be able to stand riding on horseback the four hundred and fifty leagues which I had to cover to reach the frontier of Portugal. By chance, however, I met in the house of an old acquaintance from Sorèze, who lived in Nantes, a Spanish officer named Don Raphael, who was on his way to join his regimental depot at Estramadura. We agreed to travel together, and that I would be guide as far as the Pyrenees, after which he would take over.

We went by stage-coach through the Vendée, where almost all the market towns and villages still bore the marks of fire although the civil war had been over for two years. These ruins made a sorry spectacle. We passed through La Rochelle, Rochefort and Bordeaux. From Bordeaux to Bayonne we rode in a sort of "Berlin" which never went at faster than a walking pace over the sands of Landes, so we often got out and walked alongside until we would stop to rest under a group of pine trees. Then, sitting in the shade, Don Raphael would take up his mandolin and sing. In this way we took six days to reach Bayonne.

Before crossing the Pyrenees, I had to report to the general commanding Bayonne. His name was General Ducos, an excellent man, who had served under my father. Out of concern for my safety, he wished to delay my entry into Spain for a few days, because he had just heard that a gang of robbers had plundered some travellers not far from the frontier. Even before the War of Independence and the Civil Wars, the Spanish character, at once both adventurous and lazy, had given them a noticeable taste for brigandage, and this taste was encouraged by the splitting up of the country into several kingdoms which once formed independent states, each with its own laws, usages, and frontiers. Some of these states imposed customs duties, some, such as Biscay and Navarre, did not; and the result was that the inhabitants of the customs-free countries constantly tried to smuggle dutiable goods into those whose frontiers were guarded by lines of armed and active customs officers. The smugglers, on their part, had, from time immemorial, formed bands, which employed force when cunning was insufficient, and whose occupation was not considered in any way dishonourable by the majority of Spaniards, who saw it as a just war against the imposition of customs. Preparing their expeditions, collecting intelligence, posting armed guards, hiding in the mountains, where they lie about smoking and sleeping, such is the life of the smugglers, who, as a result of the large profits to be made from a single operation, can live in comfortable idleness for several months. However, when the customs officers, with whom they have frequent skirmishes, have been victorious and confiscated their goods, these Spanish smugglers, reduced to extremes, think nothing of becoming highwaymen, a profession which they pursue with a certain magnanimity, since they never kill travellers, and always leave them the means to continue their journey. They had just done as much to an English family, and General Ducos, who wished to spare us the disagreeable experience of being robbed, had for this reason decided to delay our departure; but Don Raphael assured him that he knew enough about the habits of Spanish robbers to be certain that the safest time to travel in a province was just after a gang had committed some offence, because they then cleared off and hid for a while. So general Ducos allowed us to leave.

Draught-horses were at this time unknown in Spain, where all coaches, even the king's, were drawn by mules. There were no stage-coaches, and in the post-houses nothing but saddle horses. So that even the greatest of noblemen, who had their own coaches, were forced when they travelled to hire harness mules and go by short stages. The comfortably off took light carriages, which did not go more than ten leagues a day. The ordinary people attached themselves to caravanserais of donkey-men, who carried baggage in the same way as our carters, but no one travelled alone, partly for fear of robbers, and partly because of the mistrust with which a solitary traveller was regarded. After our arrival in Bayonne, Don Raphael, who was now in charge, said to me that as we were not such grandees that we could hire a coach, nor so poor that we had to join the donkey-men, there remained only two possibilities, either we rode on horseback or we took a seat in a carriage. Travelling on horseback, of which I have done so much, did not seem suitable, as we would have no means of carrying our baggage, so it was decided that we should go by carriage.

Don Raphael bargained with an individual who agreed to take us to Salamanca for 800 francs a head, and to lodge us and feed us on the way, at his own expense. This was double what a similar journey would have cost in France, and I had already spent a lot of money to get to Bayonne; but that was the price, and as there, was no other way for me to join my new regiment, I had to accept.

We left in an enormous and ancient four-wheeled carriage, in which three of the seats were occupied by a citizen of Cadiz, his wife and daughter, while a Benedictine Prior from the university of Salamanca completed the party.

Everything was new to me on this trip. Firstly, the harnessing, which greatly surprised me. The team consisted of six splendid mules, of which, to my astonishment, only the two on the shaft had bridles and reins, the remaining four went freely, guided only by the voices of the coachman and his "Zagal" who, agile as a squirrel, sometimes went for more than a league on foot, running beside his mules, which were at full trot, then, in a blink of an eye he would climb up on to the seat beside his master, only to get down and then up again; which he did twenty times a day; going round the coach and the harness to make sure that nothing was out of order, and while doing all this, singing to encourage his mules, each one of which he called by name. He never struck them, his voice alone being enough to urge on any mule which was not pulling its weight.

These activities, and in particular the man's singing, I found most entertaining. I also took a lively interest in what was said in the coach, for, although I did not speak Spanish, what I knew of Italian and Latin enabled me to understand much of what my fellow passengers were saying, to whom I replied in French, which they understood reasonably well. I did not smoke, but the five Spaniards, even the two ladies and the monk, soon lit up their cigars. We were all in good spirits. Don Raphael, the ladies, and even the fat monk sang together.

Normally we left in the morning. We stopped from one o'clock to three, to dine, rest the mules, and allow the heat of the day to pass, during which time one slept; what the Spanish call the siesta. Then we went on to our night stop. The meals were sufficiently plentiful, but the Spanish cuisine seemed to me, at first, to taste awful, however I got used to it; but I could never have got used to the horrible beds which we were offered at night in the pousadas or inns. They were really disgusting, and Don Raphael, who had just spent a year in France was forced to agree. To avoid this unpleasantness, on the first day of my arrival in Spain, I asked if I could sleep on a bale of straw. Sadly, I discovered that such a thing as a bale of straw was unknown in Spain, because, instead of threshing the sheaves of corn they have them trampled under foot by mules, which breaks the straw into short bits, scarcely as long as a finger. But I had the bright idea of filling a large cloth sack with this short straw, which I placed in a barn and slept on covered by my cloak; thus avoiding the vermin with which the beds and the rooms were infested. In the morning I emptied the sack and put it in the coach and each evening I refilled it so that I had a clean palliasse. Don Raphael followed my example.

We crossed the provinces of Navarre, Biscay and Alava, country of high mountains; then we crossed the Ebro and entered the immense plains of Castile. We passed through Burgos and Valladolid, and arrived, at last, after a journey lasting fifteen days, at Salamanca.

There, not without regret I parted from my good travelling companion, whom I was to meet once more in the same part of the world, during the War of Independence. General Leclerc was at Salamanca. He received me kindly, and even proposed that I should stay with him as a supernumerary aide-de-camp, but my recent experience had taught me that although the post of aide-de-camp offers one more freedom and comfort than regimental duty, this is only when one is on the establishment. As a supernumerary you are landed with all the unpleasant jobs, and you have only a very precarious position. I therefore turned down the favour which I was offered and asked to go and join my regiment. It was a good thing that I took this step, because, the following year, the general, having been given the command of the expedition to Santa Dominica, took with him, on his general staff, a lieutenant who had accepted the post which I had turned down, and all these officers and the general died of yellow fever.

I joined the 25th Chasseurs at Salamanca. The colonel was M. Moreau, an old officer and a very fine fellow. He gave me a warm welcome, as did my new comrades; and in a few days I was on the best of terms with everybody. I was introduced to the town's society, for at that time the presence of the French was highly acceptable to the Spanish, and completely opposite to what it became later. In 1801 we were their allies. We had come to fight for them against the Portuguese and the English, so we were treated as friends. The

French officers were billeted with the wealthiest inhabitants and there was competition to have them. We were received everywhere. We were overwhelmed by invitations. Being thus admitted into the family life of the Spaniards, we learned more, in a short time, about their way of living than officers who came to the peninsula during the War of Independence could have learned in several years.

I was billeted in the home of a university professor, who had given me a very nice room looking out onto the handsome Salamanca square. My regimental duties were not very onerous and left me plenty of leisure time, which I used to study the Spanish language, which is, in my opinion, the most elegant and beautiful in Europe. It was at Salamanca that I saw, for the first time, the famous General Lasalle. He sold me a horse.

The fifteen thousand French troops sent to Spain with General Leclerc formed the right wing of the Spanish Grand Army, which was commanded by the "Prince de la Paix" and we were therefore under his orders. This man (Emmanuel Godoy) was the queen's favourite and was, in effect, the king. He came to revue us on one occasion. He seemed to me to be very pleased with himself, and although he was small and undistinguished looking, he was not lacking in charm and ability.

Godoy started the army moving, and our regiment went to Toro and then to Zamora. I was sorry to leave Salamanca at first, but we were as well received in other towns, particularly in Zamora, where I stayed in the house of a rich merchant who had a superb garden, where a numerous society would gather in the evenings to make music and pass part of the night in conversation amid groves of pomegranates myrtles and lemon trees. It is difficult to appreciate fully the beauties of nature if one has not experienced the delicious nights of the southern countries.

We had, however, to tear ourselves away from the pleasant life which we were leading to go and attack the Portuguese. We crossed the border: there were a few small engagements which all went our way: the French troops went to Viseu, while the Spanish came down the Tagus and reached Alantejo: we expected to enter Lisbon soon, as conquerors. But the Prince de la Paix, who had, without much reflection, called the French troops into the peninsula, now, also without much reflection, took fright at their presence, and to get rid of them he concluded, without the knowledge of the First Consul, a peace treaty with the Portuguese, which he cunningly had ratified by the French ambassador, Lucien Bonaparte. This greatly annoyed the First Consul, and caused, from that day, a rift between the two brothers.

The French troops stayed for several months longer in Portugal, until the beginning of 1802; then we returned to Spain and successively to our previous charming stations of Zamora, Toro and Salamanca, where we were always made welcome.

On this occasion I went through Spain on horseback with my regiment, and had no longer any need to avoid the verminous beds of the pousadas, since we were lodged each evening with the most respectable citizens. A route march, when one makes it with one's own regiment and in good weather, is not without a certain charm. One has a constant change of scene, without being separated from one's comrades; one sees the countryside in the greatest detail; we talk as we travel, we dine together, sometimes well, sometimes badly, and one is in a position to observe the customs of the inhabitants.

One of our pleasures was to watch in the evenings the Spaniards, shedding their usual lethargy, dance the fandango and the bolero with a perfection of grace and agility, even in the villages. The colonel offered them the use of his band, but they, quite rightly, preferred the guitar, the castanets, and a woman's voice; an accompaniment which gave the dance its national characteristics. These improvised dances, in the open air, engaged in by the working class in the towns as well as in the country, gave us so much pleasure, even as spectators, that we were sorry to leave them.

After more than a month on the road, we recrossed the Bidassoa, and although I had happy memories of my stay in Spain, it was with pleasure that I saw France once more.

Chapter 15
Officer of Chasseurs

At this period, regiments were responsible for their own remounts, and the colonel had been authorised to buy sixty horses which he hoped to procure, bit by bit, in French Navarre, while he was takingaking the regiment to Toulouse, where we were to form the garrison. But, for my sins, we arrived at Bayonne on the day of the town fair, and the place was full of horse-copers. The colonel arranged a deal with one of them, who provided all the horses the unit needed straight away. The dealer could not be paid immediately because the funds provided by the ministry would take a week to arrive. The colonel then ordered that an officer should remain behind in Bayonne, to receive this money and pay the supplier. I was picked for this wretched task, which landed me later in a most disagreeable situation, though at the time I saw only that I had been deprived of the pleasure of travelling with my comrades. However, in spite of my feelings, I had to obey orders.

To make it easier for me to rejoin the unit, the colonel decided that my horse should go with the regiment, and that after I had completed my mission, I should take the stage-coach to Toulouse. I knew several former pupils from Sorèze who lived in Bayonne and who helped me to pass the time agreeably. The funds provided by the ministry arrived and I paid them out and was now free from all responsibility and ready to rejoin my regiment.

I had a cotton dolman, braided in the same material, and with silver buttons. I had had this strange costume made when I was on Bernadotte's staff, since it was the fashion there to wear this uniform when travelling in hot weather. I decided to wear this outfit on the journey to Toulouse, as I was not with my regiment, so I packed my uniform in my trunk and took it to the stage-coach, where I booked my seat and, unfortunately, paid in advance.

The coach was due to leave at five in the morning, so I told the porter at the hotel where I was staying to come and waken me at four, and the rascal having promised to do so, I went to bed without further ado. But he forgot; and when I opened my eyes, the sun was shining into the room and it was after eight o'clock...! What a disaster...! I was dumbfounded, and having cursed and upbraided the negligent porter, I had to think what I could do. The first difficulty was that the stage-coach ran only every second day, but that was not the major problem, which was that though the regiment had paid for my seat because I was on duty, they were not obliged to pay twice, and I had been stupid enough to pay for the whole journey in advance; so that if I took a new seat it would be at my own expense. Now at this time stage-coach fares were very costly, and I had very little money, and also, what was I to do for forty-eight hours in Bayonne, when all my belongings were on the coach...? I resolved to make the journey on foot.

I left the town without delay, and set off bravely on the road to Toulouse. I was lightly clad, and had nothing but my sabre, which I carried on my shoulder, so I covered the first stage briskly enough and spent the night at Peyrehorade.

The next day was a day of disaster. I intended to go as far as Orthez, and had already made half the journey when I was overtaken by one of these terrible storms which one has in the Midi. Rain mixed with hail fell in torrents, beating on my face; the road, already bad, became a morass in which I had the greatest difficulty in walking in boots with spurs; a chestnut tree near to me was struck by lighting.... No matter, I walked on with stoic resignation. But, behold....! In the midst of the storm I saw coming toward me two mounted gendarmes. You can easily imagine how I looked after paddling for two hours in the mud, dressed in my cotton breeches and dolman. The gendarmes belonged to the station at Peyrehorade, to which they were returning, but it seemed that they had lunched very well at Orthez, for they were somewhat drunk. The older of the two asked me for my papers; I gave him my travel permit, on which I was described as a sous-lieutenant of the 25th Chasseurs. "You! A sous-lieutenant?" shouted the gendarme, "you're too young to be an officer!" But read the description," I said, "and you will see that it says that I am not yet twenty years old. It is exact in every point." "That may be," he replied, "but it is a forgery; and the proof of that is that the Chasseur's uniform is green and you are wearing a yellow dolman. You are an escaped conscript, and I am arresting you." "All right," I said, "but when we get to Orthez and I see your lieutenant, I can easily prove that I am an officer and that this travel document is genuine."

I was not much worried by this arrest; but now the older gendarme said that he did not intend to go to Orthez. He belonged to the station at Peyrehorade, and I must follow him there. I said that I would do nothing of the kind, and that he could require this only if I had no papers, but as I had shown him my travel permit, he had no right to make me go back, and that it was his duty, according to the regulations, to accompany me to my destination, which was Orthez.

The younger gendarme, who was less full of wine, said that I was right. A lively dispute then broke out between the two of them. They hurled insults at one another and in the middle of the tempest which was all around us, they drew their sabres and charged furiously together. I was afraid I might be injured in this ridiculous combat, so I got into one of the huge ditches which ran along each side of the road, and although I was in water up to my waist, I climbed up onto the bordering field, from where I watched the two warriors skirmishing to get the better of one another.

Fortunately, the heavy, wet cloaks which they were wearing clung round their arms, and the horses, frightened by the thunder, would not go near each other, so that the riders could manage only a few ill directed blows. Eventually the older gendarme's horse fell, and he landed in the ditch. When he got out, covered in mire, he found that his saddle was broken and that he would have to continue his journey on foot; so he set out, after telling his companion that he was now responsible for the prisoner. Left alone with the more sensible of the two gendarmes, I pointed out to him that if I had anything to hide, it would be easy for me to make off into the country, as there was a large ditch between us which his horse could not cross, but that I would surrender myself to him since he had agreed not to make me go back. So I continued on my way, escorted by the gendarme, who was beginning to sober up. We had some conversation, and it became apparent that the fact that I had surrendered, when it would have been easy for me to run away, made him begin to think that I might be what I said I was. He would have let me go had he not been put in charge of me by his companion. He became more and more accommodating, and said he would not take me all the way to Orthez, but would consult the Mayor of Puyoo, which we were going to pass through.

My arrival was that of a malefactor: all the villagers, who had been driven back to the village by the storm, were at their doors and windows to see the criminal in the charge of the gendarme; however, the Mayor of Puyoo was a good, stout, sensible peasant, whom we found in his barn, threshing corn. As soon as he had read my travel permit, he said, gravely, to the gendarme, "Set this young man at liberty at once. You have no right to arrest him. An officer on a journey is designated by his documents, not by his clothes." Could Solomon have produced a better judgement? The good peasant did not stop at that, he wanted me to stay with him until the storm had passed and he offered me food. Then, while we were talking, he told me that he had once seen at Orthez a general whose name was Marbot. I told him that this was my father, and described him. Then the good man, whose name was Bordenave became even more solicitous and wanted to dry my clothes and offered me a bed for the night; but I thanked him and went on my way to Orthez, where I arrived at nightfall, completely worn out. The next day it was only with great difficulty that I could put my boots on, partly because they were wet and partly because my feet were swollen.

However I managed to drag myself as far as Pau, and being unable to go any further, I stayed there all day. I could find no other means of transport but the mail coach, and although the seats were very expensive, I took one as far as Gimont, where I was welcomed with open arms by M. Dorignac, a friend of my father, with whom I had spent several months after I left Sorèze. I rested for a few days with his family, then I took a stage-coach to Toulouse. I had spent four times the cost of the seat which I had lost through the negligence of the hotel porter at Bayonne.

On my arrival at Toulouse I was going to look around for somewhere to live, but the colonel told me that he had arranged a place for me with one of his friends, an elderly doctor named M. Merlhes, whose name I shall never forget, because this worthy man and his numerous offspring were so good to me. During the two weeks I stayed with them, I was treated as a member of the family rather than as a boarder.

The regiment was up to strength and well mounted. We had many exercises which I found very interesting; though I sometimes found myself up before squadron commander Blancheville, an excellent officer, an old soldier from whom I learned to work with precision, and I owe much to him. Blancheville, before the revolution, had been on the staff of the gendarmes of Lunéville. He was very well educated and took a great interest in young officers whom he thought capable of learning, and compelled them to study whether they liked it or not. As for the others, whom he called the block-heads, he simply shrugged his shoulders when they did not know their drill or made mistakes during exercises, but he never punished them for it. There were two or three sous-lieutenants whom he had picked out, they were MM. Gavoille, Dumonts and me. In our case he would not suffer an incorrectly given order, and punished us for the slightest mistake. As he was a very good fellow, when off duty we risked asking him why he treated us so severely. "Do you think I am so stupid that I would try to wash a black man white?" He replied, "Messers so and so are too old and lacking in talent to make it worth my while to try to improve them. As for you who have all that is required to succeed, you need to study, and study you shall!" I have never forgotten this reply, and I made use of it when I became a colonel. In fact old Blancheville had drawn our horoscopes accurately, Gavoille became a lieutenant-colonel, Dumonts a brigadier-general and I a divisional general.

On my arrival at Toulouse, I had exchanged the horse which I had bought in Spain for a delightful mount from Navarre. Now, it so happened that the prefect had arranged a race meeting in celebration of some fête or other, and Gavoille, who was a great lover of racing, had persuaded me to enter my horse. One day, when I was exercising my horse on a grass track, as he took a tight curve at full speed, he collided with the projecting wall of a garden and fell stone dead. My companions thought I had been killed or at least seriously injured, but by a miraculous piece of good luck I was unhurt. When I had been picked up, and saw my poor horse lying motionless, I was very upset, and went back sadly to my billet, where I confronted the realisation that I would have to buy another horse, and would have to ask my mother for the money to do so, although I knew she was very hard-up.

I bought a new horse, which was not as good as the Navarrais, but the general inspections, which had been reintroduced by the First Consul, were approaching, and it was essential that I was quickly remounted, the more so because we were to be inspected by General Bourcier, who had the reputation of being a stern disciplinarian.

I was detailed to go with thirty men to form an escort for him. He welcomed me warmly and spoke of my father, whom he had known well, which, however, did not prevent him from putting me on a charge the following day. The way in which this came about is quite amusing.

One of our captains, named B★★★, was a very good-looking lad, and would have been one of the most handsome men in the army if his calves had been in harmony with the rest of his person; but his legs were like stilts, which looked very odd in the tight breeches, called Hungarians, which were then worn by the Chasseurs. To get over this blemish, Captain B★★★ had acquired pads made in the shape of calves, which completed his fine appearance. You will see how these calves got me into trouble, but they were not the only cause.

The regulations laid down that the tails of officer's horses should be left flowing, as were the tails of the trooper's horses. Our colonel, M. Moreau, was always perfectly mounted, but all his horses had their tails cut, and as he feared that General Bourcier -- a stickler for the rules -- would take him to task for setting a bad example to his officers, he had, for the time of the inspection, had false tails fitted to his horses which were so realistic that, unless one knew, one would think them natural. This was all very fine. We went on manoeuvres, to which General Bourcier had invited General Suchet, the inspector of infantry, and General Gudin, the commander of the territorial division, and was accompanied by a numerous and brilliant staff.

The exercises were very long. Almost all the movements, carried out at the gallop, ended with several charges at top speed. I was in command of a section in the centre of Captain B★★★'s squadron, and it was next to the captain that the colonel took up his position. They were therefore a couple of paces in front of me when the generals came to congratulate Colonel Moreau on the fine performance of his troops. But what did I then see?.... The extreme rapidity of the movements had deranged the accessories added to the turn-out of both the colonel and Captain B★★★; the false tail of the colonel's horse had come adrift, the centre part, made of a pad of tow, was hanging down nearly to the ground and the hairs were spread over the horse's crupper in a sort of peacock's tail. As for Captain B★★★'s calves, they had slipped round to the front, and could be seen as large lumps on his shins, which produced a somewhat bizarre effect, while the captain sat up proudly on his horse, as if to say "Look at me! See how handsome I am!"

One has little gravity at the age of twenty. Mine was unable to resist the grotesque spectacle in front of me, and in spite of the presence of no less than three generals, I was unable to stop myself from bursting into laughter, however much I tried. The inspecting general, not knowing the reason for my hilarity, called me out of the ranks to reprimand me, but to reach him I had to pass between the colonel and Captain B★★★, and my eyes were once more directed to this cursed tail and the new calves sported by the captain, and I again burst out laughing. I was then put under open arrest. The generals must have thought I was crazy, but as soon as they had gone, the officers of the regiment gathered round the colonel and Captain B★★★, and soon realised what had happened. They laughed as I had done, but in easier circumstances.

In the evening, the commandant Blancheville attended a reception given by Madame Gudin. General Bourcier, who was also there, having brought up the subject of what he called my escapade, M. Blancheville explained the reasons for my unseemly laughter, an explanation which gave rise to much amusement. The laughter was increased by the entry of Captain B★★★, who having adjusted his false calves, had come to display himself in this brilliant society, without suspecting that he was one of the reasons for their hilarity. General Bourcier, appreciating that if he could not help laughing at a description of the sight which had

greeted my eyes, it was natural enough that a young sous-lieutenant could not contain himself when confronted with this ridiculous spectacle, cancelled my arrest and sent someone to look for
me. My arrival rekindled the laughter, which was increased by
the sight of Captain B★★★, who alone was unaware of the cause,
going from person to person asking what it was all about, while
everyone gazed at his calves.

Chapter 16
Disasters for My Family

Let us now turn to more serious matters. The Treaty of Lunéville had been followed by the Peace of Amiens, which put an end to the war between France and England. The First Consul decided to profit from the tranquility of Europe and the freedom of the sea to despatch a large body of troops to Dominica, which he wished to recover from the control of the blacks led by Toussaint-Louverture, a man who, without being in open revolt against the French, nevertheless adopted an air of great independence. General Leclerc was to be in command of this expedition. This general was a capable officer who had fought successfully in Egypt and Italy; but his principal distinction was that he had married Pauline Bonaparte, the First Consul's sister. Leclerc was the son of a miller from Pontoise, if one can describe as a miller, a very rich mill owner who had a considerable business. The miller had given the best of educations to his son and also to his daughter, who married General Davout.

While General Leclerc was preparing for his departure, the First Consul concentrated in Brittany those troops which he had earmarked for the expedition, and these troops naturally came under the command of the commander-in-chief of the area, which was Bernadotte.

It is well known that there was always a great rivalry between the troops of the Rhine army and those of the army of Italy. The former were greatly attached to General Moreau, and did not care for General Bonaparte, whose elevation to the head of government they had witnessed with regret. For his part, the First Consul had a great liking for the soldiers who had fought with him in Italy and Egypt, and, although the breach with Moreau was not yet openly declared, he considered that it would be in his interest to remove to as far away as possible troops devoted to this general. In consequence, the troops selected for the expedition to Dominica were almost all taken from the army of the Rhine. These men, however were perfectly happy to find themselves in Brittany, under the command of Bernadotte, a former lieutenant of Moreau's who had almost always served with them on the Rhine.

The expeditionary force was to comprise eventually some forty thousand men. The army of the west proper consisted of a similar number, so that Bernadotte, whose command extended to cover all the departments between the mouth of the Gironde and that of the Seine, had for a time under his orders an army of eighty thousand men, of whom the majority were more attached to him than to the head of the consular government.

If General Bernadotte had had more strength of character, the First Consul would have regretted putting him in such a powerful position; for I can say today, as an historical fact which will harm no one, that Bernadotte plotted against the government of which Bonaparte was the head. I shall give some details about this conspiracy which were never known to the public, and perhaps not even to General Bonaparte himself.

Generals Bernadotte and Moreau, jealous of the elevated position of the First Consul, and dissatisfied with the small part he gave them in public affairs, had resolved to overthrow him, and place themselves at the head of the government in conjunction with a civil administrator or an enlightened magistrate. To achieve this aim, Bernadotte, who, it must be said, had a talent for making himself liked by both officers and men, went about the provinces of his command, reviewing troops and using every means to increase their attachment to him. Enticements of all sorts, money, promises of promotion, were employed among the junior officers, while secretly he denigrated the government of the First Consul to the seniors. Having sown disaffection amongst most of the regiments, it would not have been difficult to push them into revolt; particularly those destined for the expeditionary force, who regarded it as a sort of deportation.

Bernadotte had as chief of staff Brigadier-general Simon, a competent but rather colourless officer. His rank put him in a position to correspond daily with unit commanders, and he used it to make his office the centre of the conspiracy. A battalion commander named Foucart was at that time attached to General Simon, who made him his principal agent. Foucart, using the excuse of official duties, travelled from garrison to garrison organising a secret league, which was joined by almost all the colonels and a crowd of senior officers, who were turned against the First Consul by accusations that he aspired to royalty; something, it seems, that he had not yet considered.

It was agreed that the garrison of Rennes, composed of several regiments, would begin the movement, which would spread like a trail of gunpowder into all divisions of the army: and as it was necessary that in this garrison there should be one unit which would start things off and get the rest moving, the 82nd Line regiment was brought to Rennes. This regiment was commanded by Colonel Pinoteau, an energetic and capable man, very brave, but something of a hothead, although he appeared outwardly phlegmatic. He was a follower of Bernadotte and one of the most enthusiastic of the conspirators. He promised to deliver his regiment, where he was extremely popular.

Everything was ready for the explosion when Bernadotte, lacking resolve and aiming, like a true Gascon, to have a catspaw to pull his chestnuts from the fire, persuaded General Simon and the other principal conspirators that it was essential that he should be in Paris when the army of Brittany proclaimed the deposition of the consul, so that he would be in a position to seize immediately the reins of government, in association with General Moreau, with whom he was going to confer about the matter. In reality, Bernadotte wished not to be compromised if the attempt failed, while maintaining himself in a position to take advantage of any success, and General Simon and the other conspirators were blind enough not to see through this ruse. The day of the armed uprising was then agreed, but the man who should have led it, because he had organised it, had cunningly absented himself.

Before Bernadotte left for Paris, a proclamation had been drawn up, addressed to the people of France as well as to the army. Several thousand copies of this were to be stuck up on the day of the event. A bookseller in Rennes, introduced by General Simon and by Foucart into the conspiracy, had undertaken to print this proclamation himself. This ensured that the proclamation would be ready for use in Brittany, but Bernadotte wanted to have a large number of these posters in Paris, for it was important to spread them throughout the capital and to send them to all the provinces as soon as the army of the west had made its move against the government, and as there was a risk of discovery if an approach was made to a Paris printer, Bernadotte devised a method of acquiring a large number of posters without compromising himself. He told my brother Adolphe, who was his aide-de-camp, that he was authorised to accompany him to Paris, and that he was to bring his horse and his carriage in anticipation of a long stay. My brother was delighted, and having packed his personal effects into the lockers of the carriage, he instructed his servant to bring the carriage, unhurriedly, to Paris while he went there by stage-coach.

As soon as my brother had left, General Simon and Commandant Foucart, delaying, under some pretext or other, the departure of my brother's servant, opened the carriage lockers and took out the personal possessions, which they replaced by packets of the proclamation. Then, having closed everything up, they sent poor Joseph on his way, without any suspicion of what he was carrying.

However, the First Consul's police had got wind of something brewing in the army of Brittany, but without knowing exactly what was going on or who was involved. The minister of police thought it was his duty to inform the prefect of Rennes who was a M. Mounier, and by the most extraordinary chance the prefect received this despatch on the very day when the revolt was due to break out, during a parade at Rennes, at mid-day. It was now eleven-thirty!

The prefect, to whom the minister had given no positive information, thought that in order to obtain some, he could do no better, in the absence of the commanding general, than to consult his chief of staff. He therefore asked General Simon to come to his office, and showed him the ministerial despatch. General Simon, believing that all had been discovered, then foolishly lost his head.

He told the prefect that there was indeed a vast conspiracy in the army, in which he had, unfortunately, played a part, of which he now repented; and thereupon he disclosed all the plans of the conspirators, and named the leaders; adding that in a few minutes the troops gathered on the parade ground, at a signal from General Pinoteau, were going to proclaim the overthrow of the consular government!

You may imagine M. Mounier's astonishment, and the concern he felt at being in the presence of a culpable general who, though at first thrown into confusion, might recover himself and recollect that he had eighty thousand men under his command, of whom eight to ten thousand were at this moment gathered not far from the prefecture. The position in which M. Mounier found himself was critical, but he extricated himself adroitly.

The general commanding the gendarmerie, Virion, had been ordered by the government to put together at Rennes a body of unmounted gendarmes, for the formation of which every regiment had supplied some Grenadiers. These soldiers, having no unifying bonds, escaped, in consequence, from the influence of the colonels of the regiments, and recognised only the orders of their new leaders, those of the gendarmerie who, in accordance with the regulations, obeyed the instructions of the prefect. M. Mounier now sent for General Virion, telling him to bring all the gendarmes. Meanwhile, fearing that General Simon might change his mind and leave him to go and place himself at the head of his troops, he soothed him with honeyed words, assuring him that his repentance and his confession would mitigate his offence in the eyes of the First Consul, and persuaded him to hand over his sword and go to the Tour Labat with the gendarmes who had at that moment arrived in the courtyard. So now the prime mover in the revolt was in prison.

While this was going on at the prefecture, the troops assembled at the Place D'armes were awaiting the hour of the parade which would also be that of the beginning of the revolt. All the colonels were in the secret, and had promised their support except the commander of the 79th, M. Goddard, who it was hoped would follow the rest.

From what a slender thread hangs the destiny of empires! Pinoteau, a strong and determined man, was due to give the signal which his regiment, the 82nd, already drawn up in battle formation on the square, was impatiently awaiting; but Pinoteau, with Foucart, had been busy all morning arranging for the despatch of proclamations, and in their preoccupation he had forgotten to shave. Mid-day arrived. Colonel Pinoteau realising that he was unshaven, hurried to put this right; but while he was engaged in this operation, General Virion, escorted by a large number of gendarmes, burst into the room, seized his sword and declared him a prisoner. He was taken to the tower to join General Simon. A few minutes later and Colonel Pinoteau would have been at the head of ten thousand men, and would undoubtedly have succeeded in starting the revolt. But taken thus by surprise he could do nothing but surrender to force.

Having made this second arrest, Virion and the prefect sent an aide-de-camp to the parade ground to tell Colonel Goddard of the 79th that they had a communication for him from the First Consul. As soon as he arrived, they told him of the discovery of the conspiracy and the arrest of General Simon and Colonel Pinoteau, and persuaded him to unite with them in putting down the rebellion. Having agreed to this, Colonel Goddard returned to the parade ground without telling anyone what he had learned, and taking his battalion to the Tour Labat, he joined the battalion of gendarmes who were guarding it. Also there were the prefect and General Virion, who arranged for ammunition to be distributed to the loyal troops. They then awaited events.

Meanwhile, the officers of the regiments which were assembled on the parade ground, surprised at the sudden departure of the 79th, and not understanding why General Pinoteau was late, sent to his home, where they were told that he had been arrested and sent to the tower. They were told at the same time of the arrest of General Simon.

This put the cat among the pigeons. The officers of the various units got together; Commandant Foucart proposed that they should march immediately to free the two prisoners and carry on with the movement. This suggestion was received with acclamation, particularly from the 82nd, who worshipped Colonel Pinoteau. They hurried to the Tour Labat, but found it surrounded by four thousand gendarmes and the battalion of the 79th. The assailants were undoubtedly the more numerous, but they had no ammunition and if they had had any, many of them would have been reluctant to fire on their comrades, simply to make a change in the members of the government. General Virion and the Prefect addressed them and urged them to return to their duty. The soldiers hesitated, and seeing this, none of the officers dared to order a bayonet attack, which was the only action which remained possible. Gradually the regiments stood down, and returned one by one to their barracks. Commandant Foucart, left alone, was taken to the tower, along with the unfortunate printer.

On learning that the insurrection at Rennes had failed, all the officers of the other regiments of the army of Brittany disavowed it; but the First Consul was not taken in by their protestations, he brought forward the date of their embarkation for Dominica and the other islands of the Antilles, where nearly all of them died, either in the fighting or of yellow fever.

As soon as he had heard the first confessions of General Simon and before the situation was fully under control, M. Mounier had sent a despatch rider to the government, and the First Consul now considered whether he should have Bernadotte and Moreau arrested. However, he suspended this measure for lack of any evidence, and to get hold of some, he ordered the examination of any travellers coming from Brittany.

While all this was going on, the good Joseph arrived at Versailles in my brother's carriage, and much to his surprise, found himself seized by the gendarmerie, and, in spite of his protests, brought before the minister of police. On learning that the carriage which this man was driving belonged to one of Bernadotte's aides-de-camp, the minister, Fouché, had all the lockers searched and found them full of proclamations, in which Bernadotte and Moreau, after denouncing the First Consul in violent terms announced his fall and their accession to power.

Bonaparte, furious with these two officers, demanded their presence. Moreau told him that as he, Moreau, had no authority over the army of the west, he would accept no responsibility for the conduct of the regiments of which it was composed; and one has to admit that this was a valid objection. It however worsened the position of Bernadotte, who, as commander-in-chief of the troops assembled in Brittany, was responsible for maintaining good order and discipline amongst them; but not only had his army engaged in conspiracy, but his chief-of-staff was a leader in the enterprise. The rebel proclamations bore Bernadotte's signature, and more than one thousand copies of this document had just been found in a carriage belonging to his aide-de-camp. The First Consul thought that such evident proofs would flatten and confound Bernadotte; but he was dealing with a true Gascon, as devious as they come!

Bernadotte expressed surprise...indignation! He knew nothing...absolutely nothing! General Simon was a villain and so was Pinoteau! He defied anyone to produce the original proclamation bearing his signature! Was it his fault if some lunatic had arranged for his name to be printed at the foot of a proclamation which he utterly and completely rejected. As for the wicked originators of all these plots, he would be the first to demand their punishment.

Bernadotte had indeed contrived to get everything directed by General Simon, without giving him a single word in writing which might compromise himself, and had left himself in a position in which he could deny everything if, in the event of the plot failing, General Simon should accuse him of being a participant. The First Consul, though convinced of Bernadotte's guilt, had no solid evidence to go on, and his council of ministers concluded that it would not be feasible to bring charges against a general who was so popular in the country and the army. Sadly, these sort of considerations did not apply to my brother Adolphe. One fine night they came to my mother's house to arrest him, and this at a time when the poor woman was already overburdened with grief.

M. de Canrobert, her eldest brother, whom she had managed to have taken off the list of émigrés, was living peaceably with her when he was picked out by a policeman as having been present at some gathering whose aim was the restoration of the previous government. He was taken to the Temple Prison, where he was detained for eleven months. My mother was taking every possible step to prove his innocence and obtain his liberty when she was struck by another terrible disaster.

My two younger brothers were pupils at the French Military School. This establishment had a huge park and a fine country house in the village of Vanves, not far from the banks of the Seine; and in the summer the pupils went there to pass some of their holidays, when those who had behaved well were allowed to bathe in the river. Now it so happened that, because of some student peccadillo, the headmaster had deprived the whole school of the pleasure of swimming; however my brother Theodore loved swimming, so he and some of his friends decided to go swimming without the knowledge of their masters. While the pupils were spread about the park playing, they went to an isolated spot where they climbed over the wall and, on a very hot day, they ran to the Seine, into which they jumped, bathed in perspiration. They were scarcely in the water, however, when they heard the college drum beating for dinner. Fearing that their escapade would be discovered by their absence from the refectory, they dressed hurriedly and rushed back by the way they had come, to arrive, breathless, at the start of the meal. In such circumstances, they should have eaten little or nothing, but schoolboys are heedless, and they ate as much as usual, with the result that they nearly all became ill. Theodore was particularly affected, and was taken to my mother's house desperately ill with pneumonia.

It was while she was going from the bedside of her mortally afflicted son to her brother's prison, that they came to arrest her first-born. An appalling situation for any mother. To make matters worse, poor Theodore died. He was eighteen years old, charming and handsome. I was desolated to hear of his death, for I was very fond of him. These dreadful misfortunes which, one after another, assailed my mother, impelled those who were my father's true friends to exert themselves on her behalf. A leading figure among them was M. Defermon, who worked almost daily with the First Consul, and who rarely failed to intercede for Adolphe and his widowed mother. Eventually, General Bonaparte said to him one day, that although he had a low opinion of Bernadotte's common sense, he did not believe that he was so lacking in judgement that in conspiring against the government, he would take into his confidence a twenty-one year old lieutenant; and besides that, General Simon had stated that it was he and Commandant Foucart who had put the proclamations in young Marbot's carriage, so that, if he was to blame at all, it was only to a very small extent. However, he, the First Consul, was not willing to release the aide-de-camp until Bernadotte came in person to ask him to do so.

When she heard of this decision taken by the First Consul, my mother hastened to Bernadotte's house and begged him to take the necessary step. He promised solemnly to do but the days and weeks rolled past without him doing anything. Eventually, he said to my mother, "What you are asking of me will be extremely painful, but no matter, I owe this to the memory of your husband, as well as to the interest I have in your children. I shall go this very evening to see the First Consul and I shall call at your house after leaving the Tuileries. I am certain I shall be able to announce the release of your son."

One can imagine with what impatience my mother waited during this long day! Every coach she heard made her heart beat. But at last it struck eleven o'clock and Bernadotte had not appeared. My mother then went round to his house, and what do you suppose she was told?....That General Bernadotte and his wife had left, to take the waters at Plombières, and would not be back for two months! In spite of his promises, Bernadotte had left Paris without seeing the First Consul. Devastated, my mother wrote to General Bonaparte. M. Defermon, who undertook to deliver the letter, was so indignant at the conduct of General Bernadotte that he could not resist telling the First Consul how he had behaved toward us. "That," said the First Consul, "is the sort of thing I would expect!"

M. Defermon, Generals Mortier, Lefebvre and Murat then urged that my brother should be freed; observing that if he had been unaware of the conspiracy, it was unjust to keep him in prison, and even if he had known something about it, he could not be expected to carry tales about Bernadotte, whose aide-de-camp he was. This reasoning impressed the First Consul, who set my brother at liberty and sent him to Cherbourg, to join the 49th Line regiment, as he did not wish him to continue as aide-de-camp to Bernadotte.

Bonaparte, who had a very long memory, probably had engraved, somewhere in his head, the words, "Marbot. Aide-de-camp of Bernadotte. Conspiracy of Rennes." So my brother was never again looked on with favour, and some time later he was sent to Pondichery.

Adolphe had spent a month in prison; Commandant Foucart was there for a year. He was cashiered and ordered to leave France. He took refuge in Holland, where he lived miserably for thirty years on earnings from French lessons, which he was reduced to giving, as he had no personal fortune.

At last, in 1832, he thought to return to his native country, and during the siege of Anvers I saw, one day, come into my room, a sort of elderly schoolmaster, very threadbare; it was Foucart, I recognised him. He told me that he did not have a brass farthing! While I offered him some assistance, I could not help reflecting on the bizarre workings of fate. Here was a man who in 1802 was already a battalion commander, and whose courage and ability would have certainly carried him to the rank of general, if Colonel Pinoteau had not decided to shave at the moment when the conspiracy of Rennes was due to come to a head. I took Foucart to Marshal Gérard, who also remembered him, and together we presented him to the Duc d'Orléans, who gave him a job in his library, at a salary of 2400 francs. He lived there for fifteen years.

As for General Simon and Colonel Pinoteau, they were imprisoned in the Isle de Ré for five or six years. Eventually, Bonaparte, having become Emperor, set them free. Pinoteau had been vegetating for some time in Rufec, his birthplace, when, in 1808, the Emperor, who was on his way to Spain, having stopped there to change horses, Pinoteau presented himself boldly before him and requested to be re-engaged in military service. The Emperor, who knew that he was an excellent officer, then placed him in command of a regiment, which he led faultlessly throughout the wars in Spain, so that after several campaigns, he was promoted to the rank of brigadier-general.

General Simon also returned to military service. He was in command of an infantry brigade in Masséna's army when we invaded Portugal. At the battle of Busaco, where Masséna made the mistake of mounting a frontal attack on the Duke of Wellington's army, which was in position on the heights of a mountain with a very difficult approach, Poor Simon, wishing, no doubt, to redeem himself and to make up for the time he had lost towards promotion, charged bravely at the head of his brigade, overcame every obstacle, clambered up the rocks under a hail of bullets, broke through the English line and was first into the enemy entrenchments. But, there, a bullet fired at close range shattered his jaw at the moment when the English second line drove back our troops, who were thrown down into the valley with considerable losses. The enemy found the unfortunate general lying in the redout among the dead and dying. His face was hardly recognisable as human. Wellington treated him with much respect, and as soon as he could be moved, he sent him to England as a prisoner of war. He was later permitted to return to France. But his terrible injury barred him from any further service. The Emperor gave him a pension, and one heard no more of him.

Chapter 17
The School of Cavalry

After the unhappy events which had just befallen her, my mother longed to re-unite her three remaining sons around her. My brother, having been ordered to join the expeditionary force which was being sent to India under the command of General Decaen, was given permission to spend two months with my mother; Félix was at the Military School, and a piece of good fortune brought me also to Paris.

The School of Cavalry was then at Versailles; every regiment sent there an officer and a non-commissioned officer, who, after completing their studies, returned to their unit to act as instructors. Now it so happened that at the moment when I was about to ask for permission to go to Paris, the lieutenant who had been at the School had completed the course, and the colonel proposed to send me to replace him. I accepted this with pleasure, for not only would it allow me to see my mother again, but it would ensure that for eighteen months I would be living only a short distance from her.

My preparations were soon made. I sold my horse and taking the stage-coach, I left the 25th Chasseurs, to which I was never to return; although not being aware of this at the time, my farewells to my comrades were lighthearted.

On my arrival in Paris, I found my mother greatly upset, not only on account of the cruel loss which we had just suffered, but also over the imminent departure of Adolphe for India, and the detention of my uncle Canrobert, which continued indefinitely.

We spent a month together as a family, at the end of which my elder brother had to report to Brest, where he was soon embarked for Pondichery in the "Marengo." As for me, I went to settle in at the School of Cavalry, whose barracks were in the great stables of Versailles.

I was lodged on the first floor, in apartments which had once been occupied by the Prince de Lambesc, the master of horse. I had a very big bedroom and an immense "salon" which looked out over the Avenue de Paris and the parade-ground. I was at first astonished that the most recently arrived pupil should be so well housed, but I soon learned that no one wanted this apartment because its huge size made it glacially cold, and few of the officer pupils could afford to keep a fire going. Happily I was not entirely without means. I had a good stove put in, and with a big screen, I made in this vast apartment a little room, which I furnished modestly, since all we were issued with was a table, a bed, and two chairs, which were quite out of place in the enormous space of my quarters. So I made myself reasonably comfortable until the return of spring, when the place seemed quite charming.

Although we were called pupils, you should not suppose that we were treated as students. We were allowed every freedom, too much freedom in fact. We were commanded by an old colonel, M. Maurice, whom we hardly ever saw, and who did not take part in anything. On three days in the week we had civilian horse-manship, under the celebrated equestrians Jardin and Coupé, and we went there when it suited us. In the afternoon, an excellent veterinarian, M. Valois, ran a course on the care of horses; but no one compelled us to study with any diligence. The other three days were devoted to military matters. In the morning, military horsemanship, taught by the only two captains in the school, and in the afternoon, drill, also taught by them. Once this parade was finished, the captains disappeared and each student went his own way.

You will appreciate that it took a keen desire to learn, to get anywhere in a school so badly run; however most of the students made progress because, being destined to become instructors in their respective regiments, their self-respect made them fear not being up to the task. So they worked reasonably hard, but not as hard as one would as a schoolboy. As for behaviour, the staff took no interest in it. As long as the students caused no trouble in the establishment itself, they were allowed to do as they pleased. They came and went at all hours. They were subject to no role call. They ate in hotels, if it suited them, slept out, and even went to Paris without asking permission. The non-commissioned pupils had a little less liberty. Two moderately strict sergeants were in charge of them, who insisted that they were back by ten o'clock at night.

Each of us wore the uniform of his regiment, so that a gathering of the whole school presented an interesting sight, as when, on the first day of every month, we paraded in full dress in order to draw up the pay roll; then you could see the uniforms of all the French cavalry regiments.

As all these officers belonged to different units, and were thrown together only for the duration of the course, there could not exist between them the close fellowship which is one of the features of regimental life. We were too numerous (ninety) for there to be a bond between all. There were coteries but no union. I did not feel any need to socialise with my new comrades. I left every Saturday for Paris, where I spent the next day and most of Monday with my mother.

I began the year 1803 at Versailles. Spring introduced some changes into my way of life. Each of the officers at the school was provided with a horse, so I devoted some of my evenings to taking long rides in the magnificent woods which surround Versailles, Marly, and Meudon.

During May, my mother was made very happy by the release of her eldest brother from the Temple prison, and the return to France of the other two, de l'Isle and de la Coste, who, having been struck off the list of émigrés came to Paris.

Chapter 18
Aide-de-Camp to Augereau

While I was on the course at the school of cavalry, great events were under way in Europe. England having broken the Treaty of Amiens, hostilities recommenced. The First Consul resolved to take the initiative by leading an army onto the soil of Great Britain, a daring and difficult undertaking, but not impossible. To put it into operation, Napoleon, who had just seized Hanover, the private property of the English monarchy, stationed on the coasts of the North Sea and the Channel, several army corps, and ordered the construction and assembly, at Boulogne and neighbouring ports, of an immense number of barges and flat-bottomed boats, on which he proposed to embark his troops.

All the armed forces were set in motion for this war. I regretted that I was not involved; and being destined to carry back to my regiment the knowledge I had acquired at the school, I saw myself condemned to spend several years in the depot with a whip in my hand, making recruits trot round on elderly horses, while my comrades were fighting at the head of troops which I had trained. I did not find this prospect very pleasant, but how was it to be changed? A regiment must always be fed with recruits, and it was certain that my colonel, having sent me to the school of cavalry to learn how to train these recruits, would not deprive himself of the services which I could render in this respect, and would keep me out of the fighting squadrons. One day, however, as I was walking down the Avenue de Paris, with my drill manual in my hand, I had a brilliant idea, which totally changed my destiny and contributed greatly to my promotion to the rank which I now occupy.

I had just learned that the First Consul, having fallen out with the court of Lisbon, had ordered the formation, at Bayonne, of an army corps destined to enter Portugal under the command of General Augereau. I knew that General Augereau owed some of his advancement to my father, so I resolved to write to him and, having explained the predicament in which I found myself, ask him to extricate me by taking me on as one of his aides-de-camp.

Having written this letter, I sent it to my mother, to see if she approved. She not only approved, but knowing that Augereau was in Paris, she decided to take the letter to him herself. Augereau received the widow of his old friend with the greatest consideration; he immediately took his carriage and went to the War Ministry, and that same evening he handed to my mother my appointment as aide-de-camp.

The following day I hurried to Paris to thank the general. He received me most kindly, and ordered me to join him at Bayonne, to where he was now going. It was now October, I had completed the first course at the school of cavalry and had little interest in starting on the second; so I was happy to leave Versailles, for I felt sure that I was starting on a new career, much more advantageous than that of a regimental instructor. I was quite right in thinking this, for nine years later I was a colonel, while those I had left at the school had hardly reached the rank of captain.

I reported promptly to Bayonne and took up my post as an aide-de-camp to the commander-in-chief. He was installed a quarter of a league from the town in the fine Château de Marac, in which the Emperor lived some years later. I was made very welcome by General Augereau and by my new comrades, his aides-de-camp, nearly all of whom had served under my father. This general staff, although it did not give to the army as many general officers as that of Bernadotte, was nevertheless very well made up. General Danzelot who was the chief-of-staff, was a highly capable man who later became the governor of the Ionian islands and then Martinique. His second in command was Colonel Albert, who at his death was general aide-de-camp to the Duc d'Orléans. The aides-de-camp were Colonel Sicard, who died at Heilsberg, Major Brame, who retired to Lille after the Peace of Tilsit, Major Massy, killed as a colonel at Moscow, Captain Chévetel and Lieutenant Mainville, the first of whom retired to his estate in Brittany and the second ended his career in Bayonne. I was the sixth and youngest of the aides-de-camp.

Finally the staff was completed by Dr. Raymond, who helped me greatly at Eylau, and Colonel Augereau, a half-brother of the general; a very quiet man, who later became a lieutenant general.

Chapter 19
The Plot to Overthrow Napoleon

At Bayonne I joined Augereau's staff. The winter, in this part of the country, is very mild; which allowed us to train and exercise troops in preparation for an attack on the Portuguese. However, the court of Lisbon having conceded all that the French government required, we gave up the idea of crossing the Pyrenees, and General Augereau was ordered to go to Brest and take command of the 7th army corps, which was earmarked for an invasion of Ireland.

General Augereau's first wife, being in Pau, he wished to visit her and take his leave of her, and he took with him three aides-de-camp, of which I was one.

Normally, a commander-in-chief had a squadron of "Guides", a detachment of which always escorted his carriage, as long as he was in a part of the country occupied by troops under his command. Bayonne did not yet have any "Guides," so they were replaced by a platoon of cavalry at each of the post-houses between Bayonne and Pau. These came from the regiment which I had just left, the 25th Chasseurs; so that from the carriage in which I was taking my ease, beside the Commander in Chief, I could see my former companions trotting beside the door.

After a stay of twenty-four hours at Pau, we returned to Bayonne, from where the general despatched me and Mainville to Brest, in order to prepare his headquarters. We took seats in the mail-coach as far as Bordeaux; but there, owing to the lack of public transport, we were forced to take to the hacks of the posting houses, which of all means of travelling, is surely the most uncomfortable. It rained. The roads were appalling. The nights pitch dark; but in spite of this, we had to press on at the gallop, as our mission was urgent. Although I have never been a very good horseman, the fact that I was accustomed to riding, and a year spent in the riding school at Versailles, gave me enough assurance and stamina to drive on the dreadful screws which we were forced to mount. I got well enough through this apprenticeship in the trade of courier, in which, you will see later, I had to perfect myself; but it was not so with Mainville, so we took two days and two nights to reach Nantes, where he arrived bruised and worn out and incapable of continuing to ride at speed. However we could not leave the commander-in-chief without lodgings when he arrived at Brest, so it was agreed that I would go on ahead, and that Mainville would follow later by coach.

On my arrival, I rented the town house of M. Pasquier, the banker, brother of the Pasquier who had been chancellor and president of the house of peers. Mainville and several of my comrades came to join me a few days later, and helped to make the necessary arrangements for the commander-in-chief to maintain the sort of state expected of him.

We began the year 1804 at Brest. The 7th Corps was made up of two divisions of infantry and a brigade of cavalry; as these troops were not encamped but were billeted in the neighbouring communes, all the generals and their staffs stayed in Brest, where the anchorages and the harbour were packed with vessels of all sorts. The admirals and senior officers of the fleet were also in the town, and other officers came there every day, so that Brest afforded a most animated spectacle. Admiral Truguet and the commander-in-chief held a number of brilliant receptions, scenes that have often been the prelude to war.

In February General Augereau left for Paris, to where the First Consul had summoned him to discuss with him the plan for the invasion of Ireland. I went with him.

On our arrival in Paris, we found a very tense political situation. The Bourbons, who had hoped that in taking the reins of government, Bonaparte would support them, and would be prepared to play the part that General Monk had once played in England, when they discovered that he had no intention of restoring them to the throne, resolved to overthrow him. To this end they concocted a conspiracy which had as its leaders three well known men, although of very different character. These were General Pichegru, General Moreau and Georges Cadoudal.

Together they conspired to overthrow Bonaparte, but the plot failed. Pichegru hanged himself in prison, Cadoudal was executed. As for General Moreau, he was sentenced to two years detention. The First Consul pardoned him on condition that he went to the United

States. He lived there in obscurity until 1813, when he went to Europe to range himself among the enemies of his country, and died fighting against the French; thus confirming all the accusations which were made against him at the time of Pichegru's conspiracy.

The French nation, weary of revolutions, and recognising the extent to which Bonaparte was needed for the maintenance of good order, raised him to the throne by declaring him Emperor on May 25th, 1804.

Almost all nations recognised the new sovereign of France. To mark the occasion, eighteen generals, selected from the most notable, were elevated to the dignity of Marshals of the Empire.

Chapter 20
The Emperor Appoints Me Lieutenant

After the trial of Moreau, we returned to Brest, from where we shortly came back to Paris, as the marshal had to assist in the distribution of the decoration of the Legion d'Honneur, an award which the Emperor had recently instituted for the recognition of all sorts of meritorious actions. In this connection I recall an anecdote which was widely circulated at the time. In order to bestow the award on all these soldiers who had distinguished themselves in the Republican armies, the Emperor took into consideration all those who had been given Armes d'Honneur, and he selected a great number of these for the Legion d'Honneur, although several of them had returned to civilian life. M. de Narbonne, a returned émigré, was living quietly in Paris in the Rue de Miromesnil, in the house next to my mother's, when, on the day that the medals were distributed, he discovered that his footman, a former soldier in Egypt, had just been decorated. Being about to dine, he sent for the footman and said to him, "It is not right that a recipient of the Legion d'Honneur should hand round plates; and it would be even less right that you should put aside your decoration to serve at table. Sit down with me and we shall dine together, and tomorrow you shall go to my country estate where you shall be a game-keeper. An occupation which is not incompatible with wearing your decoration."

When the Emperor was told of this display of good taste, he sent for M. de Narbonne, whom he had wanted to meet for a long time, having heard so much about his wit and intelligence, and was so pleased with him that he made him an aide-de-camp.

After distributing the crosses in Paris, the Emperor went, for the same purpose, to the camp at Boulogne, where the troops were drawn up in a semi-circle facing the sea. The ceremony was imposing. The Emperor appeared for the first time on a throne, surrounded by his marshals. The enthusiasm was indescribable! The

English fleet who could see what was going on, sent several light vessels in an attempt to disrupt the event by a cannonade, but our coastal batteries briskly returned their fire.

There was a story current at the time which related that, after the ceremony was over, the Emperor was returning to Boulogne followed by his marshals and an immense retinue, when he stopped in the shelter of one of these batteries, and calling to Marmont, who had served in the artillery, said "Let us see if we can remember our old trade and land a bomb on that English brig." And dismissing the corporal who was in charge of the weapon, the Emperor aimed and fired at the vessel. The bomb brushed the vessel's sails and fell into the sea. Marmont tried but with no better fortune. The Emperor then recalled the corporal to his post and the latter took aim and fired with such effect that he landed a bomb on the brig, which promptly sank, to the great delight of the onlookers, whereupon Napoleon pinned a medal to the soldier's uniform. How much truth there is in this tale, I do not know. I shared in the favours being distributed on that day. I had been a sous-lieutenant for five and a half years, and had been through several campaigns. The Emperor, at the request of Augereau promoted me to lieutenant; but for a moment I thought he was going to refuse me this rank, for remembering that a Marbot had figured in the conspiracy of Rennes, he frowned when the marshal spoke up for me and, looking closely at me he said "Is it you who...?" "No sire, it is not me who!..." I replied, thinking of my brother's association with the conspiracy at Rennes. "Ah!" he said, "you are the one who was at Genoa and Marengo. I appoint you lieutenant."

The Emperor also granted me a place at the military school of Fontainebleau for my younger brother, Félix, and from that day on he no longer confused me with my elder brother for whom he always had antipathy, though Adolphe had done nothing to deserve it.

As the troops of 7th Corps were not concentrated in an encampment, Marshal Augereau's presence in Brest was of very little use; so he was given permission to spend the rest of the summer and the autumn at his fine estate of La Houssaye, near Tournan, in Brie. I even suspect that the Emperor preferred to have him there rather than in the depths of Brittany at the head of a large army. However, any doubts which the Emperor may have had about Augereau's loyalty were without foundation, and arose from the underground plots of a General S....

S.... was a brigadier-general serving in 7th Corps. A capable officer, but over-ambitious. He was regarded as untrustworthy by his fellow generals, who did not associate with him. Angered by this rejection, and bent on revenge, he sent to the Emperor a letter in which he denounced all the generals, as well as the marshal, as conspiring against the empire. Napoleon, to his credit, did not employ any secret means to ascertain the truth: he simply passed the general's letter on to Marshal Augereau. The marshal felt sure that nothing serious was going on in his army; however as he knew that several generals and colonels had engaged in some thoughtless talk, he resolved to put an end to this sort of thing. As he did not wish to jeopardize the career of those officers to whom he intended to deliver a rebuke, he thought it would be best if his words were carried by an aide-de-camp, and he chose to take me into his confidence for this important mission.

I left La Housaye in August, in very hot weather, and rode at full speed the one hundred and sixty leagues between the château and the town of Brest, and as many again on the way back. I stayed no more than twenty-four hours in the town, so I arrived back completely worn out, for I think that there is no more exhausting job than riding rapidly on horseback from post-house to post-house. I had found things a good deal more serious than the marshal had thought; there was, in fact a considerable ferment in the army, but the message I had brought calmed down the generals, almost all of whom were devoted to the marshal.

I was beginning to recover from my exertions when the marshal said to me one morning, that the generals wanted to denounce S.... as a spy. He added that it was absolutely essential that he sent one of his aides-de-camp, and he wanted to know if I felt able to make the journey again. He said he would not order me to go, but would leave it to me to decide whether I could do it or not. If it had been merely a matter of reward or even promotion, I think I would have refused the task, but it was a question of obliging my father's friend, who had welcomed me with so much kindness, so I said that I would be ready to go in an hour's time. I was worried that I might not be able to complete the journey, because of the extremely tiring nature of this form of travel; I rested for no more than two hours out of the twenty-four, when I flung myself down on a heap of straw in the post-house stables. It was fearfully hot weather, but I managed to reach Brest and return without accident, and had the satisfaction of being able to tell the marshal that the generals would limit themselves to expressing their mistrust of S....

General S... being now discredited, deserted and went to England, and is said to have wandered over Europe for twenty years before dying in poverty.

After my second return from Brest, the marshal rewarded me by putting me in direct contact with the Emperor. He sent me to Fontainebleau to meet Napoleon and conduct him to La Houssaye, where he was to spend a day in the company of several of his marshals. It was while walking with them and discussing his plans, and the manner in which he intended to uphold his dignity and theirs, that he presented each of them with a sum of money sufficient for them to purchase a mansion in Paris. Marshal Augereau bought that of Rochechouart, in the Rue Grenelle-St-Germain, which is today occupied by the ministry of information. The mansion was superb, but the marshal preferred to stay at La Houssaye, where he kept up a great state; for over and above his aides-de-camp, each of whom had his own apartments, the number of invited guests was always considerable. One enjoyed complete liberty; the marshal allowed his guests to do as they pleased, provided that no noise reached the wing of the château occupied by his wife.

This excellent woman, who had become a chronic invalid, lived very quietly, and appeared only rarely at the table or in the salon, but when she did, far from constraining our high spirits, she took pleasure in encouraging them.

She had with her two extraordinary lady companions. The first of these always wore men's clothing, and was known by the name of Sans-Gene. She was the daughter of one of the leaders who, in 1793, defended Lyon against the forces of the convention. She escaped, with her father, both of them disguised as soldiers, and took refuge in the ranks of the 9th Dragoon regiment; where they assumed nommes de guerre and took part in campaigning.

Mlle. Sans-Gene, who combined with her masculine attire and appearance, a most manly courage, received several wounds, one of them at Castiglione, where her regiment was part of Augereau's division. General Bonaparte, who had often witnessed the prowess of this remarkable woman, when he became First Consul, gave her a pension and a position beside his wife; but life at court did not suit Mlle. San-Gene. She left Mme. Bonaparte, who by mutual consent handed her over to Mme. Augereau to whom she became secretary and reader. The second lady companion of Mme. Augereau was the widow of the sculptor Adam, and in spite of her eighty years was the life and soul of the château.

Noisy parties and practical jokes were the order of the day at this period of time, particularly at La Houssaye, whose proprietor was not happy unless he could see his guests and the younger members of his staff gay and animated. The marshal came back to Paris in November; the time for the coronation was drawing near and already the Pope, who had come for the ceremony, was at the Tuileries. A crowd of magistrates and deputations from various departments had collected in the capital, where also were all the colonels of the army, with detachments from their regiments, to whom the Emperor distributed, on the Champ de Mars, the eagles, which became so celebrated. Paris, resplendent, displayed a luxury hitherto unknown. The court of the new Emperor became the most brilliant in the world; everywhere were fêtes, balls, and joyous assemblies.

The coronation took place on the 2nd December. I accompanied the marshal at this ceremony, which I shall not describe, since the details are so well known. Some days later the marshals held a ball in honour of the Emperor and Empress. There were eighteen marshals, and Marshal Duroc, although he was only Prefect of the Palace, joined with them, which made nineteen subscribers, each one of whom paid up 25,000 francs for the expenses of the event, which therefore cost 475000 francs. The ball took place in the great ballroom of the Opera, where never before had something so magnificent been seen. General Samson of the engineers was the organiser; the aides-de-camp acted as stewards, to welcome the guests and to distribute tickets. Everyone in Paris wanted one, so the aides were overwhelmed by letters and requests. I never had so many friends! Everything went off perfectly, and the Emperor appeared very pleased. So we ended the year 1804 in the midst of celebrations, and entered the year 1805, which was to be a year of many important events.

In order that his army could participate in the general jollifications, Marshal Augereau went to Brest, in spite of the rigours of winter, and gave a number of magnificent balls, at which he entertained a succession of officers, and even a good number of soldiers. At the beginning of spring, he returned to La Houssaye to await the moment for the invasion of England.

This expedition, which was regarded as chimerical, was, however, on the point of realisation. The presence of an English squadron of about fifteen ships, cruising endlessly in the Channel, made it impossible to transport a French army to England in boats and barges which would have sunk on the least contact with a larger vessel; but the Emperor could dispose of sixty ships of the line, either French or foreign, dispersed in the harbours of Brest, Lorient, Rochefort, Le Ferrol, and Cadiz; it was a matter of concentrating them, unexpectedly, in the Channel, and crushing, by a greatly superior force, the little English squadron, to become masters of the passage, if only for three days.

To achieve this, the Emperor ordered Admiral Villeneuve, the commander-in-chief of all these forces, to gather together, from the French and Spanish ports whatever ships were available, and head, not for Boulogne, but for Martinique, to where it was certain the English fleet would follow him. While the English were making their way to the Antilles, Villeneuve was to quit the islands, and returning round the north of Scotland, was to enter the eastern end of the channel with sixty ships, which would easily overcome the fifteen which the English maintained before Boulogne, and so put Napoleon in command of the crossing; while the English, on their arrival at the Antilles, would search around for Admiral Villeneuve's fleet, and thus waste valuable time.

A part of this fine plan was now put into action. Villeneuve left, with not sixty, but some thirty ships. He reached Martinique. The English, led astray, hurried to the Antilles, which Admiral Villeneuve had left, but the French admiral, instead of returning via Scotland, made for Cadiz in order to pick up the Spanish fleet, as if thirty ships were not enough to overcome or chase away the fifteen English vessels!

That, however, is not all. Having arrived at Cadiz, Villeneuve spent a great deal of time repairing his ships; time during which the enemy fleet also returned to Europe, and established a patrolling force off Cadiz. In the end, the coming of the equinox gales having made sailing from this port difficult, Villeneuve found himself blockaded; so the ingenious plans of the Emperor came to nothing, and he, realising that the English would not be taken in a second time, gave up the idea of invading Britain, or at least postponed it indefinitely, and turned his attention to the continent.

Before I recount the principal events of this long war, and the part which I played in it, I must describe a terrible misfortune which befell the family.

My brother, Félix, who was at the military school of Fontainebleau, was a little short-sighted; he had, therefore, hesitated before taking up a military career; nevertheless, once embarked on it, he worked with such enthusiasm that he soon became a sergeant-major, a position difficult to maintain in a school. The pupils, an unruly lot, were in the habit of burying in the earth of the fortifications which they were digging, the implements which had been issued to them for the work. General Bellavene, the head of the school, a very strict man, ordered that the implements should be issued to the sergeant-majors, who would then be accountable for them.

One day, my brother, having seen a pupil bury a pick, rebuked him. The pupil replied very rudely and added that in a few days they would be leaving school, and being then the equal of his sergeant-major, he would demand satisfaction for the reprimand. My brother replied indignantly that there was no need to wait so long.

Lacking swords, they used compasses fixed to wooden batons: Jacqueminot, who later became a lieutenant-general, was my brother's second. My brother's poor eyesight put him at a disadvantage, but he succeeded in wounding his opponent, though he received in return a wound which penetrated his right arm. His companions dressed it secretly.

By an unhappy coincidence, the Emperor had come to Fontainebleau, and had decided to conduct manoeuvres for several hours, under a blazing sun. My poor brother, compelled to run without rest, his arm dragged down by the weight of his heavy musket, was overcome by the heat and his wound re-opened! He should have fallen out on the pretext of an indisposition, but he was in front of the Emperor who, at the end of the session, would distribute the commissions of sous-lieutenant, so eagerly desired. Félix made superhuman efforts to resist, but at last his strength failed him and he collapsed and was carried away in a most serious condition.

General Bellavene sent an unfeeling message to my mother, saying that if she wished to see her son, she must come immediately, for he was dying. My mother was so distressed by this news, that she was unable to make the journey. I posted there as quickly as I could, but on my arrival I was told that my brother was dead. Marshal Augereau did all that he could for us, in these unhappy circumstances, and the Emperor sent the marshal of the palace, Duroc, to convey his condolences to my mother.

All too soon another source of sadness would come to afflict her; I would be forced to leave her, as war was about to break out on the continent.

At a time when it might have been thought that the Emperor had the greatest need to be at peace with the continental powers, in order to execute his design for the invasion of England, he issued a decree whereby he annexed the state of Genoa to France. This was greatly to the advantage of the English, who profited from this decision to frighten all the peoples of the continent, to whom they represented Napoleon as aspiring to become the master of the whole of Europe. Austria and Russia declared war on us, Prussia, more circumspect, made preparations, but as yet, said nothing.

The Emperor had no doubt foreseen these reactions, and a wish to see hostilities break out perhaps underlay his seizure of Genoa; for, despairing of ever seeing Villeneuve in control of the channel, he wanted a continental war to deflect the ridicule to which his proposed invasion, threatened for three years, but never put into action, might have exposed him by displaying his impotence in the face of England. The new coalition extricated him nicely from an awkward situation.

Three years under arms had had an excellent effect on our soldiers. France had never had an army so well trained, so well organised, so keen for action, nor a leader in control of so much power and such moral and material resources, who was so skillful in their employment. So Napoleon accepted the outbreak of war with pleasure, so confident was he of conquering his enemies, and of making use of their defeat to strengthen his position on the throne; for he knew the enthusiasm which the prospect of military triumph always stirred up in the martial French spirit.

Chapter 21
I 'Lose' a Regiment of Hussars

The great army which the Emperor was about to set in motion against Austria, now had its back to that Empire, since the forces deployed on the coasts of the North Sea, the Channel and the Atlantic were facing England. On the right wing the 1st Corps, commanded by Bernadotte, occupied Hanover; the 2nd, under the orders of Marmont, was in Holland; the 3rd under Davout was in Bruges; the 4th, 5th and 6th commanded by Soult, Lannes and Ney, were encamped at Boulogne and in the surrounding district, while finally the 7th commanded by Augereau was in Brest, and formed the extreme left.

To break up this long cordon of troops and form them into a large body which could march toward Austria, it was necessary to effect an immense turn round from front to back. Each army had to make an about turn, in order to face Germany, and form columns, to march there by the shortest route. Thus the right wing became the left, and the left the right.

Obviously, to go from Hanover or Holland to the Danube, the 1st and 2nd Corps had a much shorter distance to travel than those who came from Boulogne, and they in turn were nearer than Augereau's corps, which, in order to go from Brest to the frontiers of Switzerland on the upper Rhine, had to cross the whole of France, a journey of some three hundred leagues. The troops were on the road for two months, marching in several columns; Marshal Augereau was the last to leave Brest, but he then went on ahead, and stopped first at Rennes and then successively at Alonçon, Melun, Troyes and Langres, at which stops he inspected the various regiments, whose morale was raised by his presence. The weather was superb: I spent the two months travelling endlessly in an open carriage, from one column to another, carrying the marshal's orders to the generals, and was able to stop twice at Paris to see my mother. Our equipment had gone on in advance. I had a mediocre servant, but three excellent horses.

While the Grande Armée was wending its way towards the Rhine and the Danube, the French troops stationed in northern Italy, under the command of Masséna, concentrated in the Milan area in order to attack the Austrians in the region of Venezia.

To transmit his orders to Masséna, the Emperor was obliged to send his aides-de-camp through Switzerland, which remained neutral. Now it so happened that while Marshal Augereau was at Langres, an officer who was carrying Napoleon's despatches was thrown out of his carriage and broke his collar-bone. He was taken to Marshal Augereau whom he told that he was unable to continue his mission. The marshal, knowing how important it was that the Emperor's despatches should arrive in Italy without delay, entrusted me with the task of delivering them, and also of going through Huningue, where I was to pass on his order to have a bridge built over the Rhine at this spot. I was delighted to have this mission, as it meant that I would have an interesting journey and would be sure of rejoining 7th Corps before they were in action against the Austrians.

It did not take me long to reach Huningue and Basle; I went from there to Berne and on to Rapperschwill, where I left my carriage: then, on horseback and not without some danger, I crossed the Splügen pass, at that time almost impracticable. I entered Italy at Chiavenna, and joined Marshal Masséna near Verona. I went off again without any delay, for Masséna was as impatient to see me go with his replies to the Emperor as I was to rejoin Marshal Augereau before there was any fighting. However my return journey was not as rapid as my journey out, because a very heavy fall of snow had covered not only the mountains but also the valleys of Switzerland; it had begun to freeze hard, and horses slipped and fell at every step. It was only by offering 600 francs that I was able to find two guides who were prepared to cross the Splügen with me. It took us more than twelve hours to make the crossing, walking through snow sometimes up to our knees. The guides were on the point of refusing to go any further, saying that it was too dangerous, but I was young and venturesome, and I knew the importance of the despatches which the Emperor was awaiting.

I told my guides that even if they turned back, I would go on without them. Every profession has its code of honour; that of the guides consists principally in never abandoning the traveller committed to their care. Mine then went forward, and after some truly extraordinary exertions, we arrived at the large inn situated at the foot of the Splügen as night was falling. We would have undoubtedly died if we had been trapped on the mountain, for the path, which was barely discernable, was edged by precipices which the snow prevented us from seeing clearly. I was exhausted, but a sleep restored my strength, so I left at daybreak to reach Rapperschwill, where there were carriages and passable roads.

The worst of the journey was over; so, in spite of the snow and bitter cold, I reached Basle and then Heningue, where the 7th Corps was stationed, on the 19th October. The next day we began to cross the Rhine over a bridge of boats built for that purpose; for although there was, less than half a league away in the town of Basle, a stone bridge, the Emperor had ordered Marshal Augereau to respect the neutrality of Switzerland, a neutrality which they themselves broke, nine years later, by handing the bridge to the enemies of France in 1814.

Here I was then, involved once more in a war. It was now 1805, a year which for me heralded a long series of battles which lasted continuously for ten years, for it did not end until ten years later at Waterloo. However numerous the wars of the Empire might be, nearly all French soldiers enjoyed one or even several years of respite, either because they were in a garrison in France, or they were stationed in Italy or Germany when we were at war with Spain; but, as you will see, this did not happen to me; I was continually sent from north to south, and south to north, everywhere where there was fighting. I did not spend a single one of these ten years without coming under fire and without shedding my blood in some foreign country.

I do not intend to give, here, a detailed account of the campaign of 1805. I shall limit myself to recalling the principal events.

The Russians, who were marching to the aid of Austria, were still far away, when Field-marshal Mack, at the head of eighty thousand men, advanced, unwisely, into Bavaria, where he was defeated by Napoleon, who forced him to retreat to the fortress of Ulm, where he surrendered with the greater part of his army, of which only two corps escaped the disaster.

One of these, commanded by Prince Ferdinand, managed to reach Bohemia; the other, commanded by the elderly Field-marshal

Jellachich, escaped into the Vorarlberg near Lake Constance, where, flanked by neutral Switzerland, it guarded the narrow passes of the Black Forest. It was these troops which Marshal Augereau was about to attack.

After crossing the Rhine at Huningue, 7th Corps found itself in the country of Baden, whose sovereign, along with those of Bavaria and Wurtemberg, had just concluded an alliance with Napoleon; so we were received as friends by the population of Brisgau. Field-marshal Jellachich had not dared to oppose the French in such open country, but awaited us beyond Freiburg, at the entrance to the Black Forest, the passage through which he expected us to effect only at the cost of much bloodshed. Above all, he hoped to stop us at the Val d'Enfer, a very long and narrow pass, dominated on both sides by sheer cliffs, and easy to defend. But the men of 7th Corps had now heard of the successes achieved by their comrades at Ulm and in Bavaria, and anxious to emulate them, they advanced through the Black Forest with such élan that they crossed through it in three days, in spite of the natural obstacles, the enemy resistance and the difficulty in finding food in this dreadful wilderness. The army finally broke out into fertile country and made camp around Donauschingen, a very pleasant town where there is the magnificent château of the ancient line of the princes of Furstenburg.

The marshal and his aides-de-camp were billeted in the château, in the courtyard of which is the source of the Danube; this great river demonstrates its power at the moment of its birth, for at the spot where it issues from the earth it already bears a boat.

The draught-horses for the guns and the supply wagons had been greatly fatigued by the passage through the rough and mountainous passes of the Black Forest, which a coating of frost had made even more difficult. It was therefore necessary to give them several days of rest; during which period the Austrian cavalry came from time to time to probe our outposts, which were positioned two leagues from the town; but this amounted to no more than some ineffectual fire which kept us on our toes, gave us some exercise in skirmishing, and allowed us to learn to recognise the various uniforms of the enemy. I saw, for the first time, the Uhlans of Prince Charles, Rosenberg's Dragoons and Blankenstein's Hussars.

The horses having recovered their strength, the army continued its march, and for several weeks we had a series of engagements which left us masters of Engen and Stockach.

Although I was very much involved in these various actions, I had only one accident, which, however, might have been serious. The ground was covered by snow, particularly round Stockach, where the enemy defended their position fiercely. The marshal ordered me to go and reconnoitre a spot to which he wanted to direct a column; I left at the gallop; the ground looked to me to be quite level, the snow, driven by the wind having hidden all the hollows, but suddenly my horse and I fell into a deep gully, up to our necks in snow. I was trying to get out, when two enemy Hussars appeared at the edge and fired their muskets at me. Fortunately, the snow in which my horse and I were floundering about prevented them from taking an accurate aim, and I came to no harm; but they were about to fire once more when some Chasseurs, which Marshal Augereau had sent to my aid, forced them to depart hurriedly. With some help I was able to get out of the ravine, but we had a great deal of difficulty in extricating my horse. As we were both unhurt, my comrades had a laugh at the strange appearance I presented after my bath of snow.

After we had gained control of the Vorarlberg, we captured Bregen, and drove Jellachich's Austrian corps to Lake Constance and the Tyrol. The enemy now sought the protection of the fortress of Feldkirch and its celebrated gorge, behind which they could defend themselves with advantage. We expected to have to fight a murderous battle to take this position when, to our astonishment, the Austrians offered to capitulate, an offer which Marshal Augereau was quick to accept.

During the meeting between the two marshals, the Austrian officers, humiliated by the reverse which their arms had just suffered, took malicious pleasure in giving us some very bad news which had been concealed up till this day, but which the Russians and Austrians had learned of from English sources. The Franco-Spanish fleet had been defeated by Lord Nelson on October 20th not far from Cadiz, at Cape Trafalgar. Villeneuve, our infelicitous admiral, who had failed to carry out the precise orders of Napoleon at a time when the appearance of a combined fleet in the Channel could have secured a safe passage for the troops assembled at Boulogne, learning that he was about to be replaced by Admiral Rosily, passed suddenly from an excess of circumspection to an excess of audacity. He left Cadiz and engaged in a battle which, had it turned out in our favour, would have been virtually useless, since the French army, instead of being at Boulogne to take advantage of such a success to embark for England, was two hundred leagues from the coast, fighting in Germany.

After a most desperate struggle, the fleets of France and Spain had been defeated by that of England, whose admiral, the famous Nelson, had been killed; taking to his grave a reputation as the finest seaman of the epoch. On our side we lost Rear-admiral Magon, a very fine officer. One of our vessels blew up; seventeen, as many French as Spanish, were captured. A severe storm which arose toward the end of the battle, lasted all night and the days following, and was on the verge of overwhelming both victors and vanquished, so that the English, concerned for their own safety, were forced to abandon nearly all the ships which they had captured from us; which were mostly taken back to Cadiz by the remains of their brave but unfortunate crews, though some were wrecked on the rock-bound coast.

It was during this battle that my excellent friend France d'Houdetot received a wound to his thigh which has left him with a limp. D'Houdetot, scarcely out of childhood was a naval cadet, and attached to the staff of Admiral Magon, a friend of my father. After the death of the admiral, the ship "The Algesiras," in which he served, was captured after a bloody encounter, and the English placed on board a prize crew of sixty men. But the storm separated the ship from the English fleet, and the prize crew realised that it was very unlikely that they could reach England, so they agreed to allow the French seamen to take the ship into Cadiz, with the stipulation that they would not be held as prisoners of war. The French flag was hoisted to identify the ship and the badly damaged vessel managed to reach Cadiz, though not without great difficulty. The ship which bore Admiral Villeneuve was captured and the unlucky admiral was taken to England, where he remained a prisoner for three years. Having been released on exchange, he decided to go to Paris, but, detained at Rennes, he committed suicide.

When Field-marshal Jellachich felt obliged to capitulate before the 7th French army corps, this decision seemed the more surprising since, even if defeated by us, he had the option of retiring into the Tyrol which was behind him, and whose inhabitants have for many centuries been greatly attached to the house of Austria. The thick snow which covered the country no doubt made movement difficult, but the difficulties presented would have been much greater for us, enemies of Austria, than for the troops of Jellachich, withdrawing through an Austrian province. However, if the old and hide-bound Field-marshal could not bring himself to campaign in winter, in the high mountains, his attitude was not shared by the officers under his command; for many of them condemned his pusillanimity, and spoke of rebelling against his authority. The most ardent of his opponents was General the Prince de Rohan, a French officer in the service of Austria, a bold and competent soldier. Marshal Augereau, fearing that Jellachich might take the advice offered by the Prince and retreat into the Tyrol where pursuit would be almost impossible, hastened to grant him all the conditions which he requested.

The terms of the capitulation were that the Austrian troops should lay down their arms, hand over their flags, standards, cannons and horses, but should not themselves be taken to France, and could withdraw to Bohemia after swearing not to bear arms against France for one year.

When he announced the capitulation in one of his army bulletins, the Emperor seemed a little disappointed that the Austrian soldiers had not been made prisoners of war; but he changed his mind when he realised that Marshal Augereau had no means of retaining them, as escape was so easy. In fact, during the night preceding the day when the Austrians were to lay down their arms, a revolt broke out in several brigades against Field-marshal Jellachich. The Prince de Rohan, refusing to accept the capitulation, left with his infantry division, and joined by some regiments from other divisions, he fled into the mountains, which he crossed, despite the rigours of the season: then by an audacious march, he bypassed the cantonments of Marshal Ney's troops, who occupied the towns of the Tyrol, and arriving between Verona and Venice, he fell on the rear of the French army of Italy, while this force, commanded by Masséna was following on the tail of Prince Charles, who was retiring towards Friuli. The arrival of the Prince de Rohan in Venetian territory, when Masséna was already in the far distance, could have had the most grave consequences; but fortunately a French army, coming from Naples, under the command of General Saint-Cyr, defeated the Prince and took him prisoner.

He had, at least, submitted only to force, and was right in saying that if Jellachich had been there with all his troops, the Austrians might have defeated Saint-Cyr and opened a route for themselves back into Austria.

When a force capitulates, it is customary for the victor to send to each division a staff officer to take charge, as it were, and to conduct it on the day and at the hour appointed to the place where it is to lay down its arms. Those of my comrades who were sent to the Prince de Rohan were left behind by him in the camp which he quitted, for he carried out his retreat from an area behind the fortress of Feldkirch, and in a direction away from the French camp, so that he had little fear of being stopped; but the Austrian cavalry were not in a similar situation. They were in bivouac on a small area of open ground in front of Feldkirch, and opposite and a short distance from our outposts. I had been detailed to go to the Austrian cavalry and lead them to the agreed rendezvous; this brigade did not have a general, but was commanded by a colonel of Blankenstein's Hussars, an elderly Hungarian, brave and crafty, whose name, I regret, I cannot remember, for I think highly of him although he played me a most disagreeable trick.

On my arrival at the camp, the colonel had offered me the hospitality of his hut for the night, and we had agreed to set off at daybreak, to reach the spot indicated on the shore of Lake Constance, between the town of Bregenz and Lindau, at a distance of about three leagues. I was most astonished when, at about midnight, I heard the officers mounting their horses. I hurried out of the hut and saw that the squadrons were formed up and ready to move. I asked the reason for this hasty departure, and the old colonel replied, with cool deceit, that Field-marshal Jellachich feared that some jeering directed at the Austrian soldiers by the French, whose camp one would have to pass if one took the shortest route to the beach at Lindau, might lead to fighting between the troops of the two nations. Jellachich, in consultation with Marshal Augereau, had ordered the Austrian troops to make a long detour to the right so that they would avoid our camp and the town of Breganz, and would not come into contact with our soldiers. He added that as the route was very long and the road bad, the two commanders had advanced the time of departure by some hours; he was surprised that I had not been informed of this, but suggested that the written instructions had been held up at the advance posts, owing to some misunderstanding; he carried this deception so far as to send an officer to look for this despatch, wherever it might be. The explanation given by the colonel of the Blankensteins sounded so convincing that I did not say anything, although my instinct told me that this was a little irregular; but, alone in the midst of three thousand enemy cavalry, what could I do? It was better to appear confident than to seem to doubt the good faith of the Austrian brigade. As I was unaware of the flight of the Prince de Rohan's division, it did not enter my head that the commander of the cavalry intended to evade the capitulation. I rode alongside him, at the head of the column. The Austrian had made his arrangements for the avoidance of the French camps--whose fires could be seen--so well that we did not pass near any of them. But what the old colonel had not anticipated, and was unable to avoid, was an encounter with a flying patrol, which the French cavalry usually sent out into the countryside at night, some distance from an encampment: for suddenly there was a challenge, and we found ourselves in the presence of a large column of French cavalry, which was clearly visible in the moonlight. The Hungarian colonel, without seeming the least worried, said to me "This is work for you, as an aide-de-camp; kindly come with me and explain the situation to the commander of this French unit." We went forward. I gave the pass-word, and found myself in the presence of the 7th Chasseurs a Cheval, who, knowing that the Austrian troops were expected for the laying down of arms, and recognising me as one of Marshal Augereau's aides, made no difficulty about the passage of the brigade which I was conducting. The French commander, whose troops had their sabres drawn, even took the trouble to have them sheathed, as witness to the good-will existing between the two columns, which went on their way for some distance, side by side. I closely questioned the officer in charge of the Chasseurs about the change in the time at which the Austrians were to move; but he knew nothing at all about it, something which did not raise any suspicion in my mind, for I knew that an order of this kind would not be distributed by the staff down to regimental level. So I continued to ride with the colonel for the rest of the night, finding, however that the detour we were making was very long, and the going very bad.

At last, at daybreak, the old colonel, seeing a patch of level ground, said to me, in a conversational tone of voice, that although he would soon be obliged to hand over the horses of the three regiments to the French, he wished to care for the poor animals up to the last, and to deliver them in good condition; In consequence he had ordered that they should be given a feed of oats. The brigade halted, formed up and dismounted; and when the horses had been tethered, the colonel, who alone remained on horseback, gathered in a circle around him the officers and men of the three regiments, and in a ringing voice which made the old warrior seem quite superb, he announced that the Prince de Rohan's division, preferring honour to a shameful safety, had refused to subscribe to the disgraceful capitulation whereby Field-marshal Jellachich had promised to hand over to the French, the flags and the arms of the Austrian troops, and had fled into the Tyrol; where he too would have led the brigade were it not for the fact that he feared that in that barren mountain country, there would not be enough fodder for so many horses. But now they had open country in front of them and having, by a ruse of which he was proud, gained a lead of six leagues over the French troops, he invited all those who had truly Austrian hearts to follow him across Germany to Moravia, where they could rejoin the army of their August sovereign, Francis II. Blankenstein's Hussars responded to this speech by their colonel with a resounding cheer of approval; but Rosenberg's Dragoons and the Uhlans of Prince Charles maintained a gloomy silence. As for me, although I did not yet know enough German to follow the colonel's words exactly, what I did understand, together with the tone of the orator and the position in which he found himself, allowed me to guess what was afoot, and I can promise you that I felt very crestfallen at having, although unwittingly, furthered the plans of this diabolical Hungarian.

A fearful tumult now arose in the immense circle by which I was surrounded, and I was able to appreciate the inconvenience stemming from the heterogeneous amalgamation of different peoples which makes up the Austrian Empire, and in consequence, the Austrian army. All the Hussars were Hungarian; the Blankensteins therefore approved the proposal made by a leader of their own nationality, but the Dragoons were German and the Uhlans were Polish; the Hungarian could make no nationalistic appeal to them, who, in this difficult situation listened only to their own officers; these officers declared that they thought themselves bound by the capitulation which Field-marshal Jellachich had signed and did not wish, by their departure, to worsen his position or that of their comrades who were already the hands of the French, who would be within their rights to send them all back to France as prisoners of war, if a part of the Austrian forces violated the agreement. To this the colonel replied that when the Commander-in-Chief of an army looses his head, fails in his duty and delivers his troops to the enemy, his juniors have no need to consult anything but their courage and their devotion to their country. Then the colonel, brandishing his sabre in one hand, while with the other he seized the regimental standard, cried out, "Go then Dragoons! Go! Go! Yield to the French your dishonoured standards, and the arms which the Emperor gave us for his defence. As for us, the bold Hussars, we are off to rejoin our sovereign, to whom we can once more show with honour our unstained colours, and the swords of fearless soldiers!" Then, drawing close to me, and casting a look of disdain on the Uhlans and Dragoons, he added, "I am sure that if this young Frenchman found himself in our position and had to choose between your conduct and mine, he would take the more courageous course; for the French love honour and reputation as much as their country." Having said this, the old Hungarian sheathed his sabre, dug in his spurs, and leading his regiment at the gallop, he careered into the distance, where he soon disappeared. There was some truth in both the arguments which I had heard, but that of the old Hungarian seemed the more valid because it was in conformity with the interests of his country; I then secretly approved of his behaviour, but I could not, of course advise the Dragoons and Uhlans to follow his example; that would have been to step out of my role and fail in my duty. I maintained a strict neutrality in this discussion, and when the Hussars had left, I asked the colonels of the other two regiments to follow me, and we took the road for Lindau.

On the beach beside the lake, we found Marshals Augereau and Jellachich, as well as the French forces and the Austrian infantry regiments which had not followed the Prince de Rohan. On learning from me that the Blankenstein Hussars, having refused to recognise the capitulation, were heading for Moravia both marshals flew into a rage: Marshal Augereau because he feared that these Hussars might cause havoc in the rear of the French army, since the route which they would follow would take them through areas where the Emperor, in the course of his march on Vienna, had left many dressing stations full of wounded; artillery parks, etc. But the Hungarian colonel did not think it was part of his duty to advertise his presence by any surprise attack, as he was only too anxious to get out of a country bristling with French arms. By avoiding all our positions, moving always on minor roads, hiding by day in the woods and marching rapidly at night, he managed to reach the frontier of Moravia without trouble, and joined an Austrian army corps which occupied the area. As for the troops who remained with Field-marshal Jellachich, having laid down their arms, surrendered their flags and standards and handed over their horses, they became prisoners on parole for one year, and made off in dismal silence for the interior of Germany, to make their way sadly to Bohemia. I remembered, when I saw them, the valiant words of the old colonel, and I think I saw on the faces of many of these Uhlans and Dragoons a regret that they had not followed the old warrior, and an unhappiness when they compared the heroic position of the Blankensteins with their own humiliation.

Among the trophies which Jellachich's corps was forced to hand over were seventeen flags and two standards, which Marshal Augereau, as was usual, hastened to send to the Emperor, in the care of two aides-de-camp. Major Massy and I were detailed for this task, and we left the same evening in a fine carriage with, in front of us, a wagon containing the flags and standards, in the charge of an N.C.O. We headed for Vienna via Kempten, Brauneau, Munich, Lenz and Saint-Poelten. Some leagues before this last town, following the banks of the Danube, we admired the superb Abbey of Mölk, one of the richest in the world. It was here, four years later that I ran the greatest danger, and earned the praise of the Emperor, for having performed before his eyes the finest feat of arms of my military career; as you will see when we come to the campaign of 1809.

Chapter 22
At War with Austria & Russia

In September 1805, the seven corps which made up the Grande Armée were on the march from their positions on the coast to the banks of the Danube. They were already in the countries of Baden and Wurtemberg when, on the 1st October, Napoleon, in person, crossed the Rhine at Strasburg. A part of the large force which the Russians were sending to the aid of Austria had at that moment arrived in Moravia, and the cabinet at Vienna should, with prudence, have waited until this powerful reinforcement had joined the Austrian army; but, carried away by an enthusiasm which they did not usually display, and which was inspired by Field-marshal Mack, it had despatched him, at the head of eighty thousand men, to attack Bavaria; the possession of which had been coveted by Austria for several centuries, and which French policy had always protected from invasion. The Elector of Bavaria, forced to abandon his state, took refuge with his family and his troops in Wurtzburg, from where he begged Napoleon for assistance. Napoleon entered into an alliance with him and with the rulers of Baden and Wurtzburg.

The Austrian army, under Mack, had already occupied Ulm, when Napoleon, having crossed the Danube at Donauwerth seized Augsburg and Munich. The French were now in the rear of Mack's force and had cut his communication with the Russians, who having reached Vienna, were advancing towards him by forced marches. The Field-marshal realised then, but too late, the error he had made in allowing himself to be encircled by French troops. He tried to break out, but was defeated successively in the battles of Wertingen, Gunzberg, and Elchingen, where Marshal Ney won fame. Under increasing pressure, Mack was forced to shut himself up in Ulm with all his army, less the corps of the Archduke Ferdinand and Jellachich who escaped, the former into Bohemia, and the latter to the region round Lake Constance. Ulm was then besieged by the Emperor. It was a place which, though not heavily fortified, could nevertheless have held out for a long time thanks to its position and its large garrison, and so given the Russians time to come to its relief. But Field-marshal Mack, passing from exalted over-confidence to a profound disheartenment, surrendered to Napoleon, who had now, in three weeks, scattered, captured, or destroyed eighty thousand Austrians and freed Bavaria, where he reinstalled the Elector. We shall see, in 1813, this favour repaid by the most odious treachery.

Being now the master of Bavaria, and rid of the presence of Mack's army, the Emperor increased the pace of his advance, down the right bank of the Danube towards Vienna. He captured Passau and then Linz, where he learned that 50,000 Russians, commanded by General Koutousoff, reinforced by 40,000 Austrians, whom General Kienmayer had collected, had crossed the Danube at Vienna and had taken up a position between Mölk and St. Poelten. He was told at the same time that the Austrian army commanded by Prince Charles had been defeated by Masséna in the Venetian district and was retreating via the Friuli in the direction of Vienna; and lastly that the Archduke Jean was occupying the Tyrol with several divisions. Those two princes were therefore threatening the right of the French army, while it had the Russians in front of it. To protect himself against a flank attack, the Emperor, who already had Marshal Augereau's corps in the region of Bregenz, sent Maeshal Ney to attack Innsbruk and the Tyrol, and moved Marmont's corps to Loeben, in order to block Prince Charles' route from Italy. Having taken these wise precautions to protect his right flank, Napoleon, before advancing to meet the Russians, whose advance-guard had already clashed with ours at Amstetten, near to Steyer, wished to protect his left flank from any attack from those Austrians who had taken refuge in Bohemia, under the command of Archduke Ferdinand. To effect this he gave Marshal Mortier the infantry divisions of Generals Dupont and Gazan, and ordered him to cross the Danube by the bridges at Passau and Linz, and then proceed down the left bank of the river, while the bulk of the army went down the right. However, in order not to leave Marshal Mortier too isolated, Napoleon conceived the idea of gathering together on the Danube a great number of boats, which had been captured on the tributaries of the river, and forming a flotilla which, manned by men from the guard, could move down the river, keeping level with Mortier and making a link between the troops on both banks.

You may think it a little presumptuous of me to criticise one of the operations of a great captain, but I cannot refrain from commenting that the sending of Mortier to the left bank was a move which had not been sufficiently considered, and was an error which could have had very serious consequences. The Danube, Europe's largest river, is, after Passau, so wide in winter that from one bank one cannot discern a man standing on the other; it is also very deep and very fast-flowing, and it therefore provided a guarantee of perfect safety for the left flank of the French army as it marched down the right bank. Furthermore, any attack could be made only by the Archduke Ferdinand, coming from Bohemia; but he, very pleased to have escaped from the French before Ulm, had only a few troops, and they were mostly cavalry. Even if he had wished to do so, he had not the means to mount an attack which involved crossing an obstacle such as the Danube, into which he might be driven back. Whereas, by detaching two of his divisions and allowing them to be isolated across this immense river, Napoleon exposed them to the risk of being captured or exterminated. A disaster which might have been foreseen and which very nearly came about.

Field-marshal Koutousoff, had been awaiting the French with confidence, in a strong position at St. Poelten, because he believed that they were being pursued by the army of Mack; but when he heard of the surrender of this army at Ulm, he no longer felt himself strong enough to face Napoleon alone, and being unwilling to risk his troops to save the city of Vienna, he decided to put the barrier of the Danube between himself and the victor, so he crossed the river by the bridge at Krems, which he burned behind him.

He had scarcely arrived on the left bank with all his army, when he ran into the scouts of the Gazan division, which was proceeding from Dirnstein to Krems, with Marshal Mortier at its head. Koutousoff, having discovered the presence of a French corps isolated on the left bank, resolved to crush it, and to achieve this aim he attacked it head to head on the narrow road which ran along the river bank, while seizing control of the escarpments which overlook the Danube. He sent light troops to occupy Dirnstein to cut off the retreat of the Gazan division. The position of the division was made even more critical by the fact that the flotilla of boats had dropped back and there were only two little boats available, which made it impossible to bring reinforcements from the other bank.

Attacked in front and in the rear and on one of their flanks by enemies six times their number; shut in between the rocky escarpment occupied by the Russians and the depths of the Danube, the French soldiers, crowded on the narrow roadway, did not despair. The gallant Marshal Mortier set them an example, for, when it was suggested that he should take one of the boats and go over to the right bank, where he would be with the Grande Armée, and avoid giving the Russians the glory of capturing a marshal, he replied that he would die with his men, or escape over the dead bodies of the Russians!

A savage bayonet fight ensued: five thousand French were up against thirty thousand Russians: night came to add to the horrors of the combat: Gazan's division, massed in column, managed to regain Dirnstein at a moment when Dupont's division, which had remained behind opposite Mölk, alerted by the sound of gunfire, was running to their aid. Eventually the battlefield remained in French hands.

In this hand to hand fighting, where the bayonet was almost the only weapon used, our men, more adroit and agile than the giant Russians, had a great advantage; so the enemy losses amounted to some four thousand five hundred men, while ours were three thousand only. But had our divisions not been made up of seasoned soldiers, Mortier's corps would probably have been destroyed. The Emperor was well aware of this, and hastened to recall it to the right bank. What seems to me to be proof that he realised the mistake he had made in sending this corps across the river, is the fact that, although he generously rewarded the brave regiments which had fought at Dirnstein, the official bulletins scarcely mention this sanguinary affair, and it is as if one wished to conceal the results of this operation because one could find no military justification for it.

What further confirms me in the opinion which I have taken the liberty of expressing, is that in the campaign of 1809, the Emperor, when he found himself in a similar situation, did not send any troops across the river, but, keeping all his force together, he went with it to Vienna.

But let us return to the mission with which Major Massy and I were charged.

When we arrived in Vienna, Napoleon and the bulk of the army had already left the city, which they had seized without a shot being fired. The crossing of the Danube which it was necessary to effect in order to pursue the Russians and the Austrians who were retreating into Moravia, had not been disputed, thanks to a perhaps culpable deception which was carried out by Marshals Lannes and Murat. This incident, which had such a profound effect on this well-known campaign, deserves recounting.

The city of Vienna is situated on the right bank of the Danube: a small branch of that immense river passes through the city, but the main stream is half a league away; there the Danube contains a large number of islands which are connected by a long series of wooden bridges, terminated by one which, spanning the main arm of the river, reaches the left bank at a place named Spitz. The road to Moravia runs along this series of bridges. When the Austrians are opposing the crossing of a river, they have a very bad habit of leaving the bridges intact up to the very last moment, to give them a means of mounting a counterattack against the enemy, who almost always does not allow them time to do so and takes from them the bridges which they have neglected to burn. This is what the French did during the campaign in Italy in 1796 at the memorable affairs of Lodi and Arcoli. But these examples had not served to correct the Austrians, for on leaving Vienna, which is not suited to defence, they retired to the other side of the Danube without destroying a single one of the bridges spanning this vast watercourse, and limited themselves to placing inflammable material on the platform of the main bridge, in order to set it alight when the French appeared. They had also established on the left bank, at the end of the bridge at Spitz, a powerful battery of artillery, as well as a division of six thousand men under the command of Prince D'Auersperg, a brave but not very intelligent officer. Now I must tell you that some days before the entry of the French into Vienna, the Emperor had received the Austrian general, Comte de Guilay, who came as an envoy to make peace overtures, which came to nothing. But hardly had the Emperor settled in the palace of Schoenbrunn, when General Guilay again appeared and spent more than an hour tête-a-tête with Napoleon. From this a rumour arose that an armistice had been arranged, a rumour which spread amongst the French regiments which were entering Vienna and the Austrians who were leaving to cross the Danube.

Murat and Lannes, whom the Emperor had ordered to secure the crossing of the Danube, placed Oudinot's Grenadiers behind a bushy plantation and went forward, accompanied only by some German-speaking officers. The enemy outposts withdrew, firing as they went. The French officers called out that there was an armistice, and continuing their progress, they crossed all the small bridges, without being held up. When they arrived at the main bridge, they renewed their assertion to the commander at Spitz, who did not dare to fire on two marshals, almost alone, who claimed that hostilities were suspended. However, before allowing them to go any further, he wanted to go and ask General Auersperg for orders, and while he did so, he left the post in charge of a sergeant. Lannes and Murat persuaded the sergeant that under the terms of the cease-fire, the bridge should be handed over to them, and that he should go with his men to join his officer on the left bank. The poor sergeant hesitated, he was edged back gently while the conversation continued, and by a slow but steady advance they reached, eventually, the end of the main bridge.

At this point an Austrian officer endeavored to set light to the incendiary material, but the torch was snatched from his hand, and he was told that he would be in serious trouble if he did any such thing. Next, the column of Oudinot's Grenadiers appeared and began to cross the bridge.... The Austrian gunners prepared to open fire, but the French marshals ran to the commander of the artillery and assured him that an armistice was in force, then, seating themselves on the guns, they requested the gunners to go and inform General Auersperg of their presence. General Auersperg eventually arrived and was about to order the gunners to open fire, although by now they and the Austrian troops were surrounded by the French Grenadiers, when the two marshals managed to convince him that there was a cease-fire, a principal condition of which was that the French should occupy the bridge. The unhappy general, fearing to compromise himself by the useless shedding of blood, lost his head to the point of leading away all the troops which he had been given to defend the bridges.

Without this error on the part of General Auersperg, the passage of the Danube could only have been carried out with great difficulty, and might even have been impossible; in which case Napoleon would have been unable to pursue the Russians and Austrians into Moravia, and would have failed in his campaign. That was the opinion at the time, and it was confirmed three years later when, the Austrians having burned the bridges, to secure a passage we were forced to fight the two battles of Essling and Wagram, which cost us more than thirty thousand men, whereas in 1805 Marshals Lannes and Murat took possession of the bridges without there being a single man wounded.

Was the stratagem they employed admissible? I have my doubts. I know that in war one eases one's conscience, and that any means may be employed to ensure victory and reduce loss of life, but in spite of these weighty considerations, I do not think that one can approve of the method used to seize the bridge at Spitz, and for my part I would not care to do the same in similar circumstances.

To conclude this episode, the credulity of General Auersperg was very severely punished. A court-martial condemned him to be cashiered, dragged through the streets of Vienna on a hurdle and finally put to death at the hands of the public executioner...! A similar sentence was passed on Field-marshal Mack, to punish him for his conduct at Ulm. But in both cases the death sentence was commuted to life imprisonment. They served ten years and were then released, but deprived of their position, expelled from the ranks of the nobility and rejected by their families, they died, both of them, shortly after they had been set at liberty.

The stratagem employed by Marshals Lannes and Murat having secured the crossing of the Danube, the Emperor Napoleon directed his army in pursuit of the Russians and the Austrians. Thus began the second phase of the campaign.

Chapter 23
How I Deceived the Emperor

The Russian marshal Koutousoff was heading via Hollabrunn for Brno in Moravia, in order to join the second army which was led by the Emperor Alexander in person; but on approaching Hollabrunn, he was alarmed to discover that the troops of Lannes and Murat were already occupying the town and cutting off his means of retreat. To get out of this fix, the aged marshal, making use, in his turn, of trickery, sent General Prince Bagration as an envoy to Marshal Murat, whom he assured that an aide-de-camp of the Emperor was on his way to Napoleon in order to conclude an armistice, and that, without doubt, peace would shortly follow.

Prince Bagration was a very amiable man, he knew exactly how to flatter Murat, so that he in turn was deceived into accepting an armistice, in spite of the observations of Lannes, who wished to fight but had to obey Murat, who was his superior officer.

The truce lasted for thirty-six hours; and while Murat was inhaling the incense which the crafty Russian lavished on him, Koutousoff's army made a detour and concealing its movement behind a screen of low hills, escaped from danger, and went on to take up, beyond Hollabrunn, a strong position which opened the road to Moravia and assured his retreat and his junction with the second Russian army which was encamped between Znaim and Brno. Napoleon was still in the palace of Schoenbrunn, and was furiously angry when he heard that Murat had allowed himself to be bamboozled by Prince Bagration, and had accepted an armistice without his orders, and he commanded him to attack Koutousoff immediately.

Now the situation of the Russians had changed greatly to their advantage, so they repelled the French most vigorously. The town of Hollabrunn, taken and re-taken several times, set on fire by the mortars, filled with the dead and dying, remained finally in French possession. The Russians retired in the direction of Brno;

our troops followed them and took possession of this town without a fight, although it was fortified and dominated by the well-known citadel of Spielberg.

The Russian armies and the remains of the Austrian troops were united in Moravia; the Emperor Napoleon, in order to deliver the final blow, arrived in Brno, the capital of the province.

My comrade Massy and I followed after him, but we moved slowly and with much difficulty, firstly because the post-horses were on their last legs, and then because of the great quantity of troops, guns, ammunition wagons, baggage, etc. with which the roads were obstructed. We were obliged to stop for twenty-four hours at Hollabrunn, while we waited for a passage to be cleared through the streets, destroyed by fire and littered with planks and beams and the debris of furniture, still alight. This unfortunate town had been so completely burned that we were unable to find a single house to provide shelter!

During our enforced stay, we were confronted and distressed by the most horrible and shocking spectacle. The wounded, mainly Russians, had taken refuge during the fighting in the houses which were soon set ablaze. All who could walk fled at the approach of this new danger, but the crippled and gravely injured were burned alive in the ruins! Many had attempted to escape the fire by crawling along the ground, but the flames had followed them into the streets, where one could see a multitude of these wretched victims half consumed by fire, some of them still breathing! The bodies of the men and horses killed in the battle had also been roasted, so that for several leagues around the town there was a sickening stench of burning flesh! … There are countrysides and towns which because of their situation are destined to serve as battlefields, and Hollabrun is one of them, because it offers an excellent military position; thus it was that the damage done by the fire of 1805 had scarcely been repaired, when I saw the place again, four years later, once more on fire and littered with the half-roasted bodies of the dead and dying; as you will see from my description of the campaign of 1809.

Major Massy and I left this pestilential spot as soon as we could, and went on to Znaim, where, four years later I was to be wounded; and at last we reached the Emperor at Brunn (Brno), on November 22nd, ten days before the Battle of Austerlitz.

The day after our arrival, we completed our mission and handed over the flags with the ceremony laid down by the Emperor for solemn occasions of this kind; for he missed no opportunity of displaying to the troops anything which could raise their morale and enthusiasm.

The procedure was as follows:--Half an hour before the daily parade,--which took place at eleven o'clock outside whatever residence was serving as the Emperor's palace,--General Duroc, the Grand Marshal, sent to our billet a company of Grenadiers of the Guard, with bandsmen and drummers. The town of Brunn was full of French troops, and the soldiers, as we passed, celebrated with much cheering the victory of their comrades of 7th Corps. All the guard-posts accorded us military honours, and on our entry to the courtyard of the Emperor's quarters, the units formed up for the parade beat a salute, presented arms, and cried repeatedly "Vive L'Empereur!"

The aide-de-camp on duty came to receive us and to present us to Napoleon, to whom we were introduced, accompanied always by the N.C.O.s carrying the Austrian flags. The Emperor examined these various trophies, and after dismissing the N.C.O.s. he questioned us closely about the various actions which had been fought by Marshal Augereau and on all we had seen or learned on our long journey through a countryside which had been the theatre of war. Then he told us to await his instructions, and to join the imperial suite. The Grand Marshal Duroc took charge of the flags, for which he gave us a receipt in the regular manner, informed us that horses would be placed at our disposal and invited us, for the duration of our stay, to the table over which he presided.

The French army was now massed around and before Brunn. The Russian advance-guard occupied Austerlitz, while the bulk of their army was positioned round the town of Olmutz, where were also the Emperor Alexander of Russia and the Emperor of Austria. A battle seemed inevitable, but both sides being well aware that the outcome would have an immense bearing on the destiny of Europe, each hesitated to make a decisive move. Napoleon, usually so swift to act, waited for eleven days at Brunn before launching a major attack. It is, however, true that every day of waiting increased his forces by the arrival of great numbers of soldiers who had lagged behind because of illness or fatigue, and who having now recovered, hastened to rejoin their units. I recall that, in these circumstances, I told a white lie which could have ruined my military career.

Napoleon usually treated his officers with kindness, but there was one point on which he was perhaps too strict, for he held colonels responsible for keeping their units up to full strength, something it is very difficult to do during a campaign. It was in this matter that the Emperor was most often deceived, for the corps commanders were so afraid of displeasing him that they risked being committed to facing an enemy force disproportionate to their own numbers, rather than admit that sickness, fatigue and the need to forage for food had caused many soldiers to drop out. So Napoleon, in spite of his authority, never knew the exact number of combatants available to him on the day of battle.

Now it so happened that the Emperor, in the course of one of the endless trips he made to visit the various corps of the army, saw the Chasseurs a Cheval of his guard, who were moving to a different position. He was particularly fond of this regiment, of which his "guides" from Italy and Egypt formed the nucleus. The Emperor, whose experienced eye could estimate very exactly the strength of a column, noticing that their numbers were much reduced, took out of his pocket a little notebook, and, calling for General Morland, the commander of the mounted Chasseurs a Cheval, he said to him in a stern voice, "Your regiment is down in my notes as having 1200 men, and although you have not been in action, you have no more than 800; what has happened to the others?" General Morland was a fine, brave fighting soldier, but he did not have a ready tongue, and being quite nonplussed, he said in his Franco-Alsatian dialect that he was short of only a small number of men. The Emperor maintained that he was about four hundred short, and to get to the truth of the matter he wanted to have an immediate count; but knowing that General Morland was very much liked by the officers of the imperial staff, he feared a cover-up, and thought he would be more likely to discover the truth by choosing an officer who did not belong to his entourage nor to the Chasseurs; so, seeing me, he ordered me to count the Chasseurs and to deliver to him personally a record of their numbers; having said which, he made off at the gallop. I began my task, which was made more easy because the troopers were riding past four abreast at walking pace.

Poor General Morland, who knew how close Napoleon's estimate was to the reality, was in a state of great agitation, for he foresaw that my report would call down on his head a severe reprimand. He hardly knew me, and did not dare to suggest that I might compromise myself to get him out of trouble. He was then sitting silently on his horse beside me, when, fortunately for him, his adjutant came to join him. This officer, named Fournier, had started his military career as an assistant surgeon, then, having become a surgeon-major, he felt that he had more of a vocation for the sabre than for the lancet, and had asked for and obtained permission to join the ranks of the combatant officers, and Morland, with whom he had served previously, arranged for him to join the Guard.

I had known Captain Fournier very well when he was still surgeon-major, and I was very much obliged to him, for not only had he dressed my father's wound when it was inflicted, but he had gone, like him, to Genoa, where, as long as my father lived, he had come several times a day to care for him: if the doctors charged with the duty of fighting the typhus epidemic had been as assiduous and zealous as Fournier, my father, perhaps, would not have died. I had often thought this, so I gave the warmest of welcomes to Fournier, whom I did not at first recognise in the pelisse of a captain of Chasseurs.

General Morland, seeing the pleasure we had in meeting one another, thought he might profit from our mutual friendship to persuade me not to reveal to the Emperor by how many men he was short. He took his adjutant aside and conferred with him for a time; then Fournier came, and in the name of our former friendship, he begged me to extricate General Morland from a most unpleasant situation by concealing from the Emperor the extent to which the regiment was under strength. I refused firmly and continued to count. The Emperor's estimate was very close, for there were only a few over eight hundred Chasseurs present, four hundred were missing.

I was about to leave to make my report, when General Morland and Captain Fournier renewed their pleas pointing out that the greater part of the men who had dropped behind for various reasons would rejoin them very shortly, and that it was not likely that Napoleon would engage in battle before the arrival of the divisions of Friant and Gudin, who were still at the gates of Vienna, thirty-six leagues from us and would take several days to reach us. In the interval more laggards would rejoin the unit. They added that the Emperor would be too busy to check my report. I could not pretend to myself that I was not being asked to deceive the Emperor, which was very wrong, but I felt also that I was under a great obligation to Captain Fournier for the truly tender care he had given to my dying father, I allowed myself therefore to be swayed and promised to conceal a large part of the truth.

I was scarcely alone when I realised the enormity of my error, but it was too late; the essential object now was to get out of the situation with the least harm possible. With this aim in view, I kept out of the way of the Emperor as long as he was on horseback, in case he went back to the bivouac of the Chasseurs, where their shortage of numbers striking him anew would give the lie to my report. I craftily did not return to the imperial quarters until night was approaching and Napoleon, having dismounted had gone to his apartment. Brought before him in order to make my report, I found him lying at full length on an immense map which was spread on the floor. As soon as he saw me, he called out "Well now! Marbot, how many Chasseurs are there in my guard? Are there twelve hundred as Morland claims?" "No sire" I replied. "I counted only eleven hundred and twenty, that is a shortfall of eighty." "I was sure that there was a lot missing." said the Emperor, in a tone of voice which made it plain that he had expected a much larger deficit; and to be sure if there were no more than eighty men missing from a regiment of twelve hundred which had just come five hundred leagues in winter, sleeping almost every night in bivouac, that was a very small loss. So when, on going to dinner, the Emperor passed through the room where the senior officers of the guard were gathered, all he said to Morland was, "Now you see…you are short of eighty troopers; that is almost a squadron. With eighty of these men one could stop a Russian regiment! You must take care to see that men do not drop behind." Then, passing to the commander of the foot guards, whose numbers were also much reduced, Napoleon gave him a sharp reprimand. Morland, who thought himself lucky to have got away with no more than a few observations, came over to me, as soon as the Emperor was seated at table, and thanked me warmly. He told me that some thirty troopers had just arrived, and that a courier from Vienna had met more than a hundred between Znaim and Brunn, and many more this side of Hollabrunn, which meant that within forty-eight hours the regiment would have made up most of its deficiency. I wished for this as fervently as he did, for I was well aware of the difficult spot I had landed myself in out of my consideration for Fournier. I could not sleep that night for fear of the justifiable wrath of the Emperor, if he found out that I had lied to him.

I was even more dismayed the next day when Napoleon, in the course of his usual visit to his troops, started off in the direction of the Chasseur's bivouac, for a simple question put to an officer could expose everything; but just when I thought that I was done for, I heard the sound of the band of the Russian force, camped on the high ground of the Pratzen half a league from our position. I urged my horse forward towards the head of the numerous staff by whom the Emperor was accompanied, and getting as close to him as possible, I said in a loud voice, "I am sure there is something going on in the Russian camp, their band is playing a march".... The Emperor, who heard my remark, suddenly left the path which led to the Chasseur's bivouac, and headed towards Pratzen to see what was happening in the enemy advance-guard. He stayed a long time watching, and as night was approaching, he went back to Brunn without visiting the Chasseurs. For several days I was in a mortal panic, although I learned of the arrival of successive detachments of men, but at last the coming battle and the many preoccupations of the Emperor drove from his mind the idea of making the check which I so much feared. But I had learned my lesson; so when I became a colonel and was asked by the Emperor how many men were present in the squadrons of my regiment, I always gave the exact number.

Chapter 24
My Part in One of the Emperor's Schemes

If Napoleon was often deceived, he also used deception himself to further his projects, as can be shown by the tale of this diplomatic-military comedy, in which I played a part.

In order to understand this affair, which will give you the key to the intrigues which, the following year, gave rise to the war between Napoleon and the King of Prussia, we have to go back two months to the time when the French troops, having left the coast, were proceeding by rapid marches to the Danube. The shortest route which the first corps, commanded by Bernadotte, could take to reach Hanover, on the upper Danube, lay through Anspach. This little country belonged to Prussia, but as it was quite a long way from there, from which it was separated by a number of minor principalities, it had always been regarded in previous wars as being neutral territory, through which either party could pass, provided that they paid for any goods they required and refrained from any hostile action.

Things having been established on this footing, Austrian and French armies had often passed through the Margravate of Anspach, since the time of the Directory, without informing Prussia and without the latter raising any objection. Napoleon then, taking advantage of this convention, ordered Bernadotte to go through Anspach, which he did. However, the Queen of Prussia and her court, who detested Napoleon, on hearing of this, raised an outcry, claiming that Prussian territory had been violated, and took advantage of this event to rouse the nation and call loudly for war. The King of Prussia and his minister, Count Haugwitz, alone resisted the general clamour for action. This was in October 1805, when hostilities were about to break out between France and Austria, and the Russian armies were on their way to reinforce the latter. The queen and the young Prince Louis, the king's nephew, in an attempt to persuade the king to make common cause with the Austrians and Russians, arranged for the Emperor Alexander to come to Berlin, in the hope that his presence would influence Frederick-William.

Alexander arrived in the capital of Prussia on the 25th October. He was greeted with enthusiasm by the queen, Prince Louis and the supporters of war against France. The king, besieged on all sides, allowed himself to be persuaded, but only on the condition--advised by the old Prince of Brunswick, and Count Haugwitz--that his army should not be committed to a campaign until the outcome of the conflict between the French and the Austrians on the Danube had been determined. This partial adherence to their cause pleased neither Alexander nor the queen, but for the time being they could obtain nothing more explicit. A melodramatic scene was played out at Potsdam, where the Emperor of Russia and the King of Prussia, having descended, by the light of torches, into the sepulchral vaults of the palace, swore, in the presence of the court, eternal friendship, on the tomb of Frederick the Great; (an oath which did not prevent Alexander from incorporating into the Russian Empire, eighteen months later, one of the Prussian provinces, which Napoleon awarded him under the treaty of Tilsit, and this in the presence of his friend Frederick-William.) The Russian Emperor now went back to Moravia, to place himself at the head of his army, for Napoleon was advancing rapidly towards Vienna, which he shortly occupied.

When he heard of the King of Prussia's reluctance and the compact made at Potsdam, Napoleon, in order to deal with the Russians before the Prussians had made up their minds, installed himself for the encounter with the former in Brunn, where we now were.

It is said, quite rightly, that ambassadors are privileged spies. The King of Prussia, who heard daily of fresh victories won by Napoleon, was anxious to find out what the true position was between the warring parties; so he decided to send Count Haugwitz, his minister, to the French headquarters, with instructions to assess the situation. Now it was necessary to find an excuse for doing this, so he entrusted Count Haugwitz with a reply to a letter which Napoleon had sent to him, complaining about the agreement concluded between the Prussians and the Russians at Potsdam. Count Haugwitz arrived at Brunn some days before the Battle of Austerlitz, and would dearly have liked to stay there until he knew the result of the major engagement which was in prospect, in order to advise his sovereign to do nothing if we were victorious, or to attack us if we should be defeated. You do not have to be a soldier to see from a map what damage a Prussian army, coming from Breslau in Silesia, could do by going through Bohemia to fall on our rear around Regansberg.

As Napoleon knew that Count Haugwitz sent a courier every evening to Berlin, he decided that it would be by this means that he would inform the Prussians of the defeat of Field-marshal Jellachich's army corps, news of which had not yet reached them. This is how it was done.

Marshal of the Palace Duroc, after telling us what we were to do, had all the Austrian flags which we had brought from Bregenz secretly replaced in the lodgings which Massy and I occupied; then, some hours later, when the Emperor was in conversation with Count Haugwitz in his study, we re-enacted the ceremony of the handover of the flags in exactly the same way as it had been done on the first occasion. The Emperor hearing the band playing in the courtyard, feigned astonishment, and went to the windows followed by the ambassador. Seeing the flags carried by the N.C.Os he called for the duty aide-de-camp and asked him what was going on. The aide-de-camp having told him that we were two of Marshal Augereau's aides who had come to hand over to him the flags of Jellachich's Austrian corps captured at Bregenz, we were led inside; there Napoleon, without blinking an eyelid, and as if he had never seen us before, took the letter from Augereau, which had been re-sealed, and read it, although he had been aware of its contents for four days. Then he questioned us, making us go into the smallest details. Duroc had warned us to speak out loudly, as the ambassador was a little hard of hearing, this advice was of no use to Major Massy, who was the leader of the mission, since he was suffering from a cold and had almost completely lost his voice, so it was I who replied to the Emperor, and taking a lead from him, I painted in the most vivid colours the defeat of the Austrians, their despondency, and the enthusiasm of the French. Then, presenting the trophies one after the other, I named the Austrian regiments to which they had once belonged. I laid particular stress on two of them, because I knew that their capture would have a powerful effect on the ambassador, "Here," I said "is the flag of the infantry regiment of his Majesty the Emperor of Austria, and there is the standard of the Uhlans, commanded by the Archduke Charles, his brother." Napoleon's eyes twinkled, and he seemed to say, "Well done young man!" At last he dismissed us, and as we left we heard him say to the ambassador, "You see, monsieur le Comte, my armies are everywhere triumphant.... The Austrian army is no more, and soon the same fate will befall the Russians." Count Haugwitz seemed deeply impressed, and Duroc said to us, after we had left the room, "The count will write tonight to Berlin, to tell his government of the destruction of Jellachich's force, which will put a damper on the war party, and give the king new reasons for holding off. Which is what the Emperor very much wants."

This comedy having been played out, The Emperor, to be rid of a dangerous onlooker who could give an account of the disposition of his forces, suggested to Count Haugwitz that it was not very safe for him to remain between two armies which were about to come to blows, and persuaded him to go to Vienna to M. Tallyrand, his minister for foreign affairs, which he did that same evening.

The following day the Emperor said nothing to us about the scene which had been enacted the previous evening, but wishing, no doubt, to give some sign of his satisfaction with the manner in which we had played our parts, he asked Major Massy, kindly, about the progress of his cold, and he pinched my ear, which with him was a sort of caress.

Chapter 25
The Battle of Austerlitz

Now the dénouement of the great drama was approaching and both sides were preparing for the coming struggle. Nearly all military authors so overload their narrative with details that they confuse the mind of the reader, to the extent that, in most of the published works on the wars of the Empire which I have read, I have been unable to understand the description of several of the battles in which I myself have taken part, and the various phases of which I know. I think that to preserve clarity in the description of an action, one needs to limit oneself to indicating the respective positions of the two armies, prior to the engagement, and to recounting only the principal and decisive events in the combat. This is what I shall attempt to do.

The coming battle is known as the Battle of Austerlitz, although it took place some distance from the village of that name: the reason for this is that, on the eve of the battle, the Emperors of Austria and Russia had slept in the Château of Austerlitz, out of which Napoleon drove them.

You will see on the map that a stream, the Goldbach, which rises on the far side of the road to Olmutz, flows into a pool called Menitz. This stream, which runs in a little valley with quite steep banks, separated the two armies. The right of the Austro-Russian forces lay on a wooded escarpment, situated behind the posthouse of Posoritz, on the far side of the Olmutz road; their centre occupied Pratzen and the vast plateau of that name, and their left was near the meres of Satschan and the neighbouring marshes. The Emperor placed his left flank on a little hill, very difficult of access, which our men who had been in Egypt called the Santon (a holy man's grave) because it was surmounted by a small chapel, the roof of which had the appearance of a minaret. The French centre was near the pool of Kobolnitz, and the right was at Telnitz. The Emperor had put very few troops there in order to tempt the

Russians into the marshy ground, where he had prepared their defeat by concealing in Gross-Raigern, on the road to Vienna, the corps of Marshal Davout.

On the 1st December, the eve of the battle, Napoleon left Brunn in the morning and spent all day examining the positions; in the evening he set up his headquarters behind the French centre, at a spot from where could be seen the camps of both armies and the area which would form their battlefield the next day. There was no building in the vicinity but a dilapidated barn, and it was there that were placed the Emperor's tables and maps, while he himself took up a position by a huge fire, surrounded by his numerous staff and his guards. Happily there was no snow, although it was very cold. I bedded down on the ground and fell into a deep sleep; but soon we had to remount our horses to accompany the Emperor, who was about to visit his troops. There was no moon, and the obscurity of the night was increased by a thick mist which made progress difficult. The troopers of the Emperor's escort had the idea of lighting torches made of pinewood and straw which were most useful. The soldiers, seeing the approach of a group of mounted men thus illuminated, could easily distinguish the imperial staff, and in an instant, as if by magic, one saw all our camp lit up by torches carried by the men who greeted the Emperor with cheer, made all the louder because the next day would be the anniversary of his coronation, a coincidence which seemed to them to be a good augury. The enemy must have been greatly astonished when, from the height of the neighbouring slope, they saw in the middle of the night, the light of sixty thousand torches and heard the repeated cheers of "Vive l'Empereur!" mingled with the sound of the regimental bands. All was gaiety, light and movement in our camp, while, on the Austro-Russian side, all was dark and silent.

The next day, the 2nd December, the cannons were heard at daybreak. We have seen that the Emperor had deployed few troops on his right wing; a bait which he dangled before the enemy, who would see the apparent possibility of taking Telnitz easily, and then crossing the Goldbach and going on to Gross-Raigern in order to control the road from Brunn to Vienna and so cut off our line of retreat. The Austro-Russians fell headlong into the trap, and, thinning out the rest of their line, they clumsily piled up a considerable force in the lower part of Telnitz, and in the narrow, marshy defiles around the meres of

Satschan and Menitz. They thought, for some unknown reason, that Napoleon was considering withdrawing, without facing a battle, so to hasten this move they decided to attack us at the Santon on our left and at our centre before Puntowitz, so that, being defeated at these two points, and forced to retreat, we would find the road to Vienna cut by the Russian troops. But on our left Marshal Lannes not only repelled all the enemy attacks on the Santon, but drove them back across the Olmutz road as far as Blasiowitz, where the more level ground allowed Murat's cavalry to make several very effective charges, which compelled the Russians to retire hurriedly to the village of Austerlitz.

While our left was achieving this brilliant success, the centre, consisting of the troops of Marshals Soult and Bernadotte, who had been placed by the Emperor in the valley of the Goldbach where they were hidden by a thick mist, advanced towards the slope on which stood the village of Pratzen. It was at this moment that the bright "Sunshine of Austerlitz" appeared, the memory of which Napoleon was pleased so frequently to recall. Marshal Soult took not only the village of Pratzen but also the great plateau of that name, which is the high point of the surrounding country, and, in consequence, the key to the battlefield. Here took place, before the eyes of the Emperor, a very sharp engagement in which the Russians were defeated; but a battalion of the 4th Line regiment, commanded by Prince Joseph, Napoleon's brother, went too far in pursuit of the enemy and was charged and over-run by the horse-guards and Cuirassiers of the Grand-duke Constantin, the brother of Alexander, who captured their Eagle. A force of Russian cavalry advanced rapidly to support the momentary success of the horse-guards; but Napoleon sent against them the Mamelukes, the light cavalry and the mounted Grenadiers of his guard, led by Marshal Bessières and General Rapp, and a most sanguinary mêlée ensued. The Russian squadrons were overcome and driven back beyond the village of Austerlitz with great losses. Our cavalry captured many standards and prisoners, among whom was Prince Repnin, the commander of the horse-guards. This regiment, made up of the most glittering youth of the Russian nobility, suffered many casualties. The boastful threats which they had made concerning the French were known to our men, who in reply said that they would give the ladies of St. Petersburg something to cry about.

The painter Gérard, in his picture of the Battle of Austerlitz, has taken as his subject the moment when General Rapp, leaving the battle, wounded and covered in his own and the enemies' blood, is presenting to the Emperor the flags which have been captured as well as Prince Repnin, his prisoner. I was present at this memorable scene, which the painter has reproduced with remarkable exactness. All the heads are portraits, even that of the brave trooper, who without complaining, though shot through the body, fell dead at the feet of the Emperor as he presented the standard which he had just captured. Napoleon, to honour the memory of this brave Chasseur, ordered the painter to include him in his composition. One can see also in this picture a Mameluke, who carries in one hand an enemy flag, and with the other holds the bridle of his wounded horse. This man, named Mustapha, known in the guards for his courage and ferocity, had set off, during the charge, in pursuit of the Grand-duke Constantin, who was only able to get rid of him by firing a pistol shot which mortally wounded his horse. Mustapha, grieved at having only a standard to offer the Emperor, said in his broken French, when he presented it, "Ah! If me catch Prince Constantin, me cut off head and bring to Emperor!" Napoleon replied indignantly, "You be quiet! You wicked savage!"

Let us now finish the story of the battle. While Marshals Lannes, Soult and Murat attacked the centre and right of the Austro-Russians and drove them back beyond the village of Austerlitz, the enemy left, having fallen into the trap which the Emperor had prepared for them, attacked the village of Telnitz and took possession of it, then, crossing the Goldbach, they prepared to occupy the road to Vienna; but they had greatly underestimated the skill of Napoleon in thinking that he would neglect to defend his route of retreat in case of misfortune. Marshal Davout's divisions were concealed in Gross-Regairn and from that point he fell on the Russians as soon as he saw that their massed troops were held up in the defiles between the meres of Telnitz, Menitz and the rivulet.

The Emperor, whom we left on the plateau of Pratzen, free of the right and centre of the enemy, who were retreating in disorder beyond Austerlitz, came down from the heights of Pratzen and hurried with Marshal Soult's corps and all his guard, infantry, cavalry and artillery, towards Telnitz; where he attacked in the rear the enemy columns which Marshal Davout was attacking in front. From this moment, the cumbersome masses of the Austro-Russians, crammed together on the narrow pathways which ran alongside the Goldbach, finding themselves between two fires, fell into indescribable confusion. The ranks broke down and each man sought his own safety in flight. Some rushed into the marshes around the meres, but our infantry followed them; others tried to escape down the road which runs between the two meres, but our cavalry charged them with fearful slaughter; the largest body of men, principally Russians, tried to get across the frozen meres, and already a great number were on the ice of Lake Satschan when Napoleon ordered his gunners to fire on them. The ice broke in many places with a loud cracking sound and we saw a host of Russians with their horses wagons and guns slide slowly into the depths. The surface of the lake was covered with men and horses struggling amid the ice and water. A few were saved, helped by poles and ropes which our men held out to them from the bank, but many were drowned.

The number of combatants at the Emperor's disposal in this battle was sixty-eight thousand men. The Austro-Russians had ninety-two thousand. Our losses in killed and wounded were about eight thousand, the enemy stated that their losses in killed wounded and drowned amounted to fourteen thousand. We took eighteen thousand prisoners and captured one hundred and fifty cannons, as well as a great number of flags, standards, etc.

After giving orders to pursue the enemy in all directions, the Emperor went to his new headquarters in the post-house at Posoritz, on the Olmutz road. He was highly delighted as you may imagine, although he several times expressed regret that the only Eagle we had lost was that of the fourth line regiment, of which his brother, Prince Joseph, was colonel. The fact that this had been captured by the regiment of the Grand-duke Constantin, the Emperor of Russia's brother, made the loss even more annoying.

Napoleon soon had a great consolation; Prince Jean of Lichtenstein came, on behalf of the Emperor of Austria, to request a meeting, and Napoleon, realising that this would lead to peace and remove the fear of having the Prussians attack the French rear before he had rid himself of his present enemies, readily agreed to the proposal.

Of all the units of the Imperial Guard, the regiment of Mounted

Chasseurs was the one which suffered the most casualties in the great charge made on the Pratzen plateau against the Russian Guard. My poor friend Fournier was killed, as was General Morland. It is said that Napoleon intended to have the body of General Morland interred in a mausoleum which he meant to have built in the centre of the Esplanade des Invalides, and that it was preserved in a cask of rum for that reason. But the mausoleum was never built, and it is alleged that the general's body was still in a room in the school of medicine when Napoleon lost his Empire in 1814.

I was not wounded at Austerlitz, although I was often exposed to danger, notably during the mêlée with the Russian cavalry on the Pratzen plateau. The Emperor had sent me to take some orders to General Rapp, whom I found it very difficult to reach amid the appalling confusion of the embattled soldiery. My horse was crushed up against that of a Russian horse-guard and our sabres were about to clash when we were separated by other combatants; I came away with a large bruise. However, the next day I ran into a more serious danger, one that one does not expect to meet on the field of battle.

On the morning of the 3rd of December, the day after the battle, the Emperor mounted his horse and went round all the places where action had taken place on the previous day. Having arrived at the mere of Satschan, Napoleon dismounted and was chatting round a fire with a number of marshals, when we saw, some hundred paces from the bank, a large slab of ice on which lay a poor Russian sergeant, who was unable to help himself because of a bullet wound in his thigh. Seeing the large group on the bank, the soldier raised his voice and pleaded for help, saying that when the fighting was over we were all brother soldiers. When his interpreter translated this, Napoleon was touched and ordered General Bertrand to do what he could to rescue the wretched Russian.

Several men of the escort, and even two staff officers, attempted to reach the Russian using two tree trunks which they pushed into the water, but they ended up by falling in with all their clothes on, and having difficulty in getting out. It then occurred to me to say that they should have entered the water naked, so that their movements would not be hampered, and they would not have to wear wet clothing. This observation was repeated to the Emperor, who said that I was right, and that the others had shown zeal without forethought. I have no wish to make myself out to be better than I am; I can assure you that, having just taken part in a battle where I had seen thousands of dead and dying, my emotions were blunted, I did not feel sufficiently philanthropic to risk pneumonia by struggling amongst the ice floes to save the life of an enemy soldier, however much I deplored his unhappy lot; but the Emperor's remark stung me into action, it seemed to me ridiculous that I should offer advice which I was not prepared to put into action. I jumped off my horse, stripped off my clothes and leapt into the lake.

I had been very active during the day, and was warm; the water felt bitterly cold, but I was young and vigourous, a very good swimmer, and encouraged by the presence of the Emperor, I was making towards the Russian, when my example and probably the praise I received from the Emperor, persuaded a lieutenant of artillery named Roumestain to come after me.

While he was undressing, I pushed on, but I had more difficulty than I had foreseen in forcing my way through the thin layer of new ice which was forming on the water, the sharp edges of which inflicted many scrapes and scratches. The officer who followed me was able to make use of the sort of path which I had made, and when he reached me, he volunteered to take the lead, to give me some relief. We eventually reached the large block of ice on which the Russian lay, but it was only with the greatest difficulty that we managed to push it near enough to the shore for the man to be rescued. We were both so cold and exhausted that we had to be lifted out of the water, and we were hardly able to stand. My good comrade Massy, who had watched me with much anxiety during this swim, had had the forethought to warm his horse's blanket before the fire, which he wrapped round me as soon as I was out of the water. After I had dried myself and dressed, I wanted to lie beside the fire, but Doctor Larrey was against this and told me to walk around, something I was unable to do without the aid of two troopers. The Emperor came to congratulate the two of us on the courage with which we had undertaken the rescue of the wounded Russian, and calling for his Mameluke, Roustan, whose horse was always loaded with provisions, he poured out for us a tot of rum each, and asked us, laughing, how we had enjoyed the bath.

As for the Russian sergeant, after his wound had been dressed by Doctor Larrey, Napoleon gave him several gold coins. He was wrapped in warm coverings and put in one of the houses of Telnitz which was acting as a dressing station; the next day he was taken to the hospital at Brunn. The poor lad blessed the Emperor as well as Roumestain and me, and wanted to kiss our hands. He was a Lithuanian, that is to say, born in a former province of Poland, which is now part of Russia. As soon as he had recovered, he announced that he wished now to serve no one but Napoleon. He was sent back to France with our own wounded and subsequently joined the Polish legion. In the end he became a sergeant in the lancers of the guard, and each time I met him, he gave me a warm greeting.

The ice-cold bath which I had taken and the almost superhuman efforts I had made to rescue the Russian could have cost me dear had I been less young and strongly built; for Lieutenant Roumestain, who did not possess the latter of these two advantages to the same extent, was taken that same evening with a severe chest infection. He had to be taken to the hospital at Brunn, where he spent several months between life and death. He never recovered completely, and his poor health forced him to resign from the service some years later.

As for me, although I felt very weak, I mounted my horse when the Emperor left to go to the château of Austerlitz, where his headquarters had been set up. Napoleon never went anywhere except at the gallop; in my bruised state this pace was hardly suitable, however I followed on, since night was approaching, and I feared to be left behind, and anyway, if I had ridden at a walk, I would have been overcome by the cold.

When I arrived at the courtyard of the château of Austerlitz, I had to be helped off my horse. A violent shivering took me, my teeth chattered and I felt very ill. Colonel Dahlmann, a major in the Mounted Chasseurs, who had just been promoted to replace Colonel Morland, remembering, no doubt, the service I had rendered to the latter, took, me into one of the château's barns, where he had established himself with his officers. There, after giving me some hot tea, his medical officer massaged me with warm oil, I was wrapped in several blankets and put into an enormous pile of hay with only my face exposed. A gentle warmth crept slowly back into my benumbed limbs; I slept very soundly and thanks to these ministrations and my twenty-three years, I awoke the next day fully recovered and able to mount my horse and to observe a spectacle of great interest.

Chapter 26
My Mission to Darmstadt

The defeat suffered by the Russians had thrown their army into such confusion that all those who had escaped from the disaster of Austerlitz, hastened to Galicia to get out of reach of the victor. The rout was complete: the French took a great number of prisoners, and found the roads covered with cannons and abandoned baggage. The Emperor of Russia, who had believed he was marching to certain victory, withdrew, stricken with grief, and authorised his ally, Francis II to treat with Napoleon. In the evening following the battle, the Austrian Emperor, in order to save his country from total ruin, had sent a request for an interview to the French Emperor, and when Napoleon had agreed to this, he went to the village of Nasiedlowitz. The meeting took place on the 4th of December, near the Poleny mill, between the lines of the French and the Austrian outposts. I was at this memorable conference.

Napoleon left the château of Austerlitz early in the morning, accompanied by his large staff. He arrived first at the rendezvous, dismounted and strolled around until he saw the Emperor of Austria arrive. He went over to him and embraced him warmly....A spectacle which might well inspire some philosophical reflection! A German Emperor coming to humble himself and solicit peace from a little Corsican gentleman, recently a second lieutenant of artillery, whose talents, good fortune and the courage of the French armies had raised to the pinnacle of power and made arbiter of the destiny of Europe.

Napoleon did not abuse the position in which the Austrian Emperor found himself; he was attentive and extremely polite, as far as could be judged from the distance which was respectfully maintained by the two general staffs. An armistice was arranged between the two sovereigns which stipulated that both parties should send plenipotentiaries to Brunn in order to negotiate a peace treaty between France and Austria. The two Emperors embraced once more on parting; the Germans returned to Nasiedlowitz, and Napoleon returned to spend the night at Austerlitz. He spent two days there, during which time he gave Major Massy and me our final audience, and charged us to tell Marshal Augereau all that we had seen; he gave us at the same time some despatches for the court of Bavaria, which had returned to Munich, and informed us that Marshal Augereau had left Bregenz and that we would find him at Ulm. We went back to Vienna and continued our journey, travelling day and night in spite of the heavy falls of snow.

I shall not go into any details of the political changes which resulted from the Battle of Austerlitz and the Peace of Presburg. The Emperor went to Vienna and from there to Munich, where he had to assist at the marriage of his step-son, Eugène de Beauharnais to the daughter of the King of Bavaria. It seems that the despatches which we carried to this court were concerning this marriage; for we could not have had a better reception. However, we stayed only a few hours in Munich and went on to Ulm, where we found Marshal Augereau and 7th Corps, and where we stayed for a fortnight.

In order to move 7th Corps gradually nearer to the electorate of Hesse, a close ally of Prussia, Napoleon ordered it to move to Heidelburg, where we arrived about the end of December and saw the beginning of the year 1806. After a short stay in this town, 7th Corps went to Darmstadt, the capital of the landgrave of Hesse-Darmstadt, a prince much attached to the King of Prussia by family ties as well as politics. Although this prince had, on accepting Hanover, concluded a treaty of alliance with Napoleon, he had done so with reluctance, and was suspicious of the approach of the French army.

Marshal Augereau, before taking his troops into the country of Darmstadt, considered it his duty to inform the landgrave, by letter, of his intentions, and he chose me to effect its delivery. The journey was one of only fifteen leagues; I made it in a night; but on my arrival at Darmstadt I found that the landgrave, to whom it had been suggested that the French intended to make him a prisoner, had left his residence and retired to another part of his state from where he could easily take refuge in Prussia. This created a difficulty for me, however, having heard that his wife was still in the palace, I asked to be presented to her.

The princess, whose person greatly resembled the portraits of the Empress Catherine of Russia, had, like her, a masculine character, great capability, and all the qualities necessary to control a vast empire. She also governed her husband as she did her states; she was a masterful woman, and when she saw the letter in my hands, addressed to the landgrave, she took it without further ado, as if it had been addressed her. She then told me quite frankly, that it had been on her advice that her husband had left on the approach of the French, but that she would arrange for him to come back if the marshal would give her an assurance that he did not have any orders to make an attempt on the liberty of the prince. I understood that the arrest and death of the Duc d'Enghien had frightened all those princes who thought that Napoleon might have some reason to complain about their alliances. I protested, as much as I could, the innocence of the French government's intentions, and offered to go back to Heidelburg and ask Marshal Augereau for the assurances which she required, an offer which she accepted.

I left, and returned the next day with a letter from the marshal, couched in such conciliatory terms that the landgravine, after saying that she relied on the honour of a French marshal, went immediately to Giessen, where the landgrave was, and brought him back to Darmstadt, where they both received Marshal Augereau most graciously, when he came to set up his headquarters in the town. The marshal was so grateful for the confidence which they had placed in him that several months later, when the Emperor gathered up all the little European states and reduced their number to thirty-two, out of which he formed the confederation of the Rhine, he not only contrived to preserve the landgravate but gained for the landgrave the title of Grand-Duke and an enlargement of his state which increased the population from scarcely five hundred thousand to over one million. Some months later, the new Grand-Duke allied his army to ours to combat the Russians, and requested that they should serve in Marshal Augereau's corps. The prince owed not only his preservation but his elevation to his wife's courage.

Although I was still very young, I thought that Napoleon had made a mistake in reducing the number of the little German principalities.

The fact is that in previous wars against France, the eight hundred princes of the Germanic region had been unable to act in unison; there were some who provided no more than a company, others only a platoon, and some just one soldier; so that a combination of all these different contingents made up an army wholly lacking cohesion, which broke up at the first reverse. But when Napoleon had reduced the number of the principalities to thirty-two, centralisation began to appear in the German forces. Those rulers who remained, with states increased in size, formed a small well-organised army. This result was what the Emperor had intended, in the expectation of using for his own ends all the military resources of the country; something which he was in fact able to do as long as we were successful. But on the first setback, the thirty-two sovereigns, by agreement among themselves, united in opposition to France, and their coalition with the Russians overthrew the Emperor Napoleon, who was thus punished for not following the ancient policies of the kings of France.

We spent part of the winter at Darmstadt, where there were fêtes, balls and galas. The grand-duke's troops were commanded by a competent general named De Stoch. He had a son of my age, a charming young man with whom I struck up a close friendship, and to whom I shall refer again.

We were only some ten leagues from Frankfurt-on-main. This town, still free, and immensely rich as a result of its commerce, had been for a long time a hot-bed of all the plots contrived against France, and the place of origin of all the false stories about us which circulated in Germany. So that, the day after Austerlitz, and while the news was spreading that there had been an engagement, the result of which was not yet known, the inhabitants of Frankfurt were sure that the Russians had won, and several papers indulged their hatred to the point of saying that the disaster which had overtaken our army was so great that not a single Frenchman had survived!... The Emperor, to whom all this was reported, appeared to take no notice until, seeing the likelihood of a break with Prussia, he gradually moved his armies to the frontiers of that kingdom. Then, to punish the impertinence of the Frankfurters, he ordered Marshal Augereau to leave Darmstadt without warning, and to establish himself with his army corps in Frankfurt and its surroundings.

The Emperor decreed that the city, on the entry of our troops, should give, as a welcome, a louis d'or to each soldier, two to the corporals, three to the sergeants, ten to second lieutenants and so on! The inhabitants were also to lodge and feed the soldiers and pay messing expenses of six hundred francs daily for the marshal, four hundred for a divisional general, three hundred for a brigadier-general and two hundred for the colonels. The senate was instructed to pay every month, one million francs into the treasury in Paris. The authorities of Frankfurt, appalled by these exorbitant demands, hurried to the French envoy; but he replied "You claimed that not a single Frenchman escaped from the arms of the Russians; the Emperor Napoleon wishes to put you in a position to count the number making up a single corps of his army. There are six more of the same size, and the guard to follow." This reply plunged the inhabitants into consternation, for however great their wealth, they would be ruined if this state of affairs continued for any length of time. But Marshal Augereau made an appeal for clemency on behalf of the citizens, and he was told he could act as he thought best; so he took it on himself to station in the town only his general staff and one battalion. The remaining troops were spread around other neighbouring principalities. The Frankfurters were greatly relieved by this, and to show their gratitude to Marshal Augereau they treated him to a great number of fêtes. I was billeted with a rich merchant named M. Chamot. I spent nearly eight months there, during which time he and his family looked after me very well.

Chapter 27
My Mission to Berlin

While we were in Frankfurt, a very distressing event affecting an officer of 7th Corps, landed me with a double mission, the first part of which was very unpleasant and the second most agreeable, indeed brilliantly so.

As a result of a brain fever, Lieutenant N... of the 7th Chasseurs became completely childish. Marshal Augereau detailed me to take him to Paris, first to Marshal Murat, who had an interest in the matter, and then, if I was asked to do so, to the Quercy. As I had not seen my mother since leaving for the campaign of Austerlitz, and I knew that she was not far from St. Céré, in the Château de Bras, which my father had bought shortly before his death, I welcomed with pleasure a mission which would allow me not only to be of service to Marshal Murat but also to go and spend several days with my mother. Marshal Augereau lent me a fine carriage and I set off on the road to Paris. But the heat and insomnia so excited my poor companion that he went from a state of idiocy to one of mania and nearly killed me with a blow from a coach spanner. I have never made a more disagreeable journey. I arrived at last in Paris, and I took Lieutenant N... to Murat, who was staying for the summer at the Chateau de Neuilly. The marshal asked me to take the lieutenant to Quercy. I agreed to do so, in the hope of being able to see my mother again, but I pointed out that I could not leave for twenty-four hours, because Marshal Augereau had given me some despatches for the Emperor, whom I was going to meet at Rambouillet, to where I reported officially the same day.

I do not know what was in the despatches which I was carrying, but they made the Emperor very thoughtful. He sent for M. de Tallyrand and left with him for Paris to where he ordered me to follow him and present myself to Marshal Duroc that evening.

I waited for a long time in one of the salons of the Tuileries, until Marshal Duroc, coming out of the Emperor's study, the door of which was left half open, called for an orderly officer to get ready set off on a long mission. But Napoleon called out, "Duroc, that will not be necessary; we have Marbot here, who is going to rejoin Augereau; he can push on to Berlin. Frankfurt is half way there." So Marshal Duroc told me to prepare to go to Berlin with the Emperor's despatches. This was disappointing as it meant that I had to give up all hope of seeing my mother; but I had to resign myself. I hurried to Neuilly to tell Murat what had happened and as I believed that my new mission was very urgent, I returned to the Tuileries; but Marshal Duroc dismissed me until the next day. I was there at dawn: I was dismissed until evening; then the evening of the next day, and so on for more than a week. However, I remained patient, because each time I presented myself, Marshal Duroc kept me for only a minute, which allowed me time to get around Paris. I had been given quite a large sum of money for the purpose of buying myself new uniform, so as to appear well turned out before the king of Prussia, into whose hands I was personally to deliver a letter from the Emperor. You will understand that Napoleon neglected no detail when it came to enhancing the standing of the French army in the eyes of foreigners.

I left at last, after taking the despatches from the Emperor, who advised me that I should make sure that I carefully examined the Prussian troops, their bearing, their arms, their horses, etc. M. de Tallyrand gave me a packet for M. Laforest, the French ambassador in Berlin, to whose embassy I was to go. On my arrival at Maintz, which at that time was still part of French territory, I was told that Marshal Augereau was at Wiesbaden. I reported to him there and greatly surprised him by telling him that I was going to Berlin on the Emperor's orders. He congratulated me and told me to continue my journey. I travelled night and day, in superb July weather, and arrived in Berlin somewhat weary. At this period the Prussian roads were not yet metalled, one went almost always at walking pace over loose soil into which the coaches sank deeply, raising clouds of unbearable dust.

I was given a warm welcome by M. Laforest, at whose embassy I stayed. I was presented to the king and queen, and also to the princes and princesses. When the king received the letter from Napoleon, he seemed much affected. He was a fine figure of a man, with a benevolent expression, but lacking that animation which suggests a decisive character. The queen was really very pretty; she had only one blemish, she always wore a large scarf, in order, it was said, to conceal an ulcerated swelling on her neck. For the rest, she was graceful and her expression, calm and spiritual, was evidence of a firm personality.

I was very well received, and since the reply which I was to take back to the Emperor seemed so difficult to draft that it took more than a month, the queen was pleased to invite me to the balls and fêtes which she gave during my stay.

Of all the members of the royal family, the one who treated me in the most friendly manner, or so it seemed, was Prince Louis, the king's nephew.

I had been warned that he hated the French, and in particular, their Emperor, but as he was passionately interested in military matters, he questioned me endlessly about the siege of Genoa, the battles of Marengo and Austerlitz and also about the organisation of our army. Prince Louis was a most handsome man, and in respect of spirit, ability and character, the only one of the royal family who bore any resemblance to Frederick the Great. I made the acquaintance of several members of the court, mainly with the officers whom I followed daily to parades and manoeuvres. I spent my time in Berlin very pleasantly. The ambassador showed me much attention; but in the end I discovered that he wanted me to play, in a delicate affair, a role for which I was unsuited, so I became very reserved.

Now, let us examine the position of Prussia vis-à-vis France. The despatches which I had brought concerned this matter, as I later found out.

In accepting from Napoleon the gift of the electorate of Hanover, the patrimony of the English royal family, the cabinet in Berlin had alienated not only the anti-French party but almost all of the Prussian nation. Germanic pride was wounded by the victories won by the French over the Austrians, and Prussia feared that its commerce would be ruined by the war which had just been declared against it by the cabinet in London. The queen and Prince Louis made use of these turbulent emotions to persuade the king to make war on France by allying himself with Russia who, though abandoned by Austria, still hoped to take revenge for its defeat at Austerlitz. The Emperor of Russia was further encouraged in his plans by a Pole, his favourite aide-de-camp, Prince Czartoryski.

The anti-French party, which was growing daily, was not yet able to persuade the king to break with Napoleon; but aware that it was supported by Russia, this party redoubled its efforts, and profited adroitly from the mistakes made by Napoleon in placing his brother Louis on the throne of Holland, and nominating himself as protector of the confederacy of the Rhine: acts which were represented to the Prussian king as being steps on the path to the re-establishment of the empire of Charlemagne. Napoleon, it was said, wanted finally to reduce all the sovereigns of Germany to the status of vassals.

These assertions, though greatly exaggerated, had had a considerable influence on the king's thinking. His conduct toward France became from this time, more and more equivocal, and it was this that decided Napoleon to write to him personally, without going through the usual diplomatic channels, to ask "Are you for me or against me?" This was the tenor of the letter which I had given the king. His councillors who wished to gain time for the completion of their re-armament, delayed the reply, which was the reason for my long stay in Berlin.

At last, in August, there was a general explosion of ill-feeling towards France, and one saw the queen, Prince Louis, the nobility, the army and the general populace, noisily demanding war. The king allowed himself to become involved but, although determined to end the peace he still hoped to avoid hostilities, and it seems that in his reply to the Emperor he undertook to disarm if the latter would take back to France all the troops he had in Germany, which Napoleon was unwilling to do until Prussia had disarmed. So we were in a vicious circle which could be broken only by a war.

Before I left Berlin, I witnessed the frenzy to which hatred of Napoleon raised this normally placid people. The officers whom I knew no longer dared to speak to me or even to greet me. Several French people were insulted by the populace, and finally soldiers of the Royal Guard came boastfully to sharpen their sabres on the stone steps of the French embassy. I left hurriedly for Paris, taking with me much information on what was going on in Prussia. Passing through Frankfurt, I found Marshal Augereau very sad at having heard of the death of his wife, a good, excellent woman whose loss he felt deeply, and who was mourned by all the general staff, for she had been very kind to us.

On my arrival in Paris, I delivered to the Emperor the hand-written reply from the King of Prussia. After reading it, he questioned me on what I had seen in Berlin. When I told him that the soldiers of the guard had come to sharpen their sabres on the steps of the French embassy, he clapped his hand firmly on the hilt of his sword, exclaiming indignantly, "The insolent braggarts will soon learn that our arms are in good order!"

My mission now being over, I returned to Marshal Augereau, and spent all of September in Frankfurt where, while preparing ourselves for war, we entertained ourselves as best we could, for we thought that as nothing could be more uncertain than the life of a soldier, one should enjoy it as much as is possible.

Chapter 28
At War with Prussia

While the different corps of the French army were approaching the banks of the Main, the Emperor arrived at Wurtzburg and crossed the Rhine with his Guard. The Prussians, for their part, were on the march, and going through Saxony, they compelled the elector to join forces with them. This enforced, and therefore unstable, alliance was the only one which the King of Prussia had in Germany. He was, it is true, expecting the arrival of the Russians, but their army was still in Poland behind the Niemen, more than one hundred and fifty leagues from the country where the destiny of Prussia was to be decided.

It is hard to believe the incompetence displayed, for seven years, by our enemies' governments. We saw, in 1805, the Austrians attack us on the Danube, and be defeated in isolation at Ulm, instead of waiting for Russia to join them and for Prussia to declare war on Napoleon. Now, in 1806, those same Prussians who, a year before, could have prevented the defeat of the Austro-Russians by joining them, not only declared war on us when we were at peace with Vienna, but repeated the mistake of attacking us without waiting for the Russians! Finally, in 1809, the Austrians renewed the war against Napoleon on their own, at a time when we were at peace with both Prussia and Russia! This lack of co-operation ensured a French victory. Sadly it was not so in 1813, when we were crushed by a coalition of our enemies.

In 1806 the King of Prussia was even more mistaken in taking to the field against Napoleon in the absence of the Russians, in that his troops, although well trained, were in no condition to be pitted against ours, because their composition and organisation were so bad.

In effect, at this time, Prussian captains were the owners of their company or squadron: men, horses, arms and clothing all belonged to them and the whole unit was hired out to the government for a fixed fee. Obviously, since all losses fell to their account, the captains had a great interest in sparing their companies, not only on the march but on the field of battle. As the number of men they were obliged to have was fixed and there was no conscription, they enrolled for money, first any Prussians who came forward, and then all the vagabonds of Europe, whom their recruiters enlisted in neighbouring states. But this was not enough, and the Prussian recruiters pressed many men into service, who having become soldiers against their will, were compelled to serve until they were too old to bear arms; then they were given a permit to beg, for Prussia could not afford to provide a home for old soldiers or a retirement pension. For the duration of their service these men had to be mixed with true Prussians, who had to constitute at least half of each company to prevent mutiny.

To maintain an army composed of such heterogeneous parts required an iron discipline; so the least fault was punished by beating. A large number of N.C.O.s, all of them Prussian, carried canes which they made use of frequently, and according to the current expression there was a cane for every seven men. The penalty for desertion by a foreign soldier was inevitably death. You can imagine the frightful position of these foreigners, who having enlisted in a moment of drunkenness, or been taken by force, found themselves far from their native land, under a glacial sky, condemned to be Prussian soldiers, that is slaves, for the rest of their lives! And what a life it was! Given scarcely enough to eat. Sleeping on straw. Thinly clad. Without greatcoats, even in the coldest winter, and paid a sum insufficient for their needs; they did not wait to beg until they had been given a permit on their discharge, for when they were not under the eyes of their superiors, they held out their hands, and there were several occasions both at Potsdam and Berlin when Grenadiers, even those at the palace gate, begged me for alms!

The Prussian-born officers were, in general, educated men, who performed their duties very well; but half of the officers, born outside the kingdom, were poor gentlemen from almost every country in Europe who had joined the army only to have a living, and lacking patriotism, were in no way devoted to Prussia, which the majority abandoned when there was any adversity. Finally, as promotion was only by length of service, the great majority of senior Prussian officers were old and infirm, and in no state to support the fatigues of war. It was an army thus composed and commanded which was to confront the victors of Italy, Egypt, Germany and Austerlitz. This was folly. But the cabinet in Berlin, recalling the victories which Frederick the Great had won with mercenary troops, hoped things would be the same. They forgot that times had changed.

On the 6th of October Marshal Augereau and 7th Corps left Frankfurt to head, with the rest of the Grande Armée, for the frontiers of Saxony, already occupied by the Prussians. The autumn was superb; it froze a little during the night, but by day there was brilliant sunshine. My little troupe was well organised; I had a good batman, Francois Woirland, a former soldier in the Black Legion, a real rascal and a great scrounger, but these are the best servants on a campaign, for with one of them one lacks for nothing. I had three excellent horses, good weapons, a little money and good health; so I stepped out gaily to face whatever the future might bring.

We went first to Aschaffenburg and from there to Wurtzburg, where we caught up with the Emperor, who ordered a march-past by the troops of 7th Corps, who were in good heart. Napoleon who kept a dossier about all the regiments, and who skillfully used to employ extracts from it to flatter the self-esteem of each unit, said when he saw the 44th line regiment, "Of all the units of the army you are the one with the most long service chevrons, so your three battalions I count as six!"...an announcement which was greeted by cheers. To the 7th, composed mostly of men from the lower Languedoc and the Pyrenees, the Emperor said, "There are the best marchers in the army, one never sees anyone fall behind, particularly when there is a battle to be fought." Then he added, laughingly, "But, to do you justice, I must say that you are the most brawling, thieving unit in the army!" "It's true! It's true!" replied the soldiers, each of whom had a duck, a chicken or a goose in his knapsack, an abuse which had to be tolerated, because, as I have told you, Napoleon's armies, once in the field, rarely received any rations, and had to live off the country as well as they could. This system had without doubt many defects, but it had one huge benefit, that of allowing us to move forward without being held up by convoys and supply lines, which gave us a great advantage over an enemy whose movements were subordinated to the cook-house, or the arrival of bread, and to the progress of herds of cattle, etc...etc.

From Wurtzburg, 7th Corps went to Coburg, where the marshal was lodged in the prince's palace. All his family had fled on our approach, except the celebrated Austrian Field-marshal, the Prince of Coburg. This old warrior, although he had fought for many years against the French, had enough confidence in the French character to await their coming, a confidence which was not misplaced, for Marshal Augereau sent him a guard of honour, returned promptly a visit he had received, and ordered that he was to be treated with the utmost respect.

We were not very far from the Prussians, whose king was at Erfurt. The queen was with him and rode up and down the ranks of the army on horseback, endeavouring to excite their ardour by her presence. Napoleon did not think that this was behaviour befitting a princess, and his bulletins made some wounding comments on the subject. The French and Prussian advance-guards met eventually, at Schleitz: where there took place, in view of the Emperor, a minor action in which the enemy were defeated; it was for them an ill-omened beginning.

That same day, Prince Louis, with a body of ten thousand men, found himself stationed in Saalfeld. This town is on the bank of the River Saale, in the middle of a plain which we could reach only by crossing some steep mountains. While Marshals Lannes' and Augereau's corps were moving toward Saalfeld through these mountains, Prince Louis, who had decided to await the French, should have occupied positions in this difficult country, full of narrow passes, where a few men could hold up a much greater number, but he failed to do this, probably because he was convinced that the Prussian soldiers were infinitely better than the French. He carried this scorn for all precautions so far as to place part of his force in front of a marshy stream, which would make their retreat very difficult in the event of a reverse. Old General Muller, a Swiss in the service of Prussia, whom the king had attached to his nephew as a steadying influence, made some observations which the prince took very badly, adding that there was no need to take precautions to beat the French, all that was needed was to fall on them the moment they appeared.

They appeared in the morning on the 10th; Marshal Lannes' corps leading and Marshal Augereau's behind him. This last did not arrive in time to take part in the action where, as it happened, their presence was not needed, for Marshal Lannes' troops were more than sufficient.

While waiting for his corps to emerge onto the plain, Marshal Augereau, accompanied by his staff, went up onto a little hill which overlooked the open country, from where we could follow all stages of the action.

Prince Louis could still have retreated to join the Prussian corps which occupied Jena; but having been the leading instigator of the war he perhaps felt he should not do so without a fight. He was most cruelly punished for his temerity. Marshal Lannes, making use of the heights, at the foot of which Prince Louis had imprudently deployed his troops, first raked them with grape-shot from his artillery, and when this had demoralised them, he advanced several masses of infantry, which descending rapidly from the high ground, swept like a torrent onto the Prussian battalions and instantly overwhelmed them! Prince Louis, aghast, and probably aware of his mistake, hoped to repair it by putting himself at the head of his cavalry and impetuously attacking the 9th and 10th Hussars. He had at first some success, but our Hussars having made a new and furious charge, drove the Prussians back into the marshes, while their infantry fled in disorder.

In the middle of the melée, Prince Louis found himself engaged with a sous-officier of the 10th Hussars named Guindet, who summoned him to surrender; the prince replied with a slash of his sword which cut the sous-officier's face, who thereupon ran the prince through and killed him.

After the fight and the complete rout of the enemy, the prince's body having been recognised, Marshal Lannes had it carried with honour to the château of Saalfeld, where it was handed to the princely family of that name, who were allied to the royal house of Prussia, and in whose residence the prince had spent the previous day and evening, looking forward to the coming of the French, and even, it is said, giving a ball for the local ladies. Now he was returned to them, vanquished and dead!...The next morning I saw the prince's body, laid out on a marble table, all traces of blood had been cleaned away, he was naked to the waist, still wearing his leather britches and his boots. He seemed to be asleep. He was a truly fine looking man, and I could not help indulging in some sad reflections on the uncertainty of human affairs, when I saw the remains of this young man, born on the steps of a throne, and, but lately, so loved, so courted and so powerful!

The news of the prince's death spread consternation in the enemy army, and also throughout Prussia, where he was highly popular.

7th Corps spent the day of the 11th at Saalfeld. On the 12th we went to Neustadt, and on the 13th to Kehla, where we encountered some remains of the Prussian troops defeated at Saalfeld. When Marshal Augereau attacked them, they put up little resistance and laid down their arms. Amongst those captured was the regiment of Prince Henry in which Augereau had once served as a soldier, and since, unless one was of high birth, it was very difficult to become a senior officer in the Prussian army, and as sergeants never became second lieutenants, his former company still had the same captain and the same sergeant-major. Placed by a quirk of fate in the presence of his one-time soldier, now a marshal, the Prussian captain, who remembered Augereau perfectly well, acted as a man of discretion and spoke always to the marshal as if he had never seen him before. Augereau invited him to dinner and seated him next to himself, then, learning that the officer's baggage had been seized, he lent him all the money he needed and gave him letters of introduction to take to France. What must have passed through the captain's mind! But nothing can describe the astonishment of the old Prussian sergeant-major at seeing his former soldier covered with decorations, surrounded by a numerous staff and in command of an army corps! All of which seemed like a dream! The marshal was more expansive toward this man than he had been toward the captain. Addressing the sergeant by name, he shook him by the hand, and arranged for him to be given twenty-five louis for himself and two for every soldier who had been in the ranks with him and was still there. We thought this behaviour was in the best of taste.

The marshal had expected to sleep at Kehla, which is only three leagues from Jena; but just as night was falling 7th Corps was ordered to go immediately to this last town which the Emperor had just entered, at the head of his guard and the troops of Marshal Lannes, without striking a blow.

The Prussians had abandoned Jena in silence, but some candles, forgotten in the stables, had probably started the fire, the spreading flames of which were consuming part of the unfortunate town when Marshal Augereau's corps entered it at about midnight. It was a sorry spectacle to see the inhabitants, women and old people, half naked, carrying their children and seeking to escape by flight from the scene of destruction, while our soldiers, kept in their ranks by discipline and the nearness of the enemy, remained unmoved, their arms at the ready, regarding the fire as a small matter in comparison to the dangers they would soon have to face.

The part of the town through which our troops arrived was not affected by the fire and so they could move around freely, and while they were gathering in the squares and main streets, the marshal set up his headquarters in a nice looking mansion. I was about to enter, on returning from delivering an order, when I heard loud shrieks coming from a nearby house, the door of which was open. I hurried there and guided by the cries I found my way to a well-appointed apartment where I saw two charming girls, of about eighteen to twenty years of age, dressed only in their chemises, struggling against the advances of four or five soldiers from Hesse-Darmstadt, belonging to the regiments which the landgrave had attached to the French troops of 7th Corps. Although these men, who were drunk, understood not a word of French, and I spoke little German, my appearance and my threats took them aback, and being used to beatings from their own officers, they made no retaliation to the kicks and cuffs which in my indignation I distributed freely in driving them downstairs. In this I was perhaps a little imprudent, for in the middle of the night, in a town in utter confusion there was a risk that they might turn on me and even kill me; but they ran away, and I put a platoon of the marshal's escort in one of the lower rooms.

I went up to the apartment where the two young girls had hurriedly dressed themselves, and was rewarded by their warmest expressions of gratitude. They were the daughters of a university professor, who had gone with his wife and the domestic staff to the aid of one of their sisters, who had recently given birth in that part of the town where the fire was raging, and they had been alone when the Hessian soldiers arrived. One of these young ladies said to me with great emotion, "You are going into battle at a time when you have just saved our honour. God will reward you, you may be sure that no harm will come to you." The father and the mother, who came back at this moment with the new mother and her child were at first much surprised to find me there; but when they learned the reason for my presence they too showered me with blessings. I tore myself away from the thanks of this grateful family to rejoin Marshal Augereau, who was reposing in the nearby mansion, awaiting the Emperor's orders.

Chapter 29
The Battle of Jena

The town of Jena is dominated by a height called the Landgraf-enberg, at the foot of which runs the Saale River. The approaches to Jena are very precipitous, and at that time there was only one road, which ran to Wiemar via Muhlthal, a long and difficult pass, the outlet of which was covered by a small wood and guarded by Saxon troops, allies of the Prussians; a part of whose army was drawn up in line behind them at the distance of a cannon shot.

The Emperor, having only this one route by which he could reach his enemies, expected to suffer heavy losses in a frontal attack, for there seemed to be no way in which they could be outflanked. But Napoleon's lucky star once more came to his aid, in an unexpected way, which I do not believe has been related by any historian, although I can vouch for the truth of it happening.

We have seen that the King of Prussia compelled the elector of Saxony to join forces with him. The people of Saxony saw themselves, with regret, drawn into a war which could procure them no advantage in the future, and which for the present brought desolation to the countryside, which was the theatre for the hostilities. The Prussians were therefore detested in Saxony; and Jena, a Saxon town, shared in this detestation.

A priest who belonged to the town, angered at the fire which was consuming it, and regarding the Prussians as enemies of his king and fatherland, believed he could give Napoleon the means of clearing them out of the country, by showing him a little pathway by which a body of infantrymen might climb the steep slopes of the Landgrafenberg. He led there a platoon of light infantry and some officers of the general staff. The Prussians, who thought this pathway impracticable, had not bothered to guard it, but Napoleon thought differently. As a result of the report given him by his officers, he went up himself, guided by the Saxon curé, and accompanied by Marshal Lannes; he saw that, between the heights of the path and the plain occupied by the enemy, there was a small stony plateau, and he decided to concentrate there a body of troops who would sally from it, as if from a citadel, to attack the Prussians.

The undertaking would have been of unsurmountable difficulty for anyone but a Napoleon in command of French soldiers; but he ordered the tools used by the pioneers to be taken from the wagons of the engineers and the artillery and distributed to the infantry battalions, who worked in rotation for one hour each at widening and levelling the pathway, and when they had finished their task, each battalion formed up in silence on the Landgrafenberg, while another took its place. The work was carried on by the light of torches, whose flames were confused in the eyes of the enemy with the fires in Jena.

The nights are very long at this time of year, so that we were able to make the path accessible not only for foot-soldiers but also for the wagons of the artillery, with the result that, before daybreak, the corps of Marshals Lannes and Soult, the first division of Augereau's, as well as the foot guards, were massed on the Landgrafenberg. Never has the term massed been used with more exactitude, for the chest of each man was almost touching the back of the man in front of him; but the troops were so well disciplined that, in spite of the darkness and the crowding together of more than forty thousand men, there was not the least disorder; and although the enemy were occupying villages less than half a cannon shot away, they heard nothing.

On the morning of October 14th, a thick mist covered the countryside, which favoured our movements; Augereau's second division, making a diversionary attack, advanced from Jena via Muhlthal on the road to Weimar. As the enemy believed that this was the only way by which we could come from Jena, they had placed a considerable force there; but while they prepared to conduct a vigourous defence of this pass, Napoleon, bringing down from the Landgrafenberg the troops which he had accumulated there during the night, drew them up in battle order on the plain. A light breeze having dispersed the mist, which was followed by brilliant sunshine, the Prussians were stupefied to see the lines of the French army deployed opposite them and advancing to engage them in battle. They could not understand how we had got there when they thought we were down in the valley of Jena, with no other means of reaching them but the road to Wiemar, which they were guarding so thoroughly.

The battle began immediately and the first lines of the Prussians and Saxons, commanded by Prince Hohenlohe, were forced to retreat. They advanced their reserves, but we received a powerful reinforcement. Marshal Ney's corps and Murat's cavalry which had been held up in the pass, burst out into the plain and took part in the action. However a Prussian army corps commanded by General Ruchel stopped our columns for a time; but charged by French cavalry it was almost entirely wiped out and General Ruchel was killed.

Marshal Augereau's 1st division, coming down from the Landgrafenberg, joined with the 2nd, arriving from Muhlthal, and with the troops of Marshals Lannes and Soult, they proceeded down the road to Wiemar, capturing enemy positions as they went.

The Prussian infantry, whose poor composition I have already described, fought very badly, and the cavalry not much better. One saw them on several occasions advance, with loud shouts, towards our battalions; but, intimidated by their calm bearing, they never dared charge home; at a distance of fifty paces from our line they shamefully turned about, amid a hail of bullets and the jeers of our men.

The Saxons fought with courage; they resisted Marshal Augereau's corps for a long time, and it was not until after the retreat of the Prussian troops that, having formed themselves into two large squares, they began to withdraw while continuing to fire. Marshal Augereau admired the courage of the Saxons, and to prevent further loss of life, he had just sent an envoy to persuade them to surrender, since they had no longer any hope of relief, when Prince Murat arrived with his cavalry and mounted an attack with his Cuirassiers and dragoons, who charging impetuously the Saxon squares, overwhelmed them and forced them to lay down their arms. The next day, however, the Emperor set them at liberty and restored them to their sovereign, with whom he hastened to make peace.

All the Prussian troops who had fought before Jena, retreated in a complete rout along the road to Weimar, at whose gates the fugitives, their baggage and artillery had piled up, when suddenly the squadrons of the French cavalry appeared! At the sight of them, panic spread through the crowd of Prussians, who fled in utter disorder, leaving us with a great number of prisoners, flags, guns and baggage.

The town of Weimar, called by some the new Athens, was inhabited at this period by a great number of scholars, artists and distinguished authors, who had gathered there under the patronage of the ruling duke, an enlightened protector of the arts and sciences. The noise of guns, the passage of the fugitives and the entry of the victors caused a great stir in this peaceful and studious population; but Marshals Lannes and Soult maintained a firm discipline, and apart from having to provide food for the soldiers, the town suffered no outrage. The Prince of Weimar served in the Prussian army, nevertheless his palace, where the princess, his wife, was living, was respected and none of the marshals took up residence there.

Marshal Augereau's headquarters were established at the town gates, in the house of the prince's head gardener. All the inhabitants of the house having taken flight, the general staff found nothing to eat, and had to sup on some pineapples and plums from the hothouses. This was a very light diet for people who, without food for twenty-four hours, had spent the preceding night on foot and all day fighting! But we were the victors, and that magical word enabled us to support all our privations.

The Emperor went back to sleep at Jena, where he learned of a success no less great than that which he had just achieved himself. The battle of Jena was a double battle, if one may use the expression, for neither the French nor the Prussian armies were united at Jena, they were each divided into two parts and fought two different battles: so that while the Emperor, at the head of the corps of Augereau, Lannes, Soult and Ney, his guard and the cavalry of Murat, was defeating the corps of Prince Hohenlohe and General Ruchel. The King of Prussia, at the head of his main army, commanded by the celebrated Prince of Brunswick, Marshals Mollendorf and Kalkreuth had left Weimar, and on their way to Naumburg had settled for the night at the village of Auerstadt, not far from the French corps of Davout and Bernadotte, who were in the villages around Naumburg. In order to rejoin the Emperor, who was at Apolda, in the plain beyond Jena, Davout and Bernadotte had to cross the Saale before Naumburg and traverse the narrow hilly pass of Kosen. Although Davout thought that the King of Prussia with the main body of his army was facing the Emperor, and not so close to him at Auerstadt, this vigilant warrior secured, during the night, the Kosen pass and its steep slopes which the King of Prussia and his marshals had neglected to occupy, thus making the same mistake as Prince Hohenlohe made at Jena in failing to guard the Landgrafenberg. The combined forces of Bernadotte and Davout did not amount to more than forty-four thousand men, while the King of Prussia had eighty thousand at Auerstadt.

From daybreak on the 14th, the two French marshals realised that they had to face much superior numbers; it was their duty then to act in unison. Davout, aware of this necessity, volunteered to put himself under the command of Bernadotte, but the latter jibbed at the idea of a shared victory, and unwilling to subordinate his personal interests to the welfare of his country, he decided to act on his own; and on the pretext that the Emperor had ordered him to be at Dornburg on the 13th, he decided to make his way there on the 14th, although Napoleon had written to him during the night to say that, if he was still in Naumburg, he should stay there and support Davout. Not finding the situation to his liking, Bernadotte left Davout to defend himself as best he could and, going down the Saale, he settled himself at Dornburg where, although he came across no enemies, he could see from the elevated position which he occupied, the desperate battle being fought by the gallant Davout some two leagues away. Meanwhile he ordered his men to set up their bivouacs and to start preparing a meal. His generals complained to him in vain at this culpable inaction; Bernadotte would not budge, so that Marshal Davout, with no more than twenty-five thousand men, comprising the divisions of Friant, Morland and Gudin, faced almost eighty thousand Prussians animated by the presence of their king.

The French, after emerging from the narrow pass of Kosen, formed up near the village of Hassenhausen; it was here that the real battle took place, because the Emperor was mistaken when he thought that he had before him at Jena the king and the bulk of the Prussian army. The action fought by Davout's men was one of the most terrible in our annals. His divisions, having successfully resisted all the attacks of the enemy infantry, formed into squares and repelled numerous cavalry charges, and not content with this, they advanced with such resolution that the Prussians fell back at every point leaving the ground strewn with dead and wounded. The Prince of Brunswick and General Schmettau were killed, Marshal Mollendorf was seriously wounded and taken prisoner.

The King of Prussia and his troops at first carried out their retreat towards Weimar in reasonably good order, hoping to rally there behind the forces of Prince Hohenlohe and General Ruchel, whom they supposed to have been victorious, while the latter, having been defeated by Napoleon, were for their part, on their way to seek support from the troops led by the king. Those two enormous masses of soldiers, beaten and demoralised, met on the road to Erfurt; it needed only the appearance of some French regiments to throw them into utter confusion. The rout was total, and was a just punishment for the bragging of the Prussian officers. The results of this victory were incalculable, and made us masters of almost all Prussia.

The Emperor showed his great satisfaction with Marshal Davout and with the divisions of Morand, Friant and Gudin by an order of the day, which was read out to all companies and even in the ambulances carrying the wounded. The following year Napoleon created Davout Duke of Auerstadt, although he had fought less there than in the village of Hassenhausen; but the King of Prussia had had his headquarters at Auerstadt, and the Prussians had given this name to the battle which the French called the Battle of Jena.

The army expected to see Bernadotte severely punished, but he got away with a sharp reprimand; Napoleon was afraid of upsetting his brother Joseph, whose sister-in-law, Mlle. Clary, Bernadotte had just married. We shall see later how Bernadotte's behaviour during the Battle of Auerstadt served, in a way, as a first step towards mounting the throne of Sweden.

I was not wounded at Jena, but I was tricked in a way that still rankles after forty years. At a time when Augereau's corps was attacking the Saxons, the marshal sent me to carry a message to General Durosnel, who commanded a brigade of Chasseurs, ordering him to charge the enemy cavalry. It was my job to guide the brigade along a route which I had already reconnoitred. I hurried away and put myself at the head of our Chasseurs, who threw themselves on the Saxon squadrons. The Saxons put up a stiff resistance and there was a general melée, but eventually our adversaries were forced to retreat with losses. Towards the end of the fighting, I found myself facing an officer of Hussars, wearing the white uniform of Prince Albert of Saxony's regiment. I held the point of my sabre against him and called on him to surrender, which he did, handing me his sword. As the fighting was over, I generously gave it back to him, as was the usual practice among officers in these circumstances, and I added that although his horse, under the conventions of war, belonged to me, I did not wish to deprive him of it. He gave me many thanks for this kind treatment and followed me as I returned to the marshal, very pleased with myself for bringing back a prisoner. But when we were about five hundred paces from the Chasseurs, this confounded Saxon officer, who was on my left, drew his sabre, wounded my horse on the shoulder and was about to strike me if I had not thrown myself on him. Although I had no sabre in my hand, our bodies were so close that he did not have room to swing his sabre at me, so he grabbed my epaulet, and pulled me off balance, my saddle slipped under my horse's belly and there I was with one leg in the air and my head hanging down, while the Saxon made off at full speed to rejoin the remains of the enemy army. I was furious, partly at the position I was in, and partly at the ingratitude with which this foreigner had repaid my courtesy. So when the Saxon army had been made prisoners, I went to look for my Hussar officer, to teach him a lesson, but he had disappeared.

I have said that the Duke of Hesse-Darmstadt, our new ally, had joined his troops to the Emperor's. This brigade had uniforms exactly like those of the Prussians, so several of their soldiers were killed or wounded mistakenly during the action. The young Lieutenant De Stoch, my friend, was on the point of meeting the same fate, and had already been seized by our Hussars, when, having seen me, he called out to me and I had him released.

The Emperor rewarded most generously the priest of Jena, and the elector of Saxony, having become king as a result of the victories of his ally Napoleon, rewarded him also; so that he lived very comfortably until 1814 when he took refuge in France to escape from the vengeance of the Prussians. They, however, had him taken up and shut away in a fortress where he spent two or three years. Eventually, the King of Saxony having interceded on his behalf with Louis XVIII, the latter reclaimed the priest on the grounds that he had been arrested without proper authority, and the Prussians having released him, he came to live in Paris. After the victory at Jena, the Emperor ordered a general pursuit of our enemies, and our columns took an enormous number of prisoners.

The King of Prussia had great difficulty in reaching Magdeburg and getting from there to Berlin, and it was said that the queen nearly fell into the hands of the scouts of our advance-guard.

It would take too long to detail all the disasters which befell the Prussian army; it is enough to say that of those troops who marched to attack the French, not a battalion escaped; they were all captured before the end of the month. The fortresses of Torgau, Erfurt and Wittemburg opened their gates to the victors who, having crossed the Elbe at several points -- Augereau's corps crossing near Dessau -- headed for Berlin.

Napoleon stopped at Potsdam, where he visited the tomb of Frederick the Great; then he went to Berlin where, contrary to his usual practice, he wished to make a triumphal entry. Marshal Davout's corps headed the procession; an honour to which it was entitled as it had done more fighting than the others. Then came Augereau's corps and then the guard.

Chapter 30
To the Vistula

On my return to Berlin which, when I had left it not long ago, had been so brilliant, I could not help having some sad reflections. The populace, then so self-confident, was now gloomy, downcast, and much afflicted, for the Prussians are very patriotic: they felt humiliated by the defeat of their army and the occupation of their country by the French; besides which almost every family had to mourn a relative or friend killed or captured in battle. I had every sympathy with their feelings; but I must confess that I experienced quite a different sentiment when I saw, entering Berlin as prisoners of war, walking sadly, dismounted and disarmed, the regiment of the so-called Noble Gendarmes; those same arrogant young officers who had so insolently come to sharpen their sabres on the steps of the French embassy!....Nothing could depict their shame and abasement at finding themselves defeated by those same Frenchmen whom they had boasted they would put to flight by their mere presence. They had asked that they might go round Berlin without entering it, to avoid the painful experience of filing as prisoners through the town where they were so well known and where the inhabitants had witnessed their bragging; but this is precisely why the Emperor ordered them to pass between two lines of French soldiers, who directed them down the road in which stood the French embassy. The inhabitants of Berlin did not disapprove of this little act of revenge, since they greatly disliked the Noble Gendarmes whom they accused of having pushed the king into the war.

Marshal Augereau was billeted outside the town, in the château of Bellevue, which belonged to Prince Ferdinand, the only one of Frederick the Great's brothers who was still living. This venerable old man, the father of Prince Louis who was recently killed at Saalefeld, was afflicted by grief made even more bitter by the fact that, against the opinion of all the court and also that of the son whom he mourned, he had strongly opposed the war, and had predicted the misfortunes which it would bring upon Prussia. Marshal Augereau thought it his duty to visit the prince, who had withdrawn to a dwelling in the town. He was received most politely; the unhappy father told the marshal that he had learned that his young son, Prince Auguste, the only one left to him, was at the town gate in a column of prisoners, and that he longed to embrace him before he was sent off to France. Since Prince Ferdinand's great age prevented him from going to look for his son, the marshal, sure that Napoleon would not object, told me to mount my horse right away, to go and find Prince Auguste, and to bring him back. Which I did.

The arrival of the young prince gave rise to the most moving scene. His elderly parents could not stop embracing this son, who recalled to them the loss of the other. To console them as much as lay within his power, the good marshal went to the Emperor's quarters and came back with authority for the young prince to remain, on parole, in the bosom of his family. A favour for which Prince Ferdinand was infinitely grateful.

The victory at Jena had had the most profound effect. Complete demoralisation had gripped not only the troops in the field, but the garrisons of the fortresses. Magdeburg surrendered without making any attempt at resistance; Spandau did the same; Stettin opened its gates to a division of cavalry, and the governor of Custrin sent boats across the Oder to fetch the French troops; who without this help would not have been able to take the place without several months of siege. Every day one heard of the surrender of some unit of the army or the capitulation of some fortress. The faulty organisation of the Prussian army became more evident than ever; the foreigners, in particular those who had been enlisted against their will, took the occasion to recover their liberty, and deserted in droves, or stayed behind to give themselves up to the French.

To the conquest of the Prussians, Napoleon added the confiscation of the states of the Elector of Hesse-Cassel, whose duplicity had earned him this punishment. This prince, who had been requested some time before the war to declare himself a supporter of either France or Prussia, lulled both parties with promises, with the intention of coming down on the side of the victor. An avaricious sovereign, the Elector had amassed a great fortune by selling his own people to the English, who used them to fight against the Americans in the War of Independence, in which many of them perished. Careless of his people's welfare, he had offered to join his troops to the French force on condition that the Emperor would cede to him the French American states. So no one was very sorry for the Elector, whose precipitous departure occasioned an event which is still not generally known.

Compelled to leave Hesse in a hurry, to take refuge in England, the Elector, who was regarded as one of the richest people in Europe, was unable to take with him all his wealth. So he sent for a Jew from Frankfurt by the name of Rothschild, a small-time banker and not well known, but respected for the scrupulous devotion with which he practised his religion: and it was this that decided the Elector to confide to his care some fifteen million in specie. The interest earned on this money was to belong to the banker, who was obliged to return only the capital.

When the palace of Cassel was occupied by our troops, agents of the French treasury seized a considerable quantity of valuables, mainly pictures, but did not find any money. It seemed impossible, however, that the Elector, in his hurried flight, had been able to take with him all his immense fortune. Now, as according to what are called the laws of war, the monies found in an enemy country belong to the victor, one wished to find out what had become of the treasure of Cassel. Information gathered on the subject disclosed that, before his departure, the Elector had spent a whole day with the Jew Rothschild. An imperial commission went to the latter's house, where his account books and his strong-boxes were minutely examined; but in vain, for no trace could be found of a deposit made by the Elector. Threats and intimidation produced no result, so the commission, convinced that no material interest would persuade a man so religious to perjure himself, wished to put him on oath. This he refused to accept. His arrest was considered but the Emperor was opposed to this act of violence because he thought it would be useless. Resort was then had to less honourable methods; it was proposed to the banker that he might retain half of the treasure if he would deliver the other half to the French administration; they would then give him a receipt for the full amount, accompanied by an order of seizure, proving that he had given way only to force and was thus shielded from any claim for restitution; but the upright Jew rejected this suggestion, and, tired of the struggle, they left him alone.

So the fifteen million remained in the hands of Rothschild from 1806 to the fall of the empire in 1814. Then, when the Elector had returned to his state, the Frankfurt banker handed over to him the exact sum which he had deposited. You may imagine how much interest might be earned by the sum of fifteen millions left in the hands of a Jewish Frankfurt banker for a period of eight years! It is from this time that dates the opulence of the House of the Brothers Rothschild, who owe to the probity of their founder the high financial standing which they enjoy today.

The Emperor, who was staying in the palace in Berlin, every day passed in revue the troops who arrived in succession in the town, to march from there to the Oder in pursuit of the enemy. It was while he was in Berlin that he performed a well known act of magnanimity in pardoning, for the Princess of Hatzfeld, her husband, who had used his position as burgomaster of Berlin to give the Prussian generals information about the movement of French troops; an act of espionage punishable by death. The generosity displayed by the Emperor on this occasion had a very good effect on the feelings of the Prussians.

During our stay in Berlin, I was pleasantly surprised by the arrival of my brother Adolphe, who, on learning of the fresh outbreak of hostilities on the continent of Europe had asked for and obtained from General Decaen, who commanded the French troops in India, permission to return to France, where he joined the Grande Armée. He was offered a position by General Lefebvre, but, mistakenly, in my opinion, he chose to serve as a supernumerary on the staff of Marshal Augereau, of which I was a member, a move which did neither of us any good.

I had also in Berlin another unexpected encounter. I was walking one evening with some friends along the Boulevard de Tilleuls, when I saw coming towards me a group of sous-officiers of the

1st Hussars. One of them broke away and ran to fall on my neck. It was my former tutor, the elder Pertelay who, with tears of joy cried "Te voilà, mon petit!" The officers with whom I was, were at first astonished to see a sergeant-major so familiar with an officer; but their surprise vanished when I told them of my former relations with this old soldier, who, putting his arm round me, said to his companions, "It is I who made him what you now see before you!" And the good fellow was really convinced that I owed my present position to his teaching. So at dinner, which I stood him the next day, he overwhelmed me with inconsequential advice, which he believed to be very sensible and just the thing to perfect my military education. We shall meet this type of old Hussar again in Spain.

Napoleon, who was still in Berlin, was told of the surrender of the Prince Hohenlohe who, with sixteen thousand men, had laid down his arms at Prenzlow before the troops of Marshal Lannes and the cavalry of Murat. There was no other enemy corps in the field except that of General Blücher. This general, hard pressed by the divisions of Marshals Soult and Bernadotte, violated the neutrality of Lubeck, where he sought refuge; but the French pursued him, and Blücher, one of the most ardent supporters of the war against Napoleon, was forced to give himself up as a prisoner together with the sixteen thousand men under his command.

I must here tell you something remarkable, which shows how greatly chance influences the affairs of men and empires. We have seen Marshal Bernadotte failing in his duty and standing aside at Jena when Marshal Davout was fighting, not far from him, against infinitely superior forces. Well! This disgraceful conduct served to place him on the throne of Sweden. This is how it came about.

After the battle of Jena, the Emperor, although furious with Bernadotte, ordered him to pursue the enemy because the corps which he commanded, not having fired a shot, was in better shape for battle than those who had suffered losses. Bernadotte then set out on the track of the Prussians whom he defeated first at Halle and then at Lubeck, with the help of Marshal Soult. Now as chance would have it, at the very hour when the French were attacking Lubeck, some ships carrying a division of infantry which King Gustave IV of Sweden had sent to the aid of the Prussians entered the harbour.

The Swedish troops had scarcely disembarked when, attacked by the French and abandoned by the Prussians, they were obliged to surrender to Bernadotte. Bernadotte, I can assure you, had, when he wished, the most engaging manner and very much wanted to appear before foreigners as a "Gentleman." To this end, he treated the Swedish officers in the most benevolent manner. After according them an honourable capitulation, he returned to them their horses and their baggage, saw to their needs and invited to his quarters the commander-in-chief, Count Moerner, as well as the generals and senior officers; he loaded them with kindnesses and courtesies to such an extent that, on their return to their country, they spread everywhere praise for the magnanimity of Marshal Bernadotte.

Some years later a revolution broke out in Sweden; King Gustave, whom a mental disorder had rendered unfit to rule, was removed from the throne and replaced by his aged uncle, the Duke of Sudermanie. As this new monarch had no children, the States Assembly, in order to designate a successor, chose the Prince of Holstein-Augustenburg, who took the title of Prince Royal. But he did not long enjoy this dignity, for he died in 1811 after a short illness, which was put down to poison. The states gathered once more to elect a new heir to the throne. They were hesitating between several German princes who put themselves forward as candidates when Count Moerner, one of the most influential members of the states, and the former commander of the Swedish division captured at Lubeck in 1806 by the French, proposed General Bernadotte, whose generous conduct he recalled. He praised also Bernadotte's military talents, and observed that the marshal was allied, through his wife, to Napoleon, whose support could be most useful to Sweden. A crowd of officers who had also been captured at Lubeck, joined their voices to that of General Moerner, and Bernadotte was elected almost unanimously as successor to the King of Sweden, and mounted the throne a few years later.

We shall see, further on, how Bernadotte, carried to the steps of a foreign throne by the fame which he had acquired at the head of French troops, displayed a lack of gratitude towards his native country. But now let us return to Prussia.

In one month the main forces of this kingdom, formerly in such a flourishing condition, had been destroyed by Napoleon, whose armies occupied the capital and the greater part of the provinces, and had already reached the Vistula, that great barrier between northern and central Europe. Marshal Augereau's corps remained for a fortnight in Berlin to reinforce the Guard during the long stay which the Emperor made in the town, and left about the middle of November, heading first for the Oder, which we crossed at Kostrzyn, and then on to the Vistula whose bank we reached at Bromburg (Bydgoszcz). We were now in Poland, the poorest and nastiest country in Europe...! After the Oder, no more made roads: we marched on loose gravel or appalling mud. Most of the land was uncultivated and the few inhabitants we came across were dirty to a degree which defies the imagination. The weather which had been magnificent during October and the first part of November became frightful. We no longer saw the sun, it rained or snowed continually; food became short; no more wine, almost never any beer, and what there was atrociously bad; muddy water, no bread, and billets we had to share with cattle and pigs. The soldiers used to say, "How dare the Poles call this a country?"

The Emperor himself was disillusioned, for having come intending to rebuild Poland, he had hoped that the whole population of this vast country would rise as one man at the approach of the French army. But nobody budged...! In a vain attempt to rouse some Polish enthusiasm, the Emperor had invited the famous General Kosciusko, the leader of the last insurrection, to come and join him, but Kosciusko stayed peacefully in Switzerland, to where he had retired, and to the reproaches which were addressed to him, he replied that he knew the heedless and unstable character of his compatriots too well to hope that they would ever free themselves, even with French help. Unable to attract Kosciusko, the Emperor tried to make use of his renown by addressing to the Poles a proclamation in the name of this old warrior. Not one of them took up arms, although our troops occupied several provinces and even the capital. The Poles were not willing to rebel until Napoleon had declared the re-establishment of Poland, and he was not willing to do this until they had risen against their oppressors, which they did not do.

While 7th Corps was in Bromburg, Duroc, the grand marshal of the palace, arrived in the middle of the night at Marshal Augereau's headquarters. I was sent for and told to prepare myself to accompany Marshal Duroc, who was going as an envoy to the King of Prussia at Graudentz, and who needed an officer to replace his aide-de-camp, whom he had just sent to Posnan with despatches for the Emperor. I had been chosen because it was remembered that the previous August I had been on a mission to the Prussian court and that I knew almost all the officers and the court usages.

I was soon ready. The marshal of the palace took me in his carriage and we went down the left bank of the Vistula, occupied by French troops, to cross the river by ferry opposite Graudentz. We took lodgings in the town and then presented ourselves at the citadel, where all the royal family of Prussia had taken refuge after loosing four fifths of their state. The Vistula separated the two armies. The king seemed calm and resigned; the queen, whom I had seen not long ago looking so lovely, was greatly changed and seemed overcome by grief. She could not conceal from herself the fact that having urged the king to declare war, she was the principal cause of the misfortunes of her country, whose citizens raised their voices against her. The Emperor could not have sent a more acceptable envoy to the king than Marshal Duroc, who had held the post of ambassador in Berlin, and was well known to both the king and queen who appreciated his pleasant personality. I was too small a personage to be of any account; however the king and queen recognised me and greeted me with a few polite words.

I found the Prussian officers attached to the court had greatly modified the arrogant attitude they had displayed in August. Their recent defeat had changed their opinion of the French army; nevertheless I did not wish to take advantage of this and I carefully avoided mentioning Jena and our other victories. The affairs which Marshal Duroc had to discuss with the King of Prussia related to a letter which this monarch had sent to Napoleon, requesting a peace. The meeting lasted for two days which I occupied in reading, and walking on the gloomy parade ground of the fortress. I did not wish to go up onto the ramparts, although one enjoys from there an admirable view of the Vistula, for fear that I might be suspected of examining the defence works and armaments.

In the battles which had taken place from Jena to the Vistula, the Prussians had taken about a hundred of our men prisoner, whom they employed on the earthworks of the fortress in which they were confined. Marshal Duroc had charged me with the task of distributing some aid to these poor devils, who were doubly unhappy in that they could see from the height of the fortress the French troops from whom they were separated only by the Vistula. This proximity, and the comparison of their position with that of their comrades, free and happy on the left bank, led a French prisoner, one of the élite cavalrymen of the 3rd Dragoons by the name of Harpin, to attempt to escape. This was no easy matter, for one had first to get out of the fortress and then to cross the Vistula; but what cannot be achieved by a determined man? Harpin, who was employed by the master carpenter to pile timber, had made, secretly, a little raft; he had taken a long rope and, at night, had lowered the raft to the foot of the rampart, and had then descended himself by the same means. He had already put his raft in the water and was preparing to embark when he was surprised by a patrol, taken back to the fort and confined to a dungeon. The next day the Prussian commandant, in accordance with the common custom of the Prussian army, condemned Harpin to fifty strokes of the cane. It was useless for Harpin to claim that as a Frenchman he should not be subject to Prussian regulations, his status as a prisoner made this complaint void. He had already been taken to the wooden frame to which he was to be attached, and two soldiers were preparing to administer the flogging when, having gone to fetch a book from Marshal Duroc's coach, which was standing in the parade ground, I saw Harpin struggling with some Prussians who were trying to tie him up.

Indignant at the sight of a French soldier about to be subjected to a flogging, I ran towards him, my sabre in my hand, and threatened to kill the first man to strike a blow! ... Marshal Duroc's coach was guarded by one of Napoleon's couriers, known in every post house in Europe as "Moustache." This man, of herculean strength and the courage to face anything, had accompanied the Emperor on twenty fields of battle. When he saw me in the middle of the Prussians he hurried to me, and on my instructions, he fetched four loaded pistols which were in the coach. We untied Harpin; I armed him with two of the pistols and put him in the coach, where I placed "Moustache" next to him. I then told the commandant that as this coach belonged to the Emperor, whose arms it bore, it was a sacred place of safety for the French Dragoon, entry to which was forbidden to all Prussians under penalty of a bullet in the head, and I told Harpin and "Moustache" to fire on anyone who attempted to get into the coach. The commandant, seeing me so determined, abandoned his prisoner for the moment to go and get orders from his superiors. Then, leaving Harpin and "Moustache" in the coach with pistols in their hands, I went to the king's quarters and begged one of the aides-de-camp to go and tell Marshal Duroc that I needed to speak to him about a matter which could not wait. Duroc came out and I told him what had happened.

When he heard that they wanted to flog a French soldier, he shared my indignation. He returned to the king to whom he protested warmly, adding that if the sentence were to be carried out, the Emperor by way of reprisal would flog not only the soldiers but also the Prussian officers who were his prisoners. The king was a humane man; he ordered that the dragoon Harpin should be released, and to please Napoleon, from whom he was at that moment asking peace, he offered to Marshal Duroc to release to him all the prisoners if he would undertake to send back a similar number of Prussians. Duroc having accepted this offer, I went with one of the aides-de-camp to announce the news to the prisoners, who were overjoyed. We embarked them straight away and an hour later they were across the Vistula and amongst their brothers in arms.

Marshal Duroc and I left Graudentz the next night; he approved of my conduct and told me later that he had given an account of it to the Emperor, who also approved, and who warned the Prussians that if they flogged French soldiers he would have all Prussian officers who fell into his hands, shot!

I rejoined 7th Corps at Bromburg, and we went up the left bank of the Vistula towards Warsaw. Marshal Augereau's headquarters were established at Mallochiche. The Emperor arrived at Warsaw on the 19th December, and prepared to cross the Vistula. 7th Corps then went down the left bank once more to Utrata, where for the first time on this campaign we saw the Russian outposts on the opposite bank.

Chapter 31
The Campaign in Poland

The River Vistula is fast-flowing and very wide; one expected, because of this that the Emperor would halt his winter operations there and, protected by the river, would put his troops into winter quarters until the spring. This however was not to be. Marshal Davout's and Marshal Lannes' corps crossed the river at Warsaw, Marshal Augereau and his men crossed at Utrate, from where we went on to the banks of the Ukra, a tributary of the Bug and the Vistula. The entire French army having crossed this last river, found itself face to face with the Russians, against whom the Emperor ordered an attack on the 24th December. A thaw and rain made movement extremely difficult on the clay soil, for there are no metalled roads in this country.

I shall not describe all the actions which were fought that day to force a passage across the Bug; I shall restrict myself to saying that Marshal Augereau, given the task of securing the crossing of the Ukra, ordered General Desjardins to attack with his division, Kolozomb, and General Heudelet to attack Sochocyzn. The marshal directed the attack on Kolozomb in person. The Russians, after burning the bridge which had existed at this spot, had raised earthworks on the opposite bank which they defended with cannons and numerous infantry; but they had neglected to destroy a store of planks and beams which was on the right bank, at which we had arrived. Our sappers made use of this material to construct a temporary bridge in spite of a lively fire which killed several men of the 14th Line regiment, which was at the head of our columns.

The planks of the bridge were not yet fastened and were wobbling under the feet of our infantrymen, when the colonel of the 14th, M. Savary, brother of the Emperor's aide-de-camp, risked crossing on horseback, in order to put himself at the head of his men; but he had scarcely reached the bank when a Cossack, arriving at the gallop, plunged a lance into his heart and disappeared into the woods! This was the fifth colonel of the 14th who had been killed by the enemy! You will see later the fatal destiny which always accompanied this unfortunate regiment. The passage of the Ukra was secured, the guns captured and the Russians put to flight. Desjardins' division occupied Sochoczyn, where the enemy had repulsed the attack by Heudelet's division, a repulse which was of no consequence, as it was necessary only to secure one crossing. General Heudelet however, out of misplaced pride, had ordered the attack to be renewed and was once more driven off with the loss of some thirty men killed or wounded, among them a highly thought of engineer officer. I have always disapproved of the contempt for men's lives which sometimes leads generals to sacrifice them to their desire to see their names in the bulletins.

On the 25th of December, the day following the crossing of the Ukra, the Emperor, pushing the Russians before him, headed for Golymin, having with him the Guard, Murat's cavalry and the corps of Davout and Augereau, the last of whom led the column. Marshal Lannes went off in the direction of Pultusk. There were on this day some minor encounters with the enemy who were retreating with all speed. We slept in bivouac amongst the trees.

On the 26th, 7th Corps set out once more in pursuit of the Russians. We were at a time of year when the days are at their shortest, and in this part of Poland at the end of December, it starts to get dark about two-thirty in the afternoon. It was made more gloomy as we approached Golymin by a fall of snow mixed with rain. We had not seen the enemy since morning when, on our arrival at the village of Kuskowo, very close to Golymin, our scouts, who had seen in the obscurity a large body of troops which a marsh prevented them from approaching, came to warn Marshal Augereau, who ordered Colonel Albert to go and reconnoitre, escorted by twenty-five mounted Chasseurs, whom he placed under my command.

The mission was difficult for we were in the middle of a huge, bare plain where one could easily become lost. The ground, already muddy, was intersected by areas of bog which the poor light prevented us from seeing clearly; so we advanced with caution, and found ourselves within twenty-five paces of a line of troops. We thought at first that this must be Davout's corps, which we knew was in the neighbourhood, but as no one answered our challenge, we had no doubt that these were enemy troops. However, to make quite sure, Colonel Albert ordered me to send one of my best-mounted troopers up to the line which we could distinguish in the murk: for this task I picked a bemedalled corporal named Schmit, a man of proven courage. He, having gone alone to within ten paces of a regiment whose headgear he recognised as Russian, fired a shot from his carbine into the middle of it and came back smartly.

To account for the silence which the Russians had maintained up till then, I must tell you that this unit had become separated from the main body of the army, which it was trying to rejoin, and had lost its way in the vast plains, which it knew to be occupied by French troops who were heading for Golymin. The Russian generals, in the hope that they might pass close to us in the obscurity without being recognised, had forbidden their men to speak, and in the event of an attack, even the wounded were to make no outcry. This was an order which only Russian troops would have obeyed so punctiliously that when Colonel Albert, to warn Marshal Augereau that we were in the presence of the enemy, ordered the twenty-five troopers to fire, not a cry nor a word was heard, and no one fired back!

We then saw, in spite of the poor light, a body of about a hundred horsemen who were advancing silently to cut off our retreat. We should have made off at the gallop to rejoin our columns, but some of our troopers having become stuck in the mud, we were forced to proceed less rapidly, although pursued by the Russians, who fortunately had the same trouble as we did. A fire which had broken out in a nearby farm lit up the ground and the Russians began to gallop, which compelled us to do likewise. A new danger arose in that we had left from General Desjardins' division and were returning to General Heudelet's, who had not seen us leave and opened fire on us; so that we were being driven from behind by the Russians, while a hail of bullets in front wounded several of our men and some horses. It was no use shouting "We are French. Don't shoot!" The firing continued, and one cannot blame the officers who took us for the advance guard of a Russian column who were using French, which is widely understood among foreigners, in order to deceive them in the darkness which had now fallen. We were having a bad time, when it occurred to me to call out by name to the generals, colonels and battalion commanders of Heudelet's division, names which they would know could not be known to the enemy. This was a success and we were at last received into the French line.

The Russian generals, seeing that they were discovered and wishing to continue their retreat, took a measure of which I heartily approve, and one which in similar circumstances the French have never attempted to imitate. The Russians pointed all their guns at us, and having led away all the horses, they opened a violent fire to keep us at a distance. During this time they marched off their columns, and when the ammunition was finished, the gunners withdrew and left the guns to us. Was not this better than losing many men in an effort to save the guns, which would have been continually bogged down and slowed the retreat?

The fierce Russian cannonade became increasingly harmful when it started several fires in the villages, the spreading light of which enabled the Russian gunners to pick out the masses of our troops; in particular the dragoons and Cuirassiers led by Prince Murat, whose white cloaks made them a target. These units suffered more losses than the others, and one of our generals of the Dragoons was cut in two by a cannon-ball. Marshal Augereau, after taking Kuskowa, entered Golymin, which Marshal Davout was attacking from the other side. This town was being traversed at the time by the Russian columns, who, knowing that Marshal Lannes was marching to cut off their retreat by taking Pultusk, three leagues from there, were trying to reach that spot before he did at no matter what cost. So although our soldiers were firing on them at close range, they did not reply. To do so they would have had to stop, and minutes were too precious.

Each division and each regiment marched through our fusillade without a word and without slowing their pace for a moment...! The streets of Golymin were full of wounded and dying men, yet one did not hear a sound. It was forbidden! We might have been shooting at shadows, and it was only when our soldiers attacked with the bayonet that they convinced themselves that they were dealing with men. We took thousands of prisoners, while the remainder marched into the distance.

The marshals deliberated as to whether they should pursue the enemy, but the weather was so horrible and the night so dark once one left the neighbourhood of the fires, the men so soaked and exhausted, that it was decided that they should rest until the next day.

Golymin being crowded with dead, wounded, and discarded baggage, Marshals Murat and Augereau, together with some generals and their staffs, looking for somewhere to shelter from the glacial rain, established themselves in a huge stable which was near the town. There, those who could, lay on the dung heap in an attempt to get warm and to sleep, for we had been on horseback in the most frightful weather for twenty four hours or more. The marshals and all the colonels and brass-hats were naturally in the depths of the stable where it was warmer; as for me, a humble lieutenant, who came in last, I had to bed down near the doorway, where I was more or less sheltered from the rain, but exposed to the freezing wind, since the doorway had no door. The position was most uncomfortable and added to this I was dying of hunger, not having eaten since the previous evening. But my lucky star came once more to my aid. While the well sheltered senior officers were sleeping in the warm part of the stable, and the cold was preventing us lieutenants near the doorway from doing the same, one of Prince Murat's servants arrived. I told him, in a low voice that his master was asleep; upon this he gave me a basket containing a roast goose, some bread and some wine, to give to the prince when he woke, and asked me to tell him that the mules with the provisions were expected to arrive in an hour's time. Having said which, he went off to await them.

Loaded with these provisions, I held council in undertones with Bro, Mainville, and Stoch, who, as badly placed as I, were shivering with cold and just as hungry. The conclusion reached in this deliberation was that as Prince Murat was asleep and as his provisions were due to arrive shortly, he would be able to have a meal when he woke; while we would be set on horseback and sent off in all directions without anyone asking if we had eaten or not; so without straining our consciences too much, we decided to demolish the contents of the basket, which we did with great rapidity. I don't know if this was pardonable, but what I do know is that I have had few meals which I enjoyed more.

While the troops who had been engaged at Golymin were resting, Napoleon, with all his Guard was wandering about on the plain, because, alerted by the sound of gunfire, the Emperor had hurriedly left the château where he was installed some two leagues from Golymin, with the intention of joining us by marching as the crow flies in the direction of the fires. But the ground was so soaked, the plain so intersected by bogs and the weather so awful, that it took him all night to make those two leagues, and he did not arrive on the field of battle until the fighting was long over.

On the same day as the fight at Golymin, Marshal Lannes, with no more than twenty thousand men, attacked at Pultusk some forty thousand Russians who were retreating, and inflicted immense losses on them without being able to stop them, so great was their superiority in numbers.

For the Emperor to have been able to pursue the Russians it would have required a frost to harden the ground which, on the contrary, was now so soft and sodden that one sank in at every step, and several men, notably the batman of an officer in 7th Corps, were drowned with their horses in the mud. It had now become impossible to move the artillery and to venture further into this unknown territory; besides which the troops lacked food and even boots, and they were extremely tired. These considerations decided Napoleon to place the whole army in cantonment in front of the Vistula, from the outskirts of Warsaw to the gates of Danzig. The soldiers, billeted in the villages, were at last sheltered from the weather, received some rations and were able to repair their equipment.

The Emperor returned to Warsaw to prepare for a new campaign. The divisions of Augereau's corps were spread in the villages around Plock, if one can give that name to a confused heap of lowly shacks, inhabited by unwashed Jews; but almost all the so-called towns in Poland are built like this and have similar inhabitants. The landowners, great and small, live in the country where they employ their peasants to cultivate their estates.

The marshal was lodged in Christka, a sort of château built of wood, as was customary in the country. He found in this manor some reasonable accommodation, while the aides-de-camp settled wherever they could in the rooms and barns. As for me, by ferreting around I found in the gardener's quarters a fairly good room with a fireplace; I settled in there with two friends, and leaving to the gardener and his family their very unsavoury beds, we made some out of planks and straw, on which we were very comfortable.

Chapter 32
Captain Marbot at Eylau

We celebrated at Christka the new year of 1807, which was very nearly the last year of my life. It, however, began very pleasantly for me, since the Emperor, who had not shown any favour to Augereau's staff during the Austerlitz campaign, fully repaired this oversight by heaping us with rewards. Colonel Albert was promoted to brigadier-general, Major Massy to lieutenant-colonel of the 44th Line regiment; several aides-de-camp were decorated; and finally the lieutenants, Bro, Mainville, and I, were made captains. This promotion gave me more than usual pleasure, since I had done nothing remarkable to earn it, and I was only twenty-four years old. Marshal Augereau, when he gave us our brevets of captain, said to Mainville, Bro, and me, "Let's see which of you three is the first to become a colonel." It was in fact I, who six years later commanded a regiment, while my comrades were still only captains: it is also true that in this period I had been wounded six times!

Once we had taken up winter quarters the enemy did the same, opposite to us but a considerable distance away. The Emperor expected that they would let us pass the winter in peace; however, our rest lasted only for a month; this sufficed but was not really enough.

The Russians, seeing the ground covered by snow and hardened by a very sharp frost, thought that this frigid weather would give the men from the north a great advantage over those from the south, unaccustomed to the severe cold. They resolved therefore to attack us, and in order to do this they moved, screened by the immense forest which lay between us, the greater part of the troops who faced us before Warsaw, down to the lower Vistula, opposite the cantonments of Bernadotte and Ney, whom they hoped to surprise and overrun by weight of numbers before the Emperor with the other army corps could come to their aid. But Bernadotte and Ney put up a stiff resistance, and the Emperor had sufficient time to mount an attack with a considerable force on the enemy rear who, seeing themselves at risk of being cut off from their operational base, retreated towards Konigsberg (Kaliningrad). We had therefore, on the 1st of February, to quit our billets where we were reasonably comfortable, and restarting the war, to go and sleep in the snow.

At the head of the central column, commanded by the Emperor in person, was Prince Murat's cavalry, then came Marshal Soult's corps, supported by that of Augereau, finally came the Imperial Guard. Marshal Davout's corps marched on the right flank of this huge column, and Marshal Ney's on the left. Such an agglomeration of troops heading for the same place soon strips the country-side of whatever food supplies are available, so we suffered much from hunger; only the Guard had wagons which carried food for distribution, the other corps lived on whatever they could find, that is to say they lacked practically everything.

I am not going to give any details of the actions which preceded the battle of Eylau, because Augereau's corps, which was in the second line, took no part in these various contacts, of which the most important occurred at Mohrungen, Bergfried, Guttstadt, and Valtersdorf. But at last, before the little town of Landsberg, the Russians, who had been chased for a week with a sword at their backs, decided to halt and make a stand. To do this, they placed eight élite battalions in an advantageous position, their right bounded by a village by the name of Hoff, their left by a thick wood, and their centre protected by a very steep-sided ravine, which could be crossed only by a narrow bridge. Eight cannons were placed in front of this line.

When the Emperor arrived opposite this position, he did not think it necessary to wait for the infantry of Marshal Soult, which was still several leagues behind, and attacked the Russians with some regiments of light cavalry who, dashing bravely over the bridge, crossed the ravine; but, assailed by gunfire and grape-shot, our squadrons were driven back in disorder into the gulch, from which they emerged with much difficulty. The Emperor, seeing the light cavalry repulsed, replaced them by a division of Dragoons, whose attack, received in the same manner as before, had a similar outcome. The Emperor then ordered the advance of General D'Hautpoul's terrible Cuirassiers, who crossed the bridge under a hail of grapeshot and fell on the Russian line with such ferocity that they literally flattened it. There then ensued the most frightful butchery; the Cuirassiers, enraged at the losses suffered by their comrades of the Hussars and Dragoons, almost entirely exterminated the eight Russian battalions, All were either killed or captured! The battlefield was a scene of horror. Never has a cavalry charge had such a devastating result. The Emperor demonstrated his satisfaction with the Cuirassiers by embracing their general before the whole division. General D'Hautpoul exclaimed, "To show myself worthy of this honour, I shall dedicate my life to your majesty." He kept his word, for the next day he was killed on the battlefield of Eylau. What an epoch! And what men!

The enemy army which, from a plateau beyond Landsberg, had witnessed the destruction of its rearguard, retired promptly towards Eylau, and we took possession of Landsberg. On the 7th February the Russian commander-in-chief, Benningsen, having decided to give battle, concentrated his army around Eylau, mainly in positions between us and the town. Murat's cavalry and Soult's infantry took these positions after fierce fighting, for the Russians held tenaciously to Ziegelhof, which dominates Eylau, as they wanted to make it the centre point of their line for the battle on the following day; but they were forced to retreat from the town. Night seemed to have put an end to this fighting, the prelude to the coming general action, when a fusillade of shots rang out in the streets of Eylau.

I know that military authors who have written about this campaign, claim that Napoleon ordered an attack because he did not want the town to remain in Russian hands; but I am sure that they are mistaken, and for the following reason:-

When the head of Marshal Augereau's column, coming down the road from Landsberg, drew near to Ziegelhof, the marshal climbed onto the plateau where the Emperor was already stationed, and I actually heard Napoleon say to Augereau, "It has been suggested to me that we should take Eylau this evening; but, apart from the fact that I don't like fighting at night, I do not wish to push my centre too far forward before the arrival of Davout on my right flank and Ney on my left. So I am going to wait for them until tomorrow on this plateau which, furbished with artillery, will provide a fine position for our infantry; then, when Davout and Ney are in the line, we shall march, together, against the enemy." Having said this, the Emperor ordered his bivouac to be set up at the foot of the Ziegelhof, and his guard to encamp around it.

But while Napoleon was explaining his plans to Marshal Augereau, who greatly approved of his prudence, the staff of the imperial palace, coming from Landsberg with their baggage and servants, arrived at our outposts, which were at the gates of Eylau, without anyone telling them to stop at Ziegelhof. These employees, used to seeing the imperial quarters very well guarded, and not having been warned that they were almost on top of the Russians, were interested only in selecting a good lodging for their master, and they set themselves up in the post-house, where they unpacked their equipment, stabled their horses, and began to cook. In the midst of these preparations they were attacked by a Russian patrol and would have been captured had it not been for the intervention of the guard which always accompanied the Emperor's baggage. At the sound of this outbreak of firing, the troops who were in position at the gates of the town ran to the rescue of Napoleon's equipment, which was already being pillaged by the Russian soldiers. The Russian generals, thinking that the French were attempting to seize Eylau, sent reinforcements to their side, and so a sanguinary battle was fought in the streets of the town, which ended up in our hands.

Although this attack had not been ordered by the Emperor, he saw no reason not to profit by it, and he set himself up in the Eylau post-house. The Guard and Soult's troops occupied the town which was surrounded by Murat's cavalry. Augereau's troops were positioned in Zehsen, a little hamlet in which we hoped to find some provisions, but the Russians had taken everything with them as they withdrew, so that our unhappy regiment, which had received no rations for eight days, had to make do with some potatoes and water. The equipment of the staff having been left at Landsberg, our supper was not as good as that of the soldiers, for we had no potatoes. Eventually, on the morning of the 8th, when we were about to mount our horses, one of the marshal's servants brought him some bread, and he, always generous, shared it out amongst his aides-de-camp. After this frugal meal, which for several of us was to be our last, the corps moved to the post to which it had been assigned by the Emperor.

In accordance with the plan which I explained when I started these memoirs, I shall not weary you with too detailed a description of the various phases of this terrible battle of Eylau, but will limit myself to the principal events.

On the morning of the 8th, the position of the two armies was as follows. The Russians had their left at Serpalten, their centre in front of Auklapen and their right at Schmoditten. They were awaiting the arrival of eight thousand Prussians, who were expected to go to Althoff where they would form the extreme right wing. The enemy's front line was protected by five hundred artillery pieces, of which a third at least were of large calibre. The French situation was much less favourable, since their two wings had not yet arrived. The Emperor had, at the start of the action, only a part of the force with which he had expected to do battle. Marshal Soult's corps was placed on the right and left of Eylau, the Guard in the town itself, and Augereau's corps between Eylau and Rothenen, opposite Serpalten. The enemy formed almost a semicircle about us, and the two armies occupied a terrain in which there were numerous ponds covered by snow, which neither side could see.

Neither Marshal Davout, who should have been on our right, towards Molwitten, nor Marshal Ney, who should have been on our left around Althoff, had yet appeared, when at daybreak, about eight in the morning, the Russians began the attack by a violent cannonade to which our gunners, though fewer in numbers, replied. Though fewer, they had the advantage, however of being much better trained than the Russians, and also of directing their fire at masses of men who had no cover, while the Russian cannon-balls mainly hit the walls of Eylau and Rothenen. Soon a strong enemy column advanced with the intention of capturing the town; it was vigourously repelled by the Guard and Marshal Soult's troops. At this moment, the Emperor heard, with much pleasure, that from the top of the church tower could be seen Davout's men arriving via Molwitten and marching towards Serpalten, from where they expelled the Russians and drove them back to Klein-Sausgarten.

The Russian commander, Benningsen, seeing his left beaten and his rear menaced by the audacious Davout, resolved to crush him, and directed the greater part of his force against him. It was then that Napoleon, with the object of preventing this movement by creating a diversion against the enemy centre, ordered Augereau to attack, although he foresaw the difficulties of this operation.

There are on the field of battle, circumstances when one must sacrifice some troops in order to preserve the great majority and ensure victory. General Corbineau, the Emperor's aide-de-camp, was killed by a cannon shot near to us while bringing to Marshal Augereau the order to advance. The marshal passed between Eylau and Rothenen and led his two divisions boldly against the enemy centre, and already the 14th Line regiment who made up our advance guard had seized the position which the Emperor had ordered to be taken and held at all costs, when the guns which formed a semi-circle about Augereau hurled out a storm of ball and grapeshot of hitherto unprecedented ferocity. In an instant, our two divisions were pulverised under this rain of iron! General Desjardins was killed and General Heudelet gravely wounded; however, they stood firm until the corps having been almost entirely destroyed, the remnants were compelled to retire to the cemetery of Eylau, with the exception of the 14th, who almost entirely surrounded by the enemy, remained on the little hill which they had occupied. The situation was made even worse by a gale of wind which blew a heavy snowfall into our faces, and reduced visibility to about fifteen paces, so that several French batteries opened fire on us, as well as the Russians. Marshal Augereau was wounded by a bullet.

The devotion of 7th Corps, however, produced a good result, for, relieved by our attack, Marshal Davout was able not only to maintain his position, but to take Klein-Sausgarten and even push his advance-guard as far as Kuschitten, in the enemy's rear. Then, in an attempt to deliver a knock-out blow, Napoleon despatched, between Eylau and Rothenen, the squadrons commanded by Murat. This terrifying mass fell on the Russian centre, overwhelming them, cutting them down with their sabres and throwing them into the greatest confusion. The valiant General D'Hautpoul was killed at the head of his Cuirassiers, as was General Dahlmann, who had succeeded General Morland in the command of the Chasseurs of the Guard. The success of our cavalry allowed us to carry the day. Eight thousand Prussians, escaped from pursuit by Marshal Ney, and arriving at Althoff, tried to mount a new attack by advancing, one does not quite know why, on Kuschitten instead of Eylau, but Davout drove them off, and the arrival of Ney's corps at Schmoditten towards the end of the day, made Benningsen fear that his line of communication would be cut, and so he ordered a retreat in the direction of Konigsberg, leaving the French masters of the horrible battlefield covered with dead and dying. Since the invention of gunpowder one has not seen such a terrible effect, for in relation to the numbers engaged at Eylau, in comparison to all the battles, ancient or modern, the proportion of losses was highest. The Russians had twenty-five thousand casualties, and although the figure for French losses has been given as ten thousand, it is my belief that it was at least twenty thousand. A total of forty-five thousand men, of whom more than half died!

Augereau's corps was almost entirely destroyed. Out of fifteen thousand combatants under arms at the beginning of the action, there remained by evening only three thousand, under the command of Lieutenant colonel Massy: the marshal, all the generals and all the colonels had been either killed or wounded.

It is difficult to understand why Benningsen, knowing that Davout and Ney had not yet arrived, did not take advantage of their absence to attack Eylau at daybreak with the numerous troops of the centre of his army, instead of using precious time in bombarding us; for his superior strength would certainly have made him master of the town before the arrival of Davout, and the Emperor would then have regretted having moved so far forward instead of consolidating his position on the plateau of Ziegelhof and awaiting the arrival of his flank forces, as he had intended the evening before.

The day after the battle the Emperor followed the Russians to the gates of Konigsberg; but that town was fortified and it was thought unwise to attack it with troops weakened by a sanguinary battle, and what is more, almost all the Russian army was in Konigsberg and the surrounding country.

Napoleon spent several days at Eylau, partly to collect the wounded and partly to reorganise his forces. The survivors of Augereau's corps were spread amongst other units and the marshal was given leave to return to France for the treatment of his wound. The Emperor, seeing that the bulk of the Russian army was now at a distance, put his troops into billets in the towns and villages in front of the lower Vistula. There was no interesting event during the rest of the winter, except the taking of Danzig by our troops. Hostilities in the open country would not begin again until the month of June, as we shall see later.

Chapter 33
I Try to Save the Eagle of the 14th!

I did not want to interrupt the story of the battle of Eylau to tell you what happened to me in this terrible conflict; a sad tale, to understand which we must go back to the autumn of 1805 when the officers of the Grande Armée were equipping themselves in preparation for the Battle of Austerlitz. I had two good horses and was looking for a third of a better quality, a charger. This was something difficult to find, for although horses were infinitely cheaper than they are today, they were still expensive, and I did not have much money; but I had a piece of very good luck.

I ran into a German scholar, named M. d'Aister, whom I had known when he was teaching at Sorèze; he was now tutor to the children of a rich Swiss banker, M. Scherer, who lived in Paris and was an associate of M. Finguerlin, who was a very wealthy man who kept up great state, and had a stable of many horses, amongst which was a charming mare called Lisette, an excellent animal from Mecklemberg, good-looking, swift as a stag, and so well schooled that a child could ride her. But this mare had a dreadful and fortunately rare vice: she bit like a bulldog, and attacked furiously anyone who displeased her, which decided M. Finguerlin to sell her. She was bought by Mme. de Lauriston, whose husband, an aide-de-camp to the Emperor, had written to her to ask her to buy him a charger.

M. Finguerlin, when he sold the mare, had omitted to mention her behaviour, and on the evening of her purchase, a groom, whom she had torn open, was found lying at her feet. Mme. de Lauriston was justly alarmed and demanded cancellation of the sale. Not only was this done, but the police, in order to prevent another such accident, required that a notice be fixed to Lisette's loose-box informing any potential buyer of her ferocity, and that any sale would be null and void unless the buyer declared in writing that he was aware of this notice.

As you may imagine, with such a recommendation, the mare was very difficult to sell; M. d'Aister told me that her owner was prepared to let her go for whatever was offered. I offered a thousand francs and M. Finguerlin handed Lisette over to me, although she had cost five thousand. For several months she gave me a great deal of trouble; it took four or five men to saddle her, and she could not be bridled without being blindfolded and having all four legs tied; but once on her back one found her a matchless ride.

However, since during the time I had owned her she had bitten several people, including me, I was thinking of getting rid of her, when, having taken into my service a man called Francis Woirland, who was scared of nothing, he, before approaching Lisette, about whose bad character I had warned him, armed himself with a very hot leg of roast mutton, and when she attempted to bite him, he offered this to her, which she seized in her teeth; but having burned her mouth and her tongue, the mare gave a cry and dropped the gigot, and from that moment she submitted herself to Woirland, whom she no longer dared to bite. I tried the same trick and achieved the same result. Lisette, as docile as a dog, allowed herself to be handled by myself and my servant; she even became a little more tractable with the grooms whom she saw every day, but woe betide any stranger passing too close to her. I could give many examples of her ferocity, but I shall limit myself to one.

While Marshal Augereau was staying at the château of Bellevue, near Berlin, the servants, having noticed that while they were at diner, someone was coming to steal the sacks of oats from the stable, asked Woirland to leave Lisette loose near the door. The thief arrived, slipped into the stable and was already carrying off one of the sacks when the mare grabbed him by the neck, dragged him into the yard and broke two of his ribs by trampling on him. People came running to the cries of the terrified thief, whom Lisette was unwilling to abandon until my servant and I persuaded her, for in her rage she would have savaged anyone else. The wickedness of this animal had got worse since the officer of the Saxon Hussars had treacherously stabbed her in the shoulder on the battlefield of Jena.

It was this mare that I was riding at the time when the remains of Marshal Augereau's corps, shattered by a hail of cannon and grape shot, were attempting to re-form in the area of the cemetery. You will recall that the 14th Line regiment had stayed alone on the little hill, which it might leave only if ordered to do so by the Emperor. The snow having stopped for a moment, one could see this gallant regiment almost completely surrounded by the enemy, waving its Eagle aloft to show that it still stood fast and needed help. The Emperor, touched by the devotion to duty of these brave men, decided to attempt their rescue; he told Marshal Augereau to send an officer with orders to them to quit the hillock, form a small square and withdraw towards us; while a brigade of cavalry would go to meet them and second their efforts.

This was before the great charge made by Murat and his cavalry, and it was almost impossible to carry out the Emperor's command because a swarm of Cossacks separated us from the 14th. It was clear that any officer sent towards the unfortunate regiment would be killed or captured before he got there. Nevertheless, an order is an order; and the marshal had to obey.

It was the custom, in the imperial army, for the aides to line up a few paces from their general, and the one in front went off first; when he had completed his mission, he joined the back of the queue, so that as each took his turn to carry orders, the dangers were shared equally. A brave captain of engineers, named Froissart, who, although not an aide-de-camp, was attached to the marshal's staff, was nearest to him and was sent off to carry the order to the 14th. He left at the gallop; we lost sight of him in the midst of the Cossacks and never saw him again, nor did we know what became of him.

The marshal, seeing that the 14th did not budge, sent another officer, named David. He suffered the same fate as Froissart, and we heard no more of him. It is likely that they were both killed, and having been stripped of their clothing their bodies were not recognisable among the many dead who covered the ground. For the third time the marshal called out "An officer to take orders! It was my turn.

When he saw before him the son of his old friend, and, I think I may dare to say, his favourite aide-de-camp, the good marshal's face fell and his eyes filled with tears, for he could not disguise from himself that he was sending me to an almost certain death;

but the Emperor's order had to be obeyed; I was a soldier; no one else could take my place, I would not have allowed something so dishonourable. So I took off! Now, while prepared to sacrifice my life, I thought it my duty to take every precaution which might save it. I had noticed that the two officers who had gone before me had left with drawn sabres, which made me think that they intended to defend themselves against the Cossacks who would attack them during the ride. This intention was in my opinion ill-advised, for they would have been forced to stop and fight a multitude of enemies who, in the end, had overwhelmed them. I adopted a different approach, and leaving my sabre in its scabbard, I thought of myself as a rider who, to win the prize in a race, goes as fast as possible by the shortest route towards the winning post without taking any notice of what is to right or left of him during his passage. Now, my winning post being the hillock occupied by the 14th, I resolved to get there without paying any attention to the Cossacks, whom I blotted out of my thoughts.

This system worked perfectly. Lisette, light as a swallow, and flying rather than galloping, rushed through space, leaping over the piled up bodies of men and horses, over ditches and the broken mountings of guns, as well as the half-extinguished bivouac fires. Thousands of Cossacks were scattered about the plain. The first ones to see me behaved like hunters who, having raised a hare, mark its presence by shouts of "Yours! Yours!" But none of them tried to stop me, firstly because I was going so fast, and also perhaps because each one thought I would be caught by his comrades who were further on. In this way I escaped from them all and arrived at the 14th without either I or my excellent mare having suffered a scratch.

I found the 14th formed in a square on top of the hillock; but the slope of the ground was so gentle that the enemy cavalry had been able to carry out a number of charges, which had been vigorously repelled, so that they were surrounded by heap of the dead bodies of horses and Russian Dragoons, which formed a sort of rampart, and now made the position almost inaccessible to cavalry; for even with the aid of our infantrymen, I had great difficulty in getting over this bloody and frightful defence work, but at last I was inside the square.

Since the death of Colonel Savary, killed during the crossing of the Ukra, the 14th had been commanded by a battalion commander; when I gave this officer the order which I carried, for him to leave his position and try to rejoin the army corps, he replied that the enemy artillery which had been firing at them for an hour had occasioned such heavy losses that the handful of soldiers which he had left would inevitably be exterminated if they went down onto the level ground; and anyway there was no time to prepare for the execution of this movement, since a Russian column, coming to attack, was now close to us. "I can see no way of saving the regiment," said the battalion commander. "Go back to the Emperor and say good-bye to him from the 14th; and take back the Eagle which we can no longer defend."

The Eagles of the infantry were very heavy, and their weight was increased by the long thick pole of oak on which they were mounted. I was bending forward and attempting to detach the Eagle from its pole, when one of the many bullets which the Russians were firing at us went through the back part of my hat, very close to my head. The shock was made worse by the fact that the hat was held on by a strong leather strap which went under my chin, and so offered more resistance to the blow. I was partially stunned by this, and found myself unable to move.

However the column of Russian infantry was now climbing the hillock; they were Grenadiers, whose headgear, garnished with metal, looked like mitres. These men, full of liquor, flung themselves on the feeble remnants of the 14th, who defended themselves bravely with their bayonets, and even when the square was broken, formed themselves into little groups and continued for a long time the unequal struggle. In my confused state, I was unable to react in any way; I was attacked by a drunken Russian soldier, who thrust his bayonet into my left arm, and then, aiming another blow at me, lost his balance and missing his mark, he slashed Lisette's haunch.

The pain of this injury aroused her ferocious instincts, she grabbed the soldier with her teeth and tore away the greater part of his face, then, kicking and biting, she forced her way through the melée and taking the path by which we had come, she went off at the gallop in the direction of the Eylau cemetery while, thanks to the Hussar's saddle in which I was seated, I remained on her back.

As we approached Eylau a new danger arose. The snow had started to fall again and in the poor visibility a battalion of the Guard took me for a Russian and opened fire on me, but although my cloak and my saddle were hit, both I and my mare were untouched. Lisette, continuing to gallop, went through the three lines of infantry like a grass-snake through a hedge, but this last burst of speed drained her resources, she was losing a lot of blood because one of the big veins in her haunch had been cut, she collapsed suddenly and fell, throwing me to the ground, where I was rendered unconscious.

I must have remained in this state for about four hours, and I was not aroused by the great charge of Murat's ninety squadrons of cavalry, which went past me and perhaps over me. When I came to, this is the dreadful position in which I found myself. I was completely naked except for my hat and my right boot. A soldier of the transport section, believing me to be dead, had despoiled me, as was customary, and in an attempt to remove my boot, was dragging at my leg, with one foot on my stomach. I was able to raise the upper part of my body and to spit out some clots of blood, my face, shoulders and chest were badly bruised, and blood from my wounded arm reddened the rest of my body. I gazed around with haggard eyes, and must have been a horrible spectacle. The transport driver made off with my possessions before I could summon my wits and address a word to him. I was too dazed and weak to move, and unable to call for help. The cold was increasing and I had little hope of surviving without some form of miracle, and something like a miracle took place.

Marshal Augereau had a valet de chambre, named Pierre Dannel, a very intelligent boy, loyal, but inclined to be cheeky; and it so happened that while we were at Houssaye, Dannel, having spoken back to his master, had been given his notice. Desolated, Dannel begged me to intercede for him, which I did with so much zeal that he was reinstated in the marshal's good graces; since when the valet had been devoted to me. Dannel had taken it on himself to come from Landsberg, on the day of the battle, to bring some victuals to his master, which he had put in a very light wagon, able to go anywhere, and containing all the things that the marshal used most frequently. This little wagon was driven by a soldier who had served in the same transport unit as the man who had stripped me. This fellow, carrying my effects, was passing the wagon which was standing at the Eylau cemetery when, recognising his old friend, he went up to him to show him the lovely booty he had taken from a dead man.

Now, while we were in cantonments by the Vistula, the marshal having told Dannel to go to Warsaw to get some provisions, I asked him to take my pelisse and have the black astrakhan with which it was trimmed, removed and replaced by grey; a style newly adopted by the aides-de-camp of Prince Berthier, who set the fashion in the army. I was still the only one of Marshal Augereau's officers who had grey astrakhan.

Dannel, who was present when the transport driver displayed his booty, easily recognised my pelisse, which made him look more closely at the other belongings of the alleged dead man, amongst which he saw my watch, marked with my father's initials, for it had been his. The valet de chambre had no doubt that I had been killed, but mourning my death, he wished to see me for the last time, and having been led there by the transport driver, he found me alive!

This good fellow, to whom I owe my life, was overjoyed. He hurried to fetch my own servant and some orderlies, who carried me into a barn where they rubbed me down with rum, while they sent for Dr. Raymond. When he at last arrived, he dressed the wound in my arm and declared that the blood which I had lost would save me.

Soon I was surrounded by my comrades including my brother. A reward was given to the transport rider who had taken my clothes, which he handed over with good grace; but as they were soaked with blood and water, Marshal Augereau had me wrapped up in clothes of his own.

The Emperor had given permission for Augereau to return to Landsberg, but his wound made it impossible for him to ride a horse; so his aides-de-camp got hold of a sledge on which they mounted the body of a carriage. The marshal, who had decided not to abandon me, had me strapped in beside him, for I was too weak to sit upright.

Before I was picked up from the battlefield, I had seen my poor Lisette near to me. Her wound had stopped bleeding and she was back on her feet, eating some straw which had been used by soldiers in their bivouacs the previous night. My servant, who was very fond of Lisette, returned to look for her; he cut strips of clothing from a dead soldier and dressed the wound on her haunch, and got her fit enough to walk to Landsberg.

The commandant of the little garrison of the town, had had the good sense to prepare quarters for the wounded. The officers of the staff were put into a large and comfortable inn, so that instead of spending the night lying naked in the snow, I was tucked into a good bed and being looked after by my brother, my companions and the worthy Dr. Raymond. The doctor had to cut the boot which the soldier had tried to pull off, and even so, he had difficulty in getting it off because my foot had swollen so much. You will see, later that this could have cost me my leg, and perhaps even my life.

We stayed in Landsberg for thirty-six hours. The rest and the care given me restored my ability to move, and when, on the second day after the battle, Marshal Augereau set off for Warsaw, I was able, though still very weak, to travel on the sledge. The journey took eight days, because we moved only in short stages; I was recovering my strength little by little, but I was aware of an icy cold in my right foot.

On our arrival at Warsaw, I was put in a large house which had been reserved for the marshal, which suited me very well, as I was unable to get out of bed. The wound of my arm was healing, the bruising of my upper body was dispersing, and my skin was resuming its normal colour, however the doctor did not know why I could not get up, and hearing me complain about my leg, he decided to have a look at it, and what do you suppose he found? My foot had become gangrenous! An accident which had occurred many years ago was the cause of this. While I was at Sorèze, my right foot had been pierced by the foil of a fencing opponent, which had lost its button. It seems that this injury had made my foot more sensitive to cold, and while I was lying on the snow it had become frostbitten, and not having been treated in time, gangrene had set in at the site of the old fencing injury, the area was covered by a scar the size of a five franc piece. The doctor looked with alarm at my foot, then, taking a bistoury, and having me held down by four servants, he picked off the scab and dug into my foot to remove the dead flesh, just as one would cut out the rotten part of an apple.

I suffered greatly, at first without complaining, though it was a different matter when the bistoury, having reached live tissue, exposed the muscles and bones, which one could see. The doctor then stood on a chair and having soaked a sponge in warm sweetened wine, he allowed it to fall, drop by drop into the hole he had made in my foot. The pain was intolerable! Nevertheless I had to endure for a week this fearful torture, but my leg was saved.

Today, when one is so prodigal with decorations and promotions, an officer who ran the risks which I had run in reaching the 14th regiment, would certainly be rewarded; but under the Empire this sort of devotion to duty was regarded as so normal that I was given no medal and never thought of asking for one.

A long rest having been judged necessary for the cure of Marshal Augereau's wound, the Emperor instructed him to go to France for treatment, and brought Marshal Masséna from Italy; to whom my brother, Bro and several of my friends were appointed. Marshal Augereau took me with him, along with his secretary and Dr.Raymond. I had to be lifted in and out of the carriage, but otherwise I felt my health improve the further we got away from those frozen wastes to a more friendly climate. My mare spent the winter in the stables of M. de Launay, the administrator of army forage supplies.

The marshal went by way of Rawa to Silesia. As long as we were in dreadful Poland, where there are no metalled roads, it took twelve and sometimes sixteen horses to drag the coach out of the bogs and swamps through which we travelled. We went always at walking pace and it was not until we reached Germany that we found ourselves in a civilised country with proper roads. We stopped at Dresden, and spent ten or twelve days at Frankfurt-on-Main, from where we had marched the previous October to attack Prussia.

We finally reached Paris about the 15th of March. I could walk with much difficulty, and had my arm in a sling, and I still felt the effects of what I had been through, but the pleasure of seeing my mother once more, and the care she devoted to me, combined with the gentle influence of the returning spring, effected my cure.

Chapter 34
To the Staff of Marshal Lannes

I spent the end of March, all of April, and the first week of May in Paris. It was during this time that I got to know the Desbrières, a family of which my marriage was soon to make me a member. I had recovered my health, and I realised that I could not stay any longer in Paris. Marshal Augereau sent me to Marshal Lannes who took me willingly onto his staff.

The Emperor, in order to keep an eye on any moves which the enemy might be tempted to make during the winter, had settled himself in the middle of the cantonments of his troops, first at Oster-ode and then at the château of Finkenstein, from where, while planning a new campaign, he governed France and directed his ministers, who, every week, sent him their reports. The portfolios holding the various documents furnished by each ministry were collected every Wednesday by M. Denniée the elder, under-secretary of state for war, who sent them off on Thursdays in the charge of a junior official whose duty it was to deliver them into the hands of the Emperor. But this system worked very badly because most of these officials had never been out of France. They did not know a word of German, nor did they understand the currency or the regulations regarding posting in foreign countries, so they did not know how to manage matters once they had crossed the Rhine. In addition, these gentlemen, being unused to fatigue, soon found themselves overcome by that of a journey of more than three hundred leagues, which lasted continuously for ten days and ten nights. One of them was so incompetent as to allow his despatches to be stolen. Napoleon was so angry at this mishap that he sent a courier to Paris to tell M. Denniée not to give the portfolios in future to officials except those who knew Germany, and who, being able to support fatigue and privation, could carry out their duties more efficiently.

M. Denniée was having great difficulty in finding anyone to fill the post, when I turned up with a letter ordering me to report to

Marshal Lannes. Delighted to have found someone to take the next lot of despatches, he warned me to be ready to leave on the coming Thursday, and gave me five thousand francs for expenses and the purchase of a carriage, which suited me very well, as I did not have much money to get me back to the army in the depths of Poland.

We left Paris about the 10th of May. Both my servant and I were armed, and if one of us left the coach the other remained on guard. We knew enough German to keep the postilions up to the mark, and as I was in uniform, they obeyed me with more alacrity than they would a civilian official. So that instead of taking the usual nine and a half or ten days over the journey, we made it in eight and a half.

The Emperor was delighted to have his despatches twenty-four hours earlier than expected, and after praising the keenness which had led me to ask to return to duty in spite of my recent wounds, he added that as I had been so efficient a courier, I could leave for Paris that same night to take back some other portfolios; a task which would not prevent me from taking part in the campaign, which could not restart before the beginning of June.

Although I had spent nothing like the five thousand francs which M. Denniée had given me, the marshal of the palace gave me the same sum to return to Paris, which I did as quickly as possible. I stayed no more than twenty-four hours in the capital, and left once more for Poland; the minister again gave me five thousand francs for this third journey; it was far more than was necessary, but that was how Napoleon wanted it. It is true that these trips were very tiring and very boring, even though the weather was fine. I was on the road day and night for nearly a month in the sole company of my servant.

I reported to the Emperor at Finkenstein, and was afraid that I might have to continue as postman until fighting broke out, when fortunately some replacements were found and the Emperor authorised me to go to Marshal Lannes, to whom I reported at Marienberg on the 25th May. He had with him Colonel Sicard, Augereau's aide-de-camp, who had been kind enough to take charge of my horses. It was with much pleasure that I saw once more my mare Lisette, who was fit enough for more service.

The fortress of Danzig, besieged by the French during the winter, had fallen into their hands. The return of the good weather soon saw campaigning recommence. The Russians attacked our cantonments on the 5th of June, and were sharply repulsed at every point. On the 10th there was a fierce encounter at Heilsberg which some historians describe as a battle. The enemy were once more defeated. I shall not go into any detail about this affair, since Marshal Lannes' corps took very little part in it, not having arrived until nightfall. We did, however, come under some heavy fire and Colonel Sicard was mortally wounded. He had already been wounded at Eylau, and although scarcely recovered from his injuries, had returned to take part in the renewed fighting. Before he died, the good colonel requested me to say his farewell to Marshal Augereau, and gave me a letter for his wife. I was very much upset by this painful scene.

The army now being in pursuit of the Russians, we passed through Eylau. The fields which we had left three months previously covered with snow and dead bodies, were now overspread by a delightful carpet of green, bedecked with flowers. What a contrast! How many soldiers lay beneath those verdant meadows? I went and sat at the place where I had fallen and been despoiled, and where I also would have died, had not a truly providential combination of circumstances come to my aid. Marshal Lannes wanted to see the hillock which the 14th had so valiantly defended. I took him there. Since the time of the battle, the enemy had been in occupation of the place; however, we found, still intact, the monument which all the corps of the French army had erected to the memory of their dead comrades of the 14th, thirty-six of whose officers had been buried in the same grave. This respect for the dead reflected honour on the Russians. I remained for a few moments on the spot where I had been hit by the bullet and wounded by the bayonet, and thought of the brave men who lay in the dust, and whose fate I had so nearly shared.

The Russians, having been defeated on the 10th of June at Heilsberg, retreated hastily and got a day ahead of the French who, by the evening of the 13th, were concentrated beyond Eylau, on the left bank of the Alle. The Russians occupied Bartenstein on the right bank of this river, which the two armies now descended on opposite sides.

Benningsen, whose stores of food and ammunition were in Konigsberg, where the Prussian corps was stationed, wanted to reach this town before the arrival of the French, but to do so he had to cross over onto the left bank of the Alle, where there were the French troops. The Russian commander hoped to reach Friedland sufficiently far ahead of the French to be able to cross the river before they could oppose him. The same reasons which made Benningsen wish to hold on to Konigsberg, made Napoleon wish to capture it. He had for several days constantly manoeuvred to out-flank the Russian left, and keep them away from the place, in the direction of which he had sent Murat, Soult and Davout to oppose the Russians if they arrived before us.

The Emperor, however, did not stick to this scheme, and foreseeing that the Russians would attempt to cross the Alle at Friedland, he aimed to occupy the town before they did, and on the night of the 13th-14th June, he despatched towards it the corps of Marshal Lannes and Mortier, and three divisions of cavalry. The rest of the army was to follow.

Marshal Lannes, who was in the van, with the Oudinot Grenadiers and a brigade of cavalry, having arrived at Posthenen, a league from Friedland, sent the 9th Hussars to reconnoitre the latter town. They were repulsed with losses, and daybreak revealed a large part of the Russian army massed on the opposite bank of the Alle on the high ground between Allenau and Friedland. They had begun to cross the old town bridge, beside which they had constructed two new ones.

The aim of the two armies was very easily understood. The Russians wanted to cross the Alle to get to Konigsberg, and the French wanted to stop them and drive them back across the river, which had very steep banks. The only crossing point was at Friedland. The Russians had difficulty in deploying from Friedland onto the open ground of the left bank, owing to the fact that the way out of the town was much restricted by a large lake, and by a stream called the Mill Stream, which ran in a very steep-sided ravine. To protect their crossing, the Russians had placed two strong batteries of guns on the right bank, which could cover the town and part of the land between Posthenen and Heinrichsdorf.

The Emperor was still at Eylau: the various corps marching towards Friedland were still several leagues away, when Marshal Lannes, having marched all night, arrived before the town. The marshal would have liked to attack the enemy immediately; but already they had thirty thousand men drawn up on the level ground before Friedland, and their lines, the right of which was opposite Heinrichsdorf, the centre at the mill stream, and the left at the village of Sortlack, were being endlessly reinforced; while Marshal Lannes had no more than ten thousand men; however, he deployed them skillfully in the village of Posthenen and the woods of Sortlack, from where he threatened the Russian's left flank, while with two divisions of cavalry he tried to stop their advance toward Heinrichsdorf, which lay on the route from Friedland to Konigsberg. There was a brisk exchange of fire before Mortier's corps arrived. Mortier, to dispute with the Russians the road to Konigsberg, while waiting for fresh reinforcements, occupied Heinrichsdorf and the area between this village and Posthenen. However, it was not possible that Lannes and Mortier with twenty-five thousand men could resist the seventy thousand Russians who would soon face them. The situation was becoming highly critical. Marshal Lannes sent a succession of officers to warn the Emperor to hasten the arrival of the army corps which he knew were coming up behind him. Mounted on my swift Lisette, I was the first to go. I met the Emperor as he was leaving Eylau; he was beaming with pleasure! He called me to his side, and as we galloped along, I had to explain to him what had happened before I left the battle. When I had finished my recital, the Emperor said to me, smiling, "Have you a good memory?" "Passable, Sir," I replied. "Well what anniversary is this, the 14th of June?" "Marengo" I said "Yes! Yes! The anniversary of Marengo," said the Emperor, "and I shall beat the Russians as I beat the Austrians!"

Napoleon was so convinced about this, that as he went along the columns, where the men greeted him with many cheers, he said to them repeatedly "Today is a lucky day, it is the anniversary of Marengo!"

Chapter 35
The Battle of Friedland

It was after eleven o'clock when Napoleon arrived on the battlefield, where several corps had already come to join Lannes and Mortier. The remainder, including the Guard, were arriving one by one. Napoleon readjusted the line: Ney was on the right, positioned in the wood at Sortlack; Lannes and Mortier formed the centre, between Posthenen and Heinrichsdorf; the left stretched out beyond this last village. The heat was overpowering. The Emperor gave the troops an hour's rest, after which, at the signal of a volley by twenty-five guns, a general attack would begin. Marshal Ney's corps had the most difficult task, for they were to come out of their hiding place in the woods of Sortlack, fight their way into Friedland, which was filled with the main forces and reserves of the enemy, seize the bridges and thus cut off the Russian's way of retreat.

It is difficult to understand why Benningsen had placed his forces in front of the narrow exit from Friedland, and with their backs to the Alle with its steep banks, in the presence of the French who commanded the open country. The explanation given later by the Russian general was that having been a day ahead of Napoleon, he did not believe that the French troops could cover in twelve hours a distance which had taken his men twenty-four hours, and he had thought that Lannes' corps was an isolated advance-guard of the French army, which he could easily crush. When this illusion had been dissipated, it was too late to bring his army back to the other bank because the narrow defile at Friedland would have caused certain disaster, so he preferred to stand and fight.

At about one in the afternoon, the twenty-five guns at Posthenen, given the order by the Emperor, fired a volley, and battle was joined all along the line. At first our left and our centre moved very slowly to give the right, commanded by Ney, time to capture the town. The marshal, emerging from Sortlack wood, took the village of that name and advanced rapidly towards Friedland, sweeping aside everything in his path; but as they moved forward from the wood and the village of Sortlack to the first houses of Friedland, Ney's troops were exposed to the fire of the Russian batteries which, positioned behind the town on the heights of the opposite bank, caused them severe losses. This fire was made more dangerous by the fact that the gunners, separated from us by the river, could aim their guns in safety, knowing that our infantry could not attack them. This serious problem could have led to the failure of the attack on Friedland, but Napoleon overcame it by sending General Senarmont with fifty guns, which he placed on the left bank of the Alle, and subjected the Russian batteries to such heavy fire that they were soon silenced. As soon as the enemy fire had ceased, Marshal Ney resumed his advance, driving the Russians back into Friedland, and mingled in confusion with them, entered the streets of the unfortunate town, where the mortar bombs had started a huge fire.

A savage bayonet fight ensued in which the Russians, crammed together and scarcely able to move, suffered enormous losses! ... At last, in spite of their courage, they were compelled to retreat in disorder and seek refuge by crossing the bridges to the other bank; but General Senarmont had moved his guns into a position from which he could fire on the bridges, which he soon broke, after killing many of the Russians who were attempting to escape across them. All those who remained in Friedland were either killed, captured or drowned while trying to cross the river.

Up until this point, Napoleon had, so to speak, made his left and his centre mark time; he now moved them rapidly forward. General Gortschakoff, who commanded the centre and right wing of the enemy, attempted, bravely, to recapture the town, (which would have been of no use, because the bridges were down, although he did not know that). He charged at the head of his men into the burning Friedland; but driven out by Ney, who was occupying the town, and forced back into the open, he found himself confronting our centre, who drove him back to the Alle at Kloschenen. The Russians defended themselves heroically and refused to surrender although completely surrounded. Many of them were killed by our bayonets, the remainder rolled down the steep banks into the river, where a large number were drowned.

The extreme right of the enemy was composed mostly of cavalry who tried during the battle to capture or outflank the village of Heinrichsdorf; but driven off by our troops, they went back to the banks of the Alle, under the command of General Lambert, who, seeing that Friedland was in the hands of the French and that the Russian left and centre were defeated, gathered all he could of the regiments of the right wing and made off from the battlefield down the side of the Alle. Nightfall prevented the French from following, so his was the only body of Russian troops to escape the disaster.

Our victory was one of the most complete; we captured all the Russian guns; we did not take a many prisoners during the action, but a great many of the enemy were killed or wounded, amounting to more than twenty-six thousand; our losses were no more than three thousand dead and four or five thousand wounded. Of all the battles fought by the Emperor, this was the only one in which the number of his troops exceeded that of the enemy. The French strength was eighty thousand and the Russian's only seventy-five thousand. The remnants of the Russian army marched in disorder all night, and retired behind the River Pregal, having destroyed the bridges.

Marshals Soult, Davout and Murat had not been involved in the battle of Friedland, but their presence induced the Russians to abandon Konigsberg, which town our troops entered. We found there an immense store of all kinds of material.

I did not suffer any injury during the battle, though I ran into a number of dangers. You saw how I left Posthenen in the morning, on Marshal Lannes' orders, to go as quickly as possible to warm the Emperor that the Russians were crossing the Alle, and that a battle appeared imminent. Napoleon was at Eylau; I had therefore to make a journy of about six leagues to reach him, which would have presented no difficulty to my excellent mare if the road had been clear, but as it was congested by the troops of various units hurrying to the aid of Marshal Lannes at Friedland, there was no way in which I could gallop along it. I therefore went across country, which meant that Lisette, having had to jump hedges, fences and ditches, was already very tired when I met the Emperor, who was just leaving Eylau. However, I had, without a moment of rest, to return with him to Friedland, and although this time the troops moved to one side to let us pass, my poor mare, having galloped over twelve leagues altogether, six of them being across country, and in very hot weather, was utterly exhausted by the time I had rejoined Marshal Lannes on the battlefield. I realised that Lisette could not continue to carry me during the action, so, taking advantage of the rest which Napoleon allowed the troops, I set out to look for my servant, in order to change horses; but in the middle of such a large collection of troops there was not much hope of finding him. It was, in fact, impossible, and I went back to the staff still mounted on the weary Lisette.

Marshal Lannes and my comrades, who saw my problem, had advised me to dismount and allow my mare a few hour's rest, when I caught sight of a Hussar leading a horse which he had captured from the enemy. I took it over, and gave Lisette to one of the troopers of the marshal's escort, so that he could take her back behind the lines, let her have some food and hand her over to my servant, when he could find him. I then got astride my new mount, took my place among the aides-de-camp, and when it came to my turn, I went off.

I was, at first, very pleased with my fresh horse, until the time came when, Marshal Ney having gone into Friedland, Marshal Lannes sent me to warn him of an enemy movement. I had barely entered the town when this devil of a horse, which had behaved so well in the open country, finding itself in a little square, where all the houses were on fire and the street covered with burning planks and furniture, in the midst of which a number of bodies were being roasted, was so frightened by the sight of the flames and the smell of burning flesh that it would go neither forward nor back, and, digging in its heels, it remained motionless, snorting loudly, and no amount of spurring would persuade it to move. Now the Russians, having gained a momentary advantage, pushed our men back to the point where I was, and from the height of a church and some neighbouring houses, they were raining down bullets, while two guns which they carried with them fired grape-shot at the soldiers among whom I was.

Many men were killed around me, which recalled to my mind the position in which I had found myself at Eylau in the middle of the 14th. As I was not anxious to be wounded again and in any case, in staying where I was I was not carrying out my mission, I simply dismounted, and abandoning my infernal mount, I slipped through the houses to contact Marshal Ney at another spot, which was pointed out by some officers.

I was with him for some fifteen minutes; there were some bullets flying around, but nothing like so many as there had been at the place where I had left my mount. The Russians were eventually driven back at bayonet point and forced to retreat toward the bridges, whereupon Marshal Ney sent me to take the good news to Marshal Lannes. To get out of the town, I took the same route as I had taken to get in, and went through the little square where I had left my horse. It had been the scene of a fierce encounter which had left many dead and dying, among whom I saw my stubborn horse, its back broken by a cannon-ball, and its body riddled by bullets!.... From there I made for the outskirts in something of a hurry because the burning houses were collapsing on all sides and I was afraid of being buried beneath the debris. At last I got out of the town and reached the edge of the lake.

The heat of the day, added to that of the fire which was raging in the streets through which I had passed, had bathed me in sweat, and I was dropping with fatigue and hunger, for I had spent a night on horseback to come from Eylau to Friedland, I had galloped back to Eylau and returned to Friedland once more, and had not eaten since the previous evening. I was not looking forward, therefore, to crossing, under a blazing sun, the large area covered with high standing corn which separated me from Marshal Lannes. But once again I had a stroke of luck. General Grouchy's division of dragoons had been engaged not far away in a sharp encounter in which, although victorious, they had lost a number of men, and the colonels had, as was usual, collected the horses of the men who had been killed and put them in the hands of a detachment which would lead them away. I saw this body of men, of which every trooper was leading four or five horses and was taking them to the lake to drink.

I spoke to the officer in charge who, encumbered by all these led horses, was only too glad to let me have one, which I promised to return to his regiment in the evening. He picked out for me an excellent beast, which had been the mount of a sous-officier killed during the charge; astride of this horse, I returned rapidly to Posthenen.

I had hardly left the edge of the lake when it became the theatre of the most savage encounter, which was due to the desperate attempt made by Gortschakoff to reopen a way of retreat by capturing the road to Friedland which was held by Marshal Ney. Caught between the marshal's troops and those of our centre, who were now advancing, Gortschakoff's Russians defended themselves bravely amongst the houses bordering the lake; so that if I had stayed there, where I had thought of resting for a while, I would have landed in the middle of this fierce outbreak of fighting. I rejoined Marshal Lannes at the moment when he was moving towards the lake to attack the rear of the Russian troops whom Ney was driving away from the front of the town, and I was able to give him some useful information about the terrain on which we were fighting.

If the French army did not take many prisoners during the battle of Friedland, it was a different matter the next day and the days following; for the Russians, pursued with a bayonet at their backs, thrown into complete disorder and utterly exhausted, were abandoning their ranks and lying down in the fields, where we captured a great number. We also collected a large quantity of artillery. All those members of Benningsen's army who escaped hurried back across the Nieman, behind which was the Russian emperor who, perhaps recalling the danger to which he had been exposed at Austerlitz, had judged it unwise to assist in person at the battle of Friedland; and two days after our victory he hastened to ask Napoleon for an armistice, to which Napoleon agreed.

Three days after the battle the French army reached the town of Tilsit and the river Nieman, which at this point is only a few leagues from the frontiers of the Russian empire.

The rear of a victorious army presents a most dismal spectacle. The path of their advance is strewn with the dead, dying, and wounded, while the survivors, soon forgetting those comrades who have fallen in the fighting, rejoice in their success and go forward cheerfully to new adventures. Our men were delighted to see the Nieman, whose opposite bank was occupied by the remains of that Russian army which they had defeated in so many engagements; and where, in contrast to their own lighthearted songs, there reigned a mournful silence. Napoleon established himself at Tilsit, and his troops encamped around the town. The Nieman separated the two armies; the French occupied the left bank and the Russians the right.

The Emperor Alexander having requested a meeting with Napoleon, this took place on the 25th of June, in a pavilion on a raft anchored in the middle of the river, in sight of the two armies which lined the banks. It was a most imposing spectacle. The two emperors arrived, each from his own side, accompanied by only five of the principal officers of their armies. Marshal Lannes, who flattered himself that he should accompany the Emperor, saw himself displaced by Marshal Bessières, an intimate friend of Prince Murat; and he never forgave the marshals for depriving him of what he considered his right.

So Marshal Lannes stayed with us on the quay at Tilsit, from where we saw the two emperors embrace on meeting, which occasioned much cheering from both camps. The next day, the 26th, in the course of a second interview which took place once more in the pavilion on the Nieman, the Russian emperor presented to Napoleon his unfortunate friend, the King of Prussia. This prince whom the fortunes of war had stripped of a vast kingdom, leaving him only the small town of Memel and some miserable villages, maintained a bearing worthy of a descendant of Frederick the Great: Napoleon greeted him politely but coolly, for he considered that he had reason to complain of his conduct, and he planned to confiscate the greater part of his states.

To facilitate the meetings of the two Emperors, the town of Tilsit was declared neutral, and Napoleon handed over half of it to the Russian emperor, who set himself up there with his Guard. The two sovereigns spent some twenty days together, during which time they decided the fate of Europe. During these proceedings, the King of Prussia was relegated to the right bank, and had no quarters in Tilsit, which he visited but rarely. One day Napoleon went to call on the Queen of Prussia, who was said to be greatly distressed. He invited her to dine with him on the following day. She accepted the invitation, no doubt with little pleasure, but realising that at a time when peace was being sought it was necessary to take every measure to soften the heart of the victor.

Napoleon and the Queen of Prussia thoroughly detested one another: she had grossly insulted him in several proclamations, and he had returned the complement in his bulletins. Their meeting, however, did not display their mutual hatred; Napoleon was respectful and attentive, the queen gracious in her attempts to captivate her former enemy; attempts made all the more determinedly as she was not unaware that the peace treaty created -- under the name of the kingdom of Westphalia -- a new state, whose territory was to be provided by the electorate of Hesse, and by Prussia itself.

The Queen was resigned to the loss of several provinces, but she could not accept the loss of the fortified city of Magdeberg, possession of which was needed for the security of Prussia. For his part, Napoleon, who planned to nominate his brother Jérôme as King of Westphalia, intended to add Magdeberg to this new state. It appears that, during the meal, the Queen deployed her not inconsiderable charms, and when Napoleon, to change the conversation, praised a superb rose which the Queen was wearing, she said to him, "Would your majesty not accept this rose in return for Magdeberg?" A more chivalrous person might have accepted, but Napoleon was too much of a realist to be won over by a pretty proposition. One may be sure that he restricted himself to admiring the beauty of the rose and also of the hand which proffered it, but he did not take the flower, which brought tears to the Queen's eyes. The conqueror, however, did not seem to notice. He kept Magdeberg and politely conducted the Queen to the boat which was to carry her to the opposite bank.

During our stay at Tilsit, Napoleon held a review of his Guard and the army in the presence of Alexander, who was impressed by the martial air and bearing of these troops. The Russian Emperor, in his turn, put on display some fine battalions of his Guard, but he did not dare to parade his line regiments, whose numbers had been so greatly reduced at Heilsberg and Friedland. As for the King of Prussia, of whose regiments there remained only the broken débris, he did not exhibit them at all.

Napoleon drew up, with Russia and Prussia, a peace treaty in which the principal articles related to the creation of the kingdom of Westphalia for the benefit of Jérôme Bonaparte. The elector of Saxony, now an ally and friend of France, was elevated to the dignity of king, and was awarded, in addition, the Grand Duchy of Warsaw, composed of a vast province of the former Poland, which was recovered from the Russians. I shall not go into the less important articles of the treaty, which resulted in the re-establishment of peace between the great powers of continental Europe.

In elevating his brother to the throne of Westphalia, Napoleon added to the mistakes he had already made in awarding the kingdom of Naples to Joseph and that of Holland, Louis. The people of these countries felt humiliated at being ruled by foreigners who had not themselves done anything of importance and who were, in fact, nonentities, who had no merit except that of being Napoleon's brothers. The dislike and distrust which these new kings attracted contributed largely to the Emperor's downfall. The conduct of the King of Westphalia in particular made very many enemies for Napoleon.

Having concluded the treaty, the two Emperors parted with mutual assurances of friendship, which at the time seemed sincere.

Chapter 36
I Smuggle the Empress' Clothes

The French army was spread out into the various provinces of Germany and Poland under the command of five marshals, in whose number Lannes had asked not to be included, since his ill-health required his return to France. If I had been his permanent aide-de-camp, I would have had to return with him, but I had an even better reason for going, and that was to rejoin Marshal Augereau, to whose staff I had not ceased to belong, my attachment to Marshal Lannes being only temporary. I made ready to return to Paris: I sold, as well as possible, my two horses, and I sent Lisette to the registrar-general, M. de Launey, who, having taken a liking to her, had asked me to let him have her when I had no further use for her. Her injuries and hard work had calmed her down, and I lent her to him for an indefinite period; he mounted his wife on her, and kept her for seven or eight years until she died a natural death.

During the twenty days which the Emperor had spent at Tilsit, he had despatched a great many officers, some to Paris, some to other parts of the empire, so that there were hardly any left available for duty. Napoleon did not want to take officers from their regiments, so he ordered a list to be made of all those who had joined the campaign voluntarily and those who did not belong to any army corps nor to the staff of any of the five marshals who were in command. I was included in this list, and felt sure that the Emperor, for whom I had already carried despatches, would choose me in preference to officers whom he did not know; and indeed, the Emperor sent for me on the 9th of July, and having given me some voluminous portfolios and some despatches for the King of Saxony, ordered me to go to Dresden and await him there. The Emperor intended to leave Tilsit that same day, but was going on a long detour to visit Konigsberg, Marienwerder, and Silesia, so that I would be several days ahead of him.

I crossed Prussia once more, and saw again several of our bat-tlefields; I went through Berlin and arrived at Dresden two days before the Emperor. The court of Saxony was aware that a peace had been agreed, and that it raised the elector to the rank of king, and awarded him the Grand Duchy of Warsaw, but they did not yet know that the Emperor was to pass through Dresden on his way to Paris; it was I who gave this information to the new king.

You may imagine the result of this! ...Immediately the court, the town, and the army were thrown into a turmoil to organise a grand reception for the great Emperor who, after having so generously restored to liberty the Saxon troops captured at Jena, had loaded their sovereign with honours! I was received with en-thusiasm; I was lodged in the château in a fine apartment, where I was magnificently cared for, and the king's aides-de-camp showed me round all the interesting sights of the palace and the town. Eventually the Emperor arrived, and in accordance with the pro-tocol, which I already knew, I hurried to hand over the portfo-lios to M. Meneval, and to ask for the Emperor's further orders. These I found agreeable, for I was instructed to carry some fresh portfolios to Paris, and the Emperor gave me a letter which I was to deliver personally to the Empress Josephine. The marshal of the palace, M. Duroc, gave me eight thousand francs to cover the expense of the journey from Tilsit to Dresden and from Dresden to Paris. I took to the road in high spirits: I had just taken part in three fine campaigns, during which I had been promoted to captain, and had been noticed by the Emperor; we were about to enjoy the delights of peace, which would allow me to spend a long time with my mother; I was fully recovered; I had never had so much money; everything conspired to make me happy, and I was very happy.

I arrived at Frankfurt-on-main, where a lieutenant colonel of the Imperial Guard named M. de L... was in command. The Emperor had given me a letter for this officer, from whom he wanted, I think, some confidential information, for M. de L... was in touch with M. Savary, who ran the secret police. This colonel invited me to dine with him, after which he conducted me back to my coach; but as I got in I noticed a fair sized pack-age which was not part of my despatches. I was about to call for my batman to get an explanation for this, when Colonel de L... stopped me, and told me, in an undertone, that the package contained some dresses in Berlin knitwear and other materials banned in France, and was destined for the Empress Josephine, who would be much obliged to me for bringing them to her! I recalled only too well the cruel anxieties I had suffered as a result of the false report which I had been persuaded to give the Emperor regarding the numerical strength of the Chasseurs a Cheval at Austerlitz, to consent to be engaged once more in some underhand business: so I flatly refused. To be sure I would have liked to please the Empress, but I was aware of the inflexible severity with which Napoleon treated those found guilty of smuggling, and after facing so many dangers, and shedding so much of my blood in battle, I had no wish to sacrifice whatever merit I had gained in the eyes of the Emperor by transgressing his laws in order to draw a smile of thanks from the Empress. To overcome my objections Colonel de L... pointed out that the package had several wrappings, of which the outermost, addressed to the minister for war, bore the seal of the 7th Light Infantry and the designation "Record of accounts." He was sure that the customs would not dare open such a package, the outer covering of which I could remove when I reached Paris and deliver the stuff to the Empress without being compromised; but in spite of all this fine reasoning, I absolutely refused to take part in this transaction and ordered the postilion to set off. When we arrived at the post-house, half way between Frankfurt and Mainz, I took my batman to task for having taken into the coach this extra package; he replied that during dinner time, M. de L... himself had put these packages into the coach: he had supposed that they contained more despatches, and had not thought that he could refuse to accept them from the hands of the commanding officer in person. "Did you say packages?" I cried. "Were there then several? He took away only one." And now, rummaging amongst the Emperor's portfolios, I found a second package of contraband which the colonel had put into my trunk without my knowledge. I was taken aback by this trickery and was tempted to throw the dresses onto the highway. However I did not dare, and I continued my journey, determined that if the contraband was seized I would explain how it had been put into my coach, and by whom the stamp of the 7th Light Infantry had been put on the wrapping; for I had no wish to face the anger of Napoleon; but as this defence would have compromised the Empress, I decided that I would use it only as a last resort, and that I would make every effort to avoid my coach being examined. A stroke of luck and a little subterfuge got me out of this dilemma.

I arrived, very worried, at the bridge over the Rhine at Mainz, which separates Germany from France, and my anxiety was increased by the sight of the great collection of customs officers and soldiers in unifor, who were waiting round this frontier. When my carriage was stopped, in the usual manner, two men arrived simultaneously at the door; one was a customs officer, to carry out a search, and the other was an aide-de-camp to Marshal Kellerman, who was in command of the station, and who wanted to know if the Emperor was on his way. This is my chance! I thought to myself, and pretending not to notice the customs officer, I replied to the aide-de-camp, "The Emperor is coming behind me." This was no lie, he was indeed following me, but at an interval of two days...which I did not think it necessary to add.

My words were heard by all around me and threw them into a state of frenzied activity. The aide-de-camp went off across the bridge at the gallop, at risk of tumbling into the Rhine in his haste to warn Marshal Kellerman. The guard took up their arms. The customs men and their superiors tried to arrange themselves in the most military manner possible in order to look good in front of the Emperor and, as my carriage got in their way, they told the postilion to clear off....So there I was! Freed from their clutches!

I went on to the posting-house and quickly changed horses; but while this was being done, a violent storm broke over Mainz and the rain began to fall in torrents. It was five o'clock in the afternoon, dinner time; but on the news of the approaching arrival of the Emperor, the general alarm was beaten throughout the town; on which signal the marshal, generals, prefect, mayor, civil and military authorities, all threw down their napkins, and hastily donning their best clothes, they went in the pouring rain through the streams of water running in the streets to take up their posts; while I, who was the cause of all this commotion, was laughing my head off as I made off at full speed drawn by three good post-horses.

In view of the fact that the Empress was willing to disobey her august spouse by wearing clothes made of prohibited material, and that a colonel was willing to slip contraband into my coach without my knowledge, the trick which I had played seemed to me to be excusable. In any case, since it was June, the soaking which I had caused these Mainz officials to undergo would do no harm except to their clothes. When I was far from Mainz, I could still hear the sound of drums, and I learned afterwards that they had stayed up all night. The Emperor arrived two days later, but as he had had an accident to his coach, the good citizens of Mainz blamed that for the delay of which their fine clothes were the victims. I was heading swiftly and happily towards Paris, when a most disagreeable accident interrupted my progress, and turned my happiness to annoyance. You will understand that when a sovereign travels, it would be impossible to supply a change of horses for the numerous carriages which precede and follow him, if the staging posts were not reinforced by horses, known as "de tournée", brought from posts established on other routes. Now, as I was leaving Dombasle, a little town this side of Verdun, a confounded postilion "de tournée" who had arrived the night before, not having noticed a steep hill which one encounters after leaving the staging post, lost control of his horses during the descent and overturned my carriage, breaking the springs and the bodywork. To make matters worse, it was a Sunday and all the population had gone to a fete in a neighbouring village, so that I could not find a workman. Those that I found the next day were so unskillful that I had to spend two mortal days in this miserable place.

I was about to set out again when an outrider having announced the arrival of the Emperor, I took the liberty of stopping his coach to tell him of the accident which I had suffered. He laughed, took back the letter for the Empress which he had given me, and went on his way. I followed him to St. Cloud, from where, after giving the portfolios to the cabinet secretary, I went to my mother's home in Paris.

I took up once more my position as aide-de-camp to Marshal Augereau, a very easy task, as it consisted of going every month to spend one or two weeks at La Houssaye, where daily life was always so amusing. Thus rolled by the end of the summer and the autumn; during which time the Emperor's policies were leading towards fresh events and storms whose terrible commotions would nearly swallow me up; me, a very small personage, who, in his carefree youth, thought of nothing but enjoying life, after having seen death at such close quarters.

ALSO FROM LEONAUR

AVAILABLE IN SOFTCOVER OR HARDCOVER WITH DUST JACKET

EW2 EYEWITNESS TO WAR SERIES
CAPTAIN OF THE 95th (Rifles) *by Jonathan Leach*

An officer of Wellington's Sharpshooters during the
Peninsular, South of France and Waterloo Campaigns
of the Napoleonic Wars.

SOFTCOVER : **ISBN 1-84677-001-7**
HARDCOVER : **ISBN 1-84677-016-5**

WFI THE WARFARE FICTION SERIES
NAPOLEONIC WAR STORIES
by Sir Arthur Quiller-Couch

Tales of soldiers, spies, battles & Sieges from the
Peninsular & Waterloo campaigns

SOFTCOVER : **ISBN 1-84677-003-3**
HARDCOVER : **ISBN 1-84677-014-9**

EWI EYEWITNESS TO WAR SERIES
RIFLEMAN COSTELLO *by Edward Costello*

The adventures of a soldier of the 95th (Rifles) in the
Peninsular & Waterloo Campaigns of the Napoleonic wars.

SOFTCOVER : **ISBN 1-84677-000-9**
HARDCOVER : **ISBN 1-84677-018-1**

MCI THE MILITARY COMMANDERS SERIES
JOURNALS OF ROBERT ROGERS OF THE RANGERS *by Robert Rogers*

The exploits of Rogers & the Rangers in his own words
during 1755-1761 in the French & Indian War.

SOFTCOVER : **ISBN 1-84677-002-5**
HARDCOVER : **ISBN 1-84677-010-6**

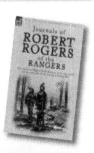

ALSO FROM LEONAUR

AVAILABLE IN SOFTCOVER OR HARDCOVER WITH DUST JACKET

RGW1 RECOLLECTIONS OF THE GREAT WAR 1914 - 18
STEEL CHARIOTS IN THE DESERT *by S. C. Rolls*

The first world war experiences of a Rolls Royce armoured car driver with the Duke of Westminster in Libya and in Arabia with T.E. Lawrence.

SOFTCOVER : **ISBN 1-84677-005-X**
HARDCOVER : **ISBN 1-84677-019-X**

RGW2 RECOLLECTIONS OF THE GREAT WAR 1914 - 18
WITH THE IMPERIAL CAMEL CORPS IN THE GREAT WAR *by Geoffrey Inchbald*

The story of a serving officer with the British 2nd battalion against the Senussi and during the Palestine campaign.

SOFTCOVER : **ISBN 1-84677-007-6**
HARDCOVER : **ISBN 1-84677-012-2**

EW3 EYEWITNESS TO WAR SERIES
THE KHAKEE RESSALAH
by Robert Henry Wallace Dunlop

Service & adventure with the Meerut Volunteer Horse During the Indian Mutiny 1857-1858.

SOFTCOVER : **ISBN 1-84677-009-2**
HARDCOVER : **ISBN 1-84677-017-3**

WF1 THE WARFARE FICTION SERIES
NAPOLEONIC WAR STORIES
by Sir Arthur Quiller-Couch

Tales of soldiers, spies, battles & Sieges from the Peninsular & Waterloo campaigns

SOFTCOVER : **ISBN 1-84677-003-3**
HARDCOVER : **ISBN 1-84677-014-9**

Lightning Source UK Ltd.
Milton Keynes UK
UKHW010725070223
416609UK00002B/680